Microsoft Press

W9-CCA-576

Microsoft®
Flight Simulator 98

Ben Chiu

PUBLISHED BY
Microsoft Press
A Division of Microsoft Corporation
One Microsoft Way
Redmond, Washington 98052-6399

Library of Congress Cataloging-in-Publication Data
Chiu, Ben, 1963-
    Microsoft Flight Simulator 98: Inside Moves / by Ben Chiu.
       p.   cm.
    Includes index.
    ISBN 1-57231-635-7
    1. Microsoft flight simulator (Computer file) 2. Airplanes-
-Piloting--Computer simulation.   I. Title.
TL712.8.C494 1997
794.8'753--dc21   97-29194
                                          CIP

Printed and bound in the United States of America.

    8 9 MLML 2 1 0 9 8

Distributed in Canada by ITP Nelson, a division of Thomson Canada Limited.

A CIP catalogue record for this book is available from the British Library.

Microsoft Press books are available through booksellers and distributors worldwide. For further information about international editions, contact your local Microsoft Corporation office or contact Microsoft Press International directly at fax (425) 936-7329. Visit our Web site at mspress.microsoft.com.

Acquisitions Editor: Kim Fryer
Project Editor: Stuart J. Stuple

Dedication

This book is dedicated in memory of William "Wild Bill" Cody, my first
flight instructor and good friend, who went down off the coast of
Los Angeles 10 years ago. If you hadn't cancelled our flight earlier
that day, I can't help feeling that I may have been lost also.
I owe you a debt that I'll never be able to repay.
Clear skies and smooth landings—rest in peace, buddy.

Ben Chiu

Acknowledgments

I would like to thank Ben Chiu, who not only wrote an excellent book,
but also accomplished this incredible feat in an ever-so-short time.
I also wish to thank the many others who contributed, behind the scenes,
to the creation of *Flight Simulator 98: Inside Moves*:

At The PC Press, Inc.: Richard Mansfield, Project Editor;
Phil Powell, Samuel Gaines, and Sylvia Graham, Copy Editors;
Kim Davis, Art Director; Kathleen Ingram, Book Coordinator,
and especially David Jackson, Editorial Assistant, who also contributed our
closing sidebar on the Microsoft Force Feedback joystick.

At Microsoft Press: Our valued colleagues,
Kim Fryer, Acquisitions Editor (and on this project, much more) and
Stuart Stuple, Project Editor and patient person.

And lastly, to the Microsoft Flight Simulator group: without their great
new game, none of this would have been possible.

Robert C. Lock,
President and Editor-in-Chief, The PC Press, Inc.

Contents

Introduction

Introducing Flight Simulator 98

Microsoft Flight Simulator 98: Inside Moves is the comprehensive guidebook of hints, tips, and strategies for the 15th-year edition of the world's most popular flight simulator—Microsoft Flight Simulator 98. This book was designed to enhance the Pilot's Handbook and the extensive help system that come with Flight Simulator—not to replace them. Given the wide scope of Flight Simulator 98 and the sheer amount of information about general aviation and flying, covering *everything* would require many volumes. That's why every effort has been made not to duplicate information found in Flight Simulator's resources, so that the maximum amount of new and valuable information could be presented within the confines of a single book.

This constraint doesn't allow us to discuss everything here, so if you detect something missing, the chances are pretty good you'll find it either in the Pilot's Handbook or Help system in Flight Simulator 98. If it isn't there, rest assured that it isn't critical for your success or enjoyment of Flight Simulator . In essence, the Pilot's Handbook and Help system tell you what things are and what they do and then provide some general information on how to use them. This book takes you to the next level by discussing the little details and tips on how things are used, when they should be used, and perhaps the most valuable of all, *why* things are done the way they're done. *Microsoft Flight Simulator 98: Inside Moves* will keep you flying high because it contains tips and strategies found nowhere else.

Flight Simulator Realism

I've lost count of how many times I've been asked how realistic a PC-based flight simulator is compared to real flying. When these questions specifically refer to Microsoft Flight Simulator (not so surprisingly, as is usually the case), my usual answer sounds something like the plot of a cheap movie or the premise of yet another predictable airplane disaster flick. Nevertheless, it's how

I truly feel: if you can learn to fly Flight Simulator 98 properly and confidently and if your survival depended on flying an actual airplane, the experience you gain from this simulation could save your life (or at least minimize the prospect of a tragic outcome).

Of course, you probably have a better chance of actually being the million dollar winner in a national sweepstakes than of finding yourself in such a predicament, but that's not the point. What I'm getting at is that PC flight simulators are extremely realistic when it comes to many of the procedural and motor skills required in real-world aviation. And I'm not the only one who thinks so, either. In fact, flight simulators have become so realistic that the Federal Aviation Administration (FAA) has approved the use of PC-based aviation training devices (PC-ATD) in instrument flight training.

On May 30th, 1997, the FAA released an Advisory Circular (AC 61-126) detailing how to qualify a PC-ATD for instrument instruction. Under this new AC, student pilots are now allowed to log ten hours of flight time for training with an approved PC-ATD under the guidance of a flight instructor. Contrary to what many believe, the PC-ATD is a new category of training device. Up until now, the only simulators certified for flight credit have been expensive, single-purpose flight simulators and flight training devices (FTD).

At the time of this writing, none of the mainstream PC-based flight sims have become PC-ATD certified (not enough time has passed to accommodate their qualification), and as far as I know, no official announcements have been made regarding anyone's intentions to seek certification. Interesting times are certainly ahead, but until then (FAA certified or not), where does that leave us?

The Essence of Flight Training

As you can probably imagine, flying is a complex subject that has a fairly steep learning curve for newcomers. Sure, anyone can buzz around in a plane and bore holes in the sky with little or no training, but becoming a pilot is in some ways like becoming a surgeon. You can learn to remove an appendix with minimal schooling, but it's knowing what to do when something goes wrong that accounts for all of the other years spent studying that profession. Flying works the same way.

Flying is really all about procedures. If you've ever been in a real cockpit during a flight, this should explain why there are so many checklists and placards found everywhere. This book will teach you to "fly by the numbers."

This is the way it's done in real life, and I believe that the evolution of this program, from the first Flight Simulator to Flight Simulator 98, has made it possible not only to teach basic fundamentals of aviation, but also to build pilot proficiency. Now, no one is saying that by the time you've finished reading this book you can go out and get your private pilot certificate without additional training. The FAA requires instruction from a Certified Flight Instructor, and you can't learn everything you need to know in a single book. But the combination of your Flight Simulator experience and the information in this book will certainly help if becoming a pilot is your goal.

Just Out for a Good Time

While there's something to be said for that inherent satisfaction of doing things just right (like when you drive a perfect lap in a racing simulation or nail a flawless putt in a golf simulation), not everyone who installs Flight Simulator does so in the serious pursuit of flight training. In addition to the academic hounds and realism/workload junkies, there are several other types of flight simulator fanatics that enjoy GA (General Aviation) simulations. One might categorize them alternately as sightseers, crash-and-burn daredevils, and of course, those just curious about aviation or what all the Flight Simulator hoopla is about. We'll discuss topics that are pertinent to just having fun as well.

This book has only one goal: to enhance your enjoyment of Flight Simulator 98. As a private pilot who flies multiengine planes, who is instrument-rated, and who just happens to be a professional computer flight simulator analyst, perhaps I'll be able to fill in the little details that'll help close the gap between most perceptions about flight simulators and real-world flying. So there you have it—no matter what your preference, this book has something to offer flight simulation fans of all interest levels.

How to Use This Book

The flexible design of Flight Simulator 98 features an enormous number of options that can easily overwhelm a budding pilot. Instead of simply reviewing what all of the instruments do and then sending you off to discover how they work in practice, I've arranged this book so topics are introduced as they become pertinent.

Microsoft
Flight Simulator 98

- Chapter One: Quick Start (including installation and interface navigation)
- Chapter Two: Preflight
- Chapter Three: Aviation Conventions
- Chapter Four: On the Flightline
- Chapter Five: Normal Procedures
- Chapter Six: Emergency Procedures
- Chapter Seven: Flight Planning
- Chapter Eight: Flying "The System"
- Chapter Nine: Just for Fun

Out of the Hangar—Quick Start

Microsoft Flight Simulator 98 is the 15th-anniversary edition of the best-selling PC game of all time. Over 3 million computer pilots from different countries (including Germany, Japan, Spain, Mexico, Holland, Belgium, Italy, Brazil, Argentina, Great Britain, Canada, and, of course, the United States) have licensed copies of this program. Flight Simulator truly circles the globe, both on the PC and in the real world.

Ever since the release of Microsoft Flight Simulator version 1.0 in November 1982, Flight Simulator has boasted leading-edge graphics and advanced computing technology. Looking back from today's standards of computing muscle, it seems almost inconceivable that version 1.0's humble wire-frame graphics could have ever been that demanding. But it was because Flight Simulator made

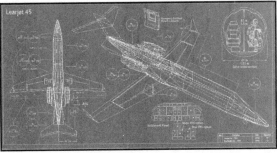

Flight Simulator 98 introduces the Learjet 45.

such high demands on hardware that Flight Simulator became *the* standard for IBM PC compatibility. Year after year, Flight Simulator has continued to lead the way. Here's a brief look at some of its many milestones:

- Version 2.0—For the PC XT and PCjr. It fit on a single 360 KB floppy disk and required 64 KB of memory to run in CGA mode or 128 KB if a mouse was used. ('84)
- Version 3.0—Featured dual player mode via modem or direct connect and introduced multiple windows so you could see two different views simultaneously. ('88)
- Version 4.0—Introduced advances such as 16-color scenery, customizable weather, random weather generation, dynamic scenery, and the addition of the Gates Learjet 25G. ('89)

Microsoft
Flight Simulator 98

Flight Simulator verson 4.0 introduced 16-color scenery.

- Version 5.0—Boasted 256 colors, some areas of photo-realistic scenery, and flight instruments. It also replaced the Gates Learjet 25G with the Learjet 35A.
- Version 5.1— Introduced CD-ROM media and even more airports. For the first time you could fly around the world.
- Flight Simulator for Windows 95—The first version designed for Windows 95 implemented some 32-bit code, plus the 737-400, as well as the Extra 300S aircraft.

Introducing Flight Simulator 98

Microsoft Flight Simulator has always pushed the limits of existing technologies, and this new version is a significant upgrade. Some of the new features in Flight Simulator 98 include:

- Full 32-bit code
- Direct3D support
- Force Feedback support
- Custom control configuration
- Virtual Cockpit (everything moves when you rotate your view)
- Multiple undockable windows
- Cessna 182S
- Learjet 45
- Bell 206 helicopter
- 8-player game play over the Internet
- Over 3,000 airports
- Several previous add-ons (Hawaii, Caribbean and Japan) are now built in.

Installing Flight Simulator 98

Before you can experience some of these improvements, you'll have to install Flight Simulator 98. First make sure your system meets the following minimum system requirements:

- Multimedia PC with 486DX/66 MHz or higher processor (Pentium recommended)
- Microsoft Windows 95 operating system or Windows NT workstation 4.0 or later
- 8 MB of memory (16 MB recommended)
- 100 MB of available hard disk space
- Double-speed CD-ROM drive
- Super VGA, 256-color monitor
- Microsoft Mouse or compatible pointing device (joystick recommended)
- Sound card with speakers or headphones required for audio

Note: *You'll see this Setup screen only during the Setup process. Afterwards you'll see the Flight Simulator screens discussed only in the next section unless you run SETUP.EXE from the Flight Simulator CD again.*

To install Flight Simulator 98:

- Close all running applications before attempting to install Flight Simulator. Setup cannot install system files or update shared files if they are in use during the Setup process.
- Insert the Flight Simulator 98 CD into your CD-ROM drive. If Autoplay (the feature that automatically runs a CD when the CD is inserted in your drive), is enabled in your version of Windows, the Flight

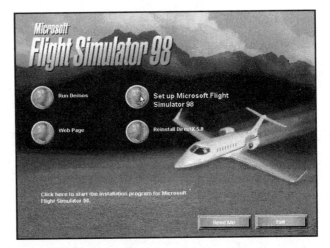

The Setup screen appears upon double-clicking the Flight Simulator 98 CD icon.

Simulator Setup screen will launch automatically. If Autoplay is disabled and the Flight Simulator Set up screen does not automatically launch, go to My Computer and double-click your CD-ROM drive's icon. Then double-click the file named SETUP.EXE.

Installing DirectX 5.0

Flight Simulator 98 requires DirectX version 5.0 or later, and it must be installed before Setup will allow you to proceed with Flight Simulator installation. DirectX is a Windows system component that improves computer access to hardware components such as graphics cards, sound cards, and input devices (such as mice and joysticks).

To install DirectX 5.0 and complete the installation of Flight Simulator:

1. Click the globe next to the words Reinstall DirectX 5.0 on the Flight Simulator 98 Setup screen.

2. Once DirectX 5.0 has been installed, you can proceed with the installation of Flight Simulator. To do this, click the globe next to the words Setup Microsoft Flight Simulator 98.

3. The Microsoft Flight Simulator 98 Install Screen will appear. Click the OK button in the lower right-hand corner of the screen.

4. The next screen that appears will ask you for your name. Type your name in the box provided. When you are finished, click the OK button at the bottom of the screen. Note that you must enter a name. If you leave the box empty, you will be notified.

5. Next, the Name Verification screen will be shown. If you entered your name correctly,

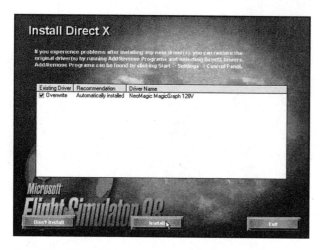

Installing DirectX 5.0 is quick and simple: click the Install button and follow the directions.

click the OK button at the bottom of the screen. If you did not enter it correctly, click the Change button. This will take you back to the screen seen in Step 4.

Flight Simulator 98 requires a name before the installation will continue.

6. Flight Simulator's Product ID number will be displayed on the next screen. You'll need this number if you call Microsoft Product Support. After installation, you can always access the number by clicking the About command on the Help menu selection. Click the OK button to continue installing Flight Simulator.

7. The next screen will ask you where you would like Setup to install Flight Simulator. For most people the default directory should be fine if you have the necessary hard disk space available on that drive. If you do, click the OK button at the lower right-hand corner of the screen.

You will be prompted to enter a path name for where you want the program installed.

8. Next you'll be asked what type of installation you'd like. The Typical Installation requires 100 MB of free hard disk space, while the Custom Installation can take up to 369 MB of hard disk space.

Flight Simulator will consume between 100 MB and 369 MB of hard drive space.

This screen updates your installation progress.

Tip: If you're new to Flight Simulator, you may want to jump ahead to Chapter Two: Preflight, for setup and configuration tips before attempting to fly.

If this is your first installation of Flight Simulator, the Typical Install is recommended. To enact the Typical Installation, click the globe next to the word Typical.

If you would like to change the default directory, click the Change button and then type in the name of the directory you'd like Setup to install Flight Simulator in. Click the OK button when you are finished to proceed with the installation.

9. Setup will begin installation.

10. After Setup has copied all of the installation files to our hard disk, you'll then be asked whether you'd like Setup to create a Flight Simulator shortcut to your desktop. If you'll be playing Flight Simulator often, this is a handy option. On the other hand, if your desktop is fairly cluttered already, you might want to skip this option. Click the Yes button to install the shortcut or click the No button to exit Setup.

Starting Flight Simulator 98 for the First Time

Once Flight Simulator is installed, the initial Setup screen you saw will change slightly. The selection that previously read Setup Microsoft Flight Simulator 98, will now read Run Microsoft Flight Simulator 98.

Click the globe labeled Run Microsoft Flight Simulator 98. The first time you run Flight Simulator and whenever you add extra scenery files, a message box will appear indicating that a database for new scenery files is being built. There's nothing to do at this point but sit back and get ready to fly!

The Opening Screen

When you start Flight Simulator, the Microsoft logo "movie" and the Flight Simulator title screen will greet you.

Next you'll be introduced to Flight Simulator's opening screen. From here you can access Flight Simulator's featured activities with a simple click of your mouse. On the left side of this screen there are four options: Learn To Fly, Select A Flight, Create A Flight, and Multiplayer. At the lower right-hand

The program has successfully been installed. Time to run Flight Simulator.

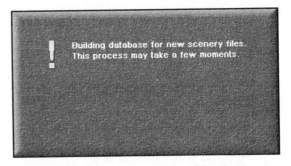

A scenery database must be built the first time the program is loaded.

Tip: *To bypass the opening movie, press the Escape key. And if you get tired of pressing the Escape key, delete the movie file MSLOGO.AVI that's found in the Flight Simulator folder. That way it won't be shown to you again unless you reinstall Flight Simulator.*

Flight Simulator 98 title screen.

The opening screen.

Tip: *If you want to bypass the opening screen in the future, uncheck the Show This screen At Startup check box at the lower left corner of the opening screen by clicking it with your mouse.*

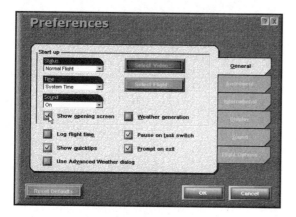

Disabling the opening screen.

corner are two buttons captioned Fly Now! and Exit.

All of the activities accessible from the opening screen can also be started directly from Flight Simulator's main window. To move directly to the main window, click the Fly Now! button.

You can re-enable the opening screen to load automatically on startup by accessing the General Preferences tab, which is located in the Preferences selection under Options on the main window menu.

To reset the opening screen to automatically load on startup:

1. From the main Flight Simulator window, click the Options menu selection.

2. Select Preferences from the menu list.

3. Click the Show Opening screen check box on the left side of the window.

Go ahead and click the Fly Now! button. We'll come back to the other activities shortly. For now, let's discuss some of the more basic features of Flight Simulator.

Navigating the Flight Simulator 98 Interface

Most everything in Flight Simulator can be accomplished by pointing and clicking—you literally point your cursor at whatever activity you want to perform and then click the mouse button. In addition to all of the general Windows 95 conventions, such as resizing a window by dragging a window border (by clicking and holding the mouse button as you move the mouse) or closing a window (by clicking on the Close Control box), many of the dials and switches on the cockpit instrument panels also work by clicking or dragging your mouse.

Adjust instrument settings by clicking on the control knob.

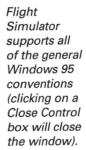

Flight Simulator supports all of the general Windows 95 conventions (clicking on a Close Control box will close the window).

For instance, you can bring up the radio stack by clicking the Avionics Master Switch on the instrument panel and adjust instrument settings by clicking on a control knob.

To learn how to operate control knobs with your mouse, first notice that when you position the mouse cursor over certain knobs on the instrument panel, the cursor changes from the usual arrow symbol to a hand symbol. The hand has a plus sign or a minus sign superimposed on it; a plus sign means that the instrument in question will increase its current setting with each mouse click, while a minus sign will decrease the current setting with each mouse click. Pointing to the right side of each knob will change the pointer to a plus sign, while pointing to the left side of the knob will cause

Clicking on the Avionics Master Switch will bring up the radio stack.

Holding the mouse over any instrument will pop up text about the instrument (Quicktips).

| ✓ Cockpit View |
| Virtual Cockpit View |
| Tower View |
| Spot View |
| Map View |
| Maximize Window |
| Undock Window |
| Close Window |
| Hide Menu Bar |
| Mouse As Yoke |

Right-click a window if you want to access a pop-up menu.

Tip: *Flight Simulator offers you the option to pause Flight Simulator anytime you use the "Cool Switch" to transfer to another application. To utilize the Pause on Task Switch option:*

1. *From the main Flight Simulator window, click the Options menu selection.*
2. *Select Preferences from the menu list.*

Toggling the Pause on Task Switch.

3. *Click the Pause on Task Switch check box on the right side of the window. When the check box is clear, Flight Simulator will no longer pause when you switch away to another program.*

a minus sign to appear instead of the pointer. You can also hold down the left mouse button to adjust some knobs continuously.

Other features associated with Flight Simulator's mouse are pop-up menus, and Quicktips.

Pop-up menus, brought into view by clicking the right mouse button, provide quick access to features and settings that are often used. Pop-up menus are window-sensitive. In other words, right-clicking on another window may bring up a different set of menu choices (appropriate to that particular window).

Quicktips are little text reminders that appear when you point your cursor at a "hot spot" (any portion of the screen representing a function that can be triggered by clicking directly on that screen item). If you forget the instrument represented by a certain hot spot, simply point your cursor at the control in question. A second later, a little window bearing the name of the instrument will appear. Quicktips like this are especially handy when you're manipulating the many flight controls that appear on an instrument panel.

Although there's little reason to do so, you can disable Quicktips by accessing the General Preferences tab found under the Preferences selection (under the Options menu).

To disable Quicktips:

1. From the main Flight Simulator window, click the Options menu selection.

2. Select Preferences from the menu list.

3. Click the Show Quicktips check box on the left side of the window. When the check box no longer displays a check mark, Quicktips will be disabled.

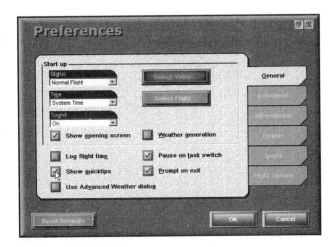

Toggling the Quicktips option.

The last two Windows conventions you should be aware of are the Fullscreen toggle and "Cool Switch" (a.k.a. Task Switch). Pressing Alt+Enter on the keyboard will cycle Flight Simulator between Fullscreen mode and windowed mode. The "Cool Switch" keys (Alt+Tab) will allow you to switch between Flight Simulator and other Windows programs. In general, you shouldn't run other programs while running Flight Simulator, because if you make too many demands of your CPU, the performance of Flight Simulator could suffer. Sometimes, however, it's unavoidable (such as when you're playing against other pilots over the Internet).

Main Activities in Flight Simulator 98

Recall that all the program activities that can be accessed on the opening screen can also be accessed directly from the Flight Simulator main window. Let's discuss the activities featured on the opening screen.

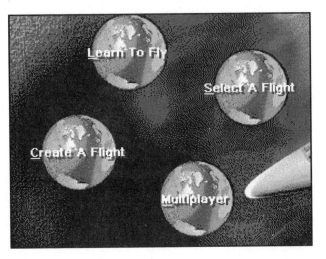

You are given four main options on the opening screen.

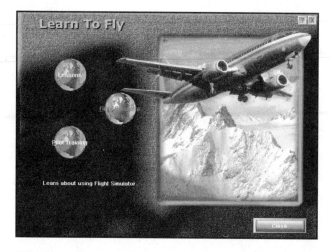

When you're ready for your virtual flight lessons, click the Learn To Fly button on the opening screen.

Learn To Fly

Appropriately enough, clicking the Learn To Fly button causes the Learn To Fly window to appear. On this window you have direct access to three key resources: Lessons, Flight Simulator Help, and Pilot Training.

- Lessons—From the Lessons window, you can select from a number of interactive flight lessons. You can fly each of these; in some, you can opt to watch as an instructor guides you through the lesson. To let the instructor fly the aircraft, click the Instructor radio button under the Aircraft Control heading at the lower left corner of the window.

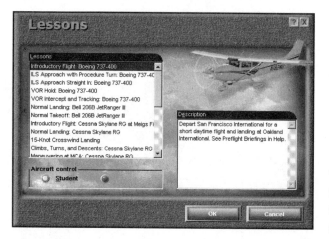

Close a lesson and begin your training.

- Flight Simulator Help— We'll talk about this shortly, under the heading Pilot's Help.
- Pilot Training—This is a separate section of Help, also covered later.

Select A Flight

The Select A Flight button on the opening screen will take you to a dialog box where you can access Flights, Challenges, and Adventures—all of which you can also call up from the Flights menu.

• Flights—The Flights window allows you to re-experience a flight previously saved to disk or sample one of the saved flights that comes loaded with Flight Simulator. This is the second quickest way to get flying (choosing Fly Now! from the opening screen is fastest). From the Flights window you can make a particular flight the startup default by selecting it from the Available Flights list and then clicking the Make This the Default Flight check box in the lower left corner of the window. (The default flight is the one automatically available every time you start Flight Simulator and select Fly Now!.)

• Challenges—Challenges are saved flights that are expressly designed to test your piloting skills (and nerves!). They are separated into four categories. In order of difficulty they are as follows: Basic, Challenging, Difficult, and Mastery.

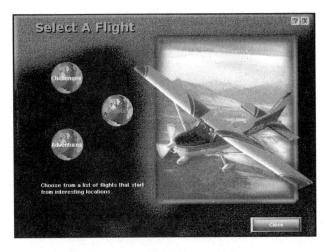

You can select a preset flight if you wish.

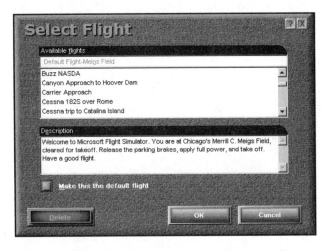

Simply click on the flight and prepare for take-off.

Note: *If you choose the Typical Install option during setup, none of the Adventure sound files will be copied to your hard disk. However, they will be read from your Flight Simulator CD if you need them later.*

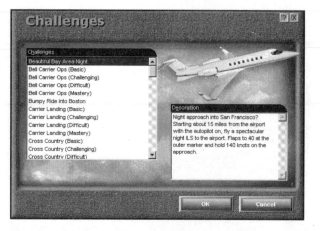

Challenges range in difficulty level.

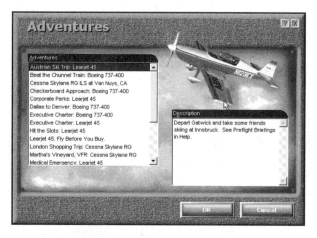

For the spontaneous adventure type.

- Adventures—Adventures are part saved flights, part Challenges, and all fun, with the added dimension of instructions from ATC (Air Traffic Control). On some trips you may even have the company of a copilot. Boys and girls, Flight Simulator Adventures are as close to real as virtual flying gets.

Create Flight

Just as the name suggests, Create Flight presents the same dialogue that's accessed from the Flight menu. From here you can custom-design a flight by choosing the aircraft, airport, weather, and time of your flight. Don't forget to save your masterpieces to share with your friends!

Multiplayer

In addition to simple multiplayer activities (modem, LAN, and direct-connect gameplay), another one of Flight Simulator's new features is its ability to let you fly with other desktop pilots via the Internet. Clicking Multiplayer brings up the Multiplayer Direct Playwizard that will take you through the process of connecting with other like-minded players.

Creating a flight.

Playing against others.

Getting Help

There are three main help resources within Flight Simulator, and you're apt to find these quite useful. Granted, knowing everything isn't always possible, but knowing where to look for the right answers is the next best thing. Let's look at each of Flight Simulator's help resources and talk a little about what kind of information they contain and how to access each of them.

Pilot's Handbook

The first and most obvious place to search for help is the printed Pilot's Handbook that's bundled with the Flight Simulator package. It includes background information about the new features in Flight Simulator and navigational charts.

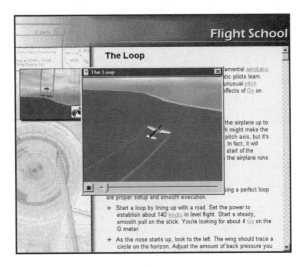

Pilot's Help

The next place to look for help is in Flight Simulator's Help system, aptly named Pilot's Help. Pilot's Help is broken down into four sections.

The Pilot's Help is a rich source of information.

Microsoft
Flight Simulator 98

To start Pilot's Help, click Help, then select the contents you need assistance with.

- Flight School—Also called Pilot Training, this section focuses on matters of basic aviation. If you want (or need) an introduction to the general principles of aerodynamics and how they relate to modern flight, here's where you can find it.
- Aircraft Handbooks—Naturally, one of Flight Simulator's main drawing cards has been its wealth of beautiful planes. This section contains specific information about those aircraft modeled in Flight Simulator.
- Preflight Briefings—Before embarking on Flight Simulator's instructive lessons and challenging adventures, look in Preflight Briefings. Each briefing contains the exact amount of information necessary to making a successful flight.
- Using Flight Simulator—This introductory section provides much of the nuts 'n' bolts information of flying with Flight Simulator. A wide variety of topics address everything from picking *your* kind of aircraft to varying the weather you'll encounter during a flight to tweaking the program to the specifications you desire.

To start Pilot's Help, select Help from the options menu. Alternately, you can access Help through Flight Simulator's context-sensitive Help feature. Anytime you see a question mark box in a window, you can click on it and a question mark will appear next to your mouse cursor. If you then click the object you have a question about, a brief description will be displayed. If there is a corresponding Help topic available, you'll be provided with a link to it.

Some tips for using Pilot's Help:

- To quickly find specific information, click the Index or Contents button at the top of the Help window.
- If you need help with a specific word or phrase, try the Glossary.
- At the bottom of each Pilot's Help page, you'll find a Related Topics section with links to other parts of Help that contain useful additional information about a similar subject.

- To print any topic, click the Print button at the top of the Help window.
- Look in the left column of the Help window for videos, animations, and pictures. To view an animation or video, click it once.

Context-sensitive help is available when you click on a question mark box.

Microsoft on the Web

As you might expect, the most up-to-date source of help and information about Flight Simulator is on the Internet. Flight Simulator provides links to Web pages in the Help menu of the main Flight Simulator window.

- Frequently Asked Questions—This links you to a list of Frequently Asked Questions (FAQ) about Flight Simulator. This is the best place to start your on-line search if you're experiencing problems. The chances are very good that someone else has had the same problem that you're experiencing.
  http://www.microsoft.com/games/fsim/rp-FAQ.htm.
- Online Support—If the FAQ doesn't contain the answer you seek, Online support can help you.
  http://www.microsoft.com/games/fsim/rp-support.htm.
- Flight Simulator Home Page— At the official Flight Simulator Home Page, you can learn about the latest news and points of interest about Flight Simulator 98. There are also many links to other popular Flight Simulator Web sites as well.
  http://www.microsoft.com/games/fsim.

You'll discover links to the following Web pages in the Help menu of the main Flight Simulator window. Internet access is required to connect to Microsoft On The Web help resources.

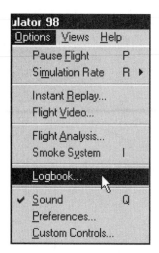

Check Before Flight

If you're a Flight Simulator veteran or just a brave soul who wants to go at it alone, there are two features that you may want to check out before taking off into the friendly skies. The first is the logbook (for keeping a detailed record of your hours in the air). The other is the Flight Video recorder (useful for making sure that no one thinks your tale of flying the LAX ILS while inverted was enhanced by your powers of imagination!).

The Logbook dialog box is located under the Options menu.

Logbook

The FAA (Federal Aviation Administration) requires only that pilots log their flight time if it is to be used to meet their requirements for a certificate, rating, or recent flight experience (also known as *flight currency*). Flight Simulator imposes no such requirements. In fact, it is rumored that there are those who refuse to log their Flight Simulator flight time as a precautionary measure—just in case their (neglected) significant other should happen to stumble across it.

Regardless of your reasons for or against keeping a log of your flight time, Flight Simulator can automatically log your flight time for you or let you manually enter it into the log.

To have Flight Simulator automatically log your flight times:

Logging your flight time.

1. From the main Flight Simulator window, click the Options menu selection.

2. Select Preferences from the menu list.

3. Click the Log Flight Time check box on the right side of the window. When the check box is clear, Flight Simulator will not automatically log your flight time.

To manually enter and/or edit your logbook:

You can add, edit, or remove log entries from this dialog box.

1. From the main Flight Simulator window, click the Options menu selection.

2. Select Logbook from the menu list.

3. You can add a log entry, edit a log entry, or delete a log entry from the Logbook window by clicking on the appropriate button.

Flight Video

Depending on what you record, Flight Videos can be a source of pride, hair-raising entertainment, sheer boredom, or utter disgrace. Of course, you'll never know the exact outcome of a flight or maneuver *before* you fly the flight or perform the maneuver, so you never really know beforehand if a flight will be worth recording. Fortunately, you aren't forced to save any Flight Videos, but if you want the option, you have to begin recording during a flight.

To record a Flight Video:

1. Select Flight Video from the Options menu.

2. At the top right-hand corner of the Flight Video window is a drop-down box labeled Recording Interval. Here you can select how

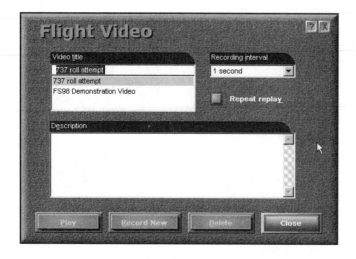

Save those fancy maneuvers to show off at parties.

often your video will be recorded. The lower the Recording Interval, the smoother the playback will be. Unfortunately, smooth playback comes at a price. With lower Recording Intervals you'll have less recording time, so you'll have to make a decision based on what you're recording and how much recording time you need.

3. Click the Record Now button at the lower half of the Flight Video

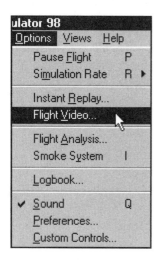

Recording a flight video.

You can add comments to the flight recording.

window when you're ready to begin recording your flight.

4. To end the recording, press the Escape key.

5. The Save Video window will appear.

From the Save Video window you have the option to either:

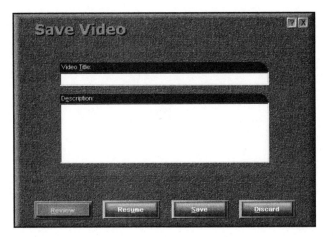

Don't forget to save.

- Review what you've recorded so far.
- Resume your recording (You can do this even after reviewing your recording.).
- Save your recording (You'll have to enter a Video Title and an optional video description.).
- Discard the recording (You'll be given the chance to change your mind before the recording is discarded.).

Tip: *To add messages that will scroll across the top of the window during video playback, press the , (comma) key while you are recording the flight. Type your message in the box provided in the Video Message box . Click OK when you are through.*

Chapter Two

PREFLIGHT

To the uninitiated, preflighting an aircraft probably seems like a ritual that a pilot uses to *bond* with the machine before flight. That conclusion is perfectly understandable considering that a pilot usually walks around the plane several times, intently looking in every nook and cranny, caressing the wings, stroking the prop, and kicking the tires. But, bonding aside, the preflight is really a safety check.

In the real world, any pilot who neglects to preflight an aircraft is literally putting his or her life in the hands of fate. It doesn't take a genius to know it's far better to find out something is wrong out on the flightline (while you're still on the ground) than it would be to make that same discovery at 8,000 feet with no airports within an hour's flight time. Although your life may never be in any danger in Microsoft Flight Simulator 98, a few minutes spent preflighting Flight Simulator now can help you avoid a lot of frustration in the long run. Sorting out configuration and setup issues before taking off into the virtual skies will help ensure pleasurable flights.

Understanding Situations

One of the oldest features of Flight Simulator has been the ability to save your flights. Saving your flight can be thought of as saving your situation. Your location, world settings, weather settings, aircraft settings, and aircraft type are saved. The choices concerning which settings are restored (when you load a flight from disk) are up to you. We'll talk about how that works a little bit later.

As useful and convenient as flight saving is, this feature is also probably one of the most confusing for new Flight Simulator 98 pilots. That's because it seems options are sometimes saved even if you don't actually save the flight, and other times they aren't saved even if you do save the flight. To help simplify the explanations, consider looking at things like this: Flight Simulator's configuration options can be categorized as either global- or

Flights	
Create Flight...	
Select Flight...	
Reset Flight	CTRL-;
Save Flight...	;
Lessons...	
Challenges...	
Adventures...	
Multiplayer	▶
Show Opening Screen	
Exit	CTRL-C

When you save a flight, you're recording information about your flying location, the weather you experience, and what kind of aircraft you're piloting.

Note: *Flight Simulator 98 automatically reverts back to your last flight situation after a crash or manual situation reset (Ctrl - ; on the keyboard). These Program Generated Temporary Flight situations only recall changes made in your aircraft type, graphics preferences, and sound preferences, but they'll revert back to the appropriate saved situation configuration settings when you load any saved situations.*

situation-oriented. The critical difference between the two is that global option changes affect all saved and unsaved situations, while saving a situation only affects that particular situation's options.

Naturally, the global options have the most influential effect on Flight Simulator because they influence all Flight Simulator flights. In this chapter we'll cover all of the global options and some of the situation options pertinent to aircraft and environment. At this point you probably want to get up in the air as soon as possible, so we'll leave the remaining situation options for later chapters.

Controller Options

The first set of global options we'll discuss are the controller options. Although it's possible to fly Flight Simulator solely by keyboard or mouse, for realism buffs nothing less than a joystick or flight yoke controller for primary flight control (ailerons and rudder) will suffice for more reasons than just authenticity alone. If you play Flight Simulator with a keyboard, functions such as elevator trim become pointless. But if you're just out to fly around and don't care about precision flight or precision landings, the keyboard or mouse will work just fine.

On the other hand, beginning desktop pilots usually find a joystick or flight yoke easier to adjust to, which probably explains why all of the real versions of the aircraft modeled in Flight Simulator use either a flight stick or flight yoke rather than a mouse or keyboard for flight control. To get a little more specific, all of the airplanes except for the Sopwith Camel and the Schweizer 2-32 sailplane use flight yokes in real life. So if you're after realism, the choices are obvious.

Of course a real Bell 206B JetRanger uses a cyclic stick. For helicopter flight, nothing less than a joystick will suffice. You'll find that attempting to use the mouse or keyboard to fly the JetRanger will be nearly impossible. A helicopter is pretty tough to fly even without handicaps, so if you're serious about flying one, you'll need a joystick.

But you may want to stay away from some of the really stiffly sprung joysticks out there. Like an airplane, flying a helicopter requires precision control, but to control a helicopter in hover requires stick movements that quickly move from one direction to another. The cyclic in a real helicopter doesn't center itself, so if your joystick is too stiff, control movements that are possible with a non-centering stick will be more difficult to perform with precision.

If you don't already own a joystick or flight yoke, or if you're considering upgrading your current controller, consider these suggestions:

If you're serious about Flight Simulator and other flight simsulators, an advanced programmable joystick such as this FLCS from ThrustMaster is a sound investment.

- Besides their fundamental features, joystick preferences are often personal choices based on feel and the user's hand size. That's why the best advice is to try out a joystick in the store before making your final selection.
- Consider buying a controller only from an established company you can trust to support you in the future. No-name or off-brand products usually end up being a waste of money in the long run.
- At the very least, get a joystick that features a view hat.
- Although Flight Simulator allows you to alter joystick button command assignments, consider

The Sidewinder 3D Pro from Microsoft combines many of the most sought-after joystick features into one neat package.

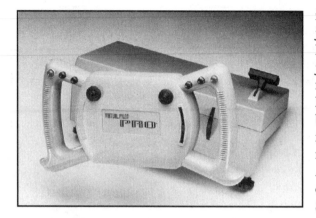

The Virtual Pilot Pro from CH Products features throttle control, elevator trim wheel, six buttons, and two view hats.

investing in a programmable joystick such as the ThrustMaster FLC. An advanced programmable joystick such as the FLCS will not only allow you to send keyboard presses for joystick button and view hat inputs, but it'll also allow you to send multiple command sequences. And it'll increase the number of commands at your fingertips. Such features come for an additional price, but if you're serious about Flight Simulator and other flight sims, this is a good investment.

- A reasonably priced, quality flight yoke is the Virtual Pilot Pro from CH Products. It features throttle control, elevator trim wheel, six buttons, and two view hats.
- The Microsoft Sidewinder 3D Pro combines many of the most sought-after features such as programmability, throttle slider, twist-action rudder control, and view hat...all in a neat package.

Do You Need a Rudder?

The need for a set of rudder pedals or a rudder controller really requires answering two questions. When it comes to airplanes, one criteria depends on your Aircraft Flight Realism setting and whether you have Auto-coordination set in Aircraft Settings. If you fly Flight Simulator's airplanes at the more user-friendly difficulty settings, the keyboard will be more than adequate for rudder control.

Note: *Aircraft Settings are only saved with flights and are not globally inclusive. This means if you want to use rudder pedals while in flight and/or fly at the Difficult Flight Realism setting with the saved situations, you'll need to open and reset each individual situation. Then you'll need to save each situation with the new settings, if you want them to remain that way.*

But when it comes to the JetRanger, just as with using a joystick to fly it, you'll have a very difficult time using the keyboard for antitorque control. It's

said that flying a helicopter is like walking, chewing gum, patting the top of your head, and rubbing your stomach all at the same time. Well, hovering is actually harder than that—and even more difficult on a computer. (More on this later.) The best recommendation for flying the helicopter is to get a set of rudder pedals or at the very least a joystick that twists for rudder control.

The second criteria is philosophical and a matter of personal preference. Using rudder pedals in a real airplane or antitorque pedals in a helicopter are all part of the experience of flying. But for some people, using a twisting joystick over a set of pedals just may not seem realistic. So that's another consideration you may want to grapple with.

If you decide pedals are the way to go, both ThrustMaster and CH Products produce excellent rudder pedal controllers. Made from aluminum and plastic, the RCS from ThrustMaster is a solid piece of equipment. The Pro Pedals from CH feature dual pedal action that'll work for both driving simulations and flight simulations.

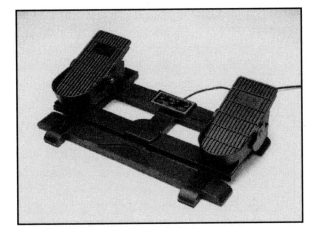

ThrustMaster's RCS is a solidly constructed set of rudder pedals.

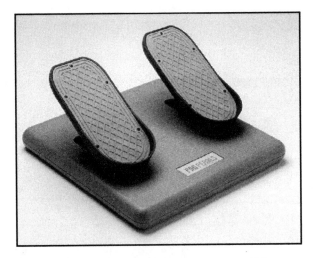

The Pro Pedals from CH Products work well for flight and driving simulations.

Throttle Jockey

Flight Simulator allows you use to use the keyboard, mouse, or throttle controller (whether it's a dedicated throttle controller or throttle wheel on a joystick) to control the throttle or helicopter collective. The keyboard is fine for

airplane throttle control, but it's rather lacking when it comes to use as a helicopter collective. Airplanes don't require quick throttle adjustments, but the keyboard simply won't cut it for hovering a helicopter. Nevertheless, despite the philosophical differences, the throttle wheel feature on some joysticks will work very well for collective control.

The old Joystick icon in Control Panel is replaced with a new icon called Game Controllers.

Controller Setup

In order to use a joystick, flight yoke, rudder device, or throttle device in Flight Simulator, it must first be installed and calibrated in the Windows 95 Control Panel. DirectX 5.0 replaces the old familiar Joystick icon in Control Panel with a new icon called Game Controllers. Although the look may have changed, it generally operates the same way as the old Joystick version.

Please see the Windows 95 manual and your joystick manufacturer's documentation for specific instructions about installing your particular controller. Here are some general instructions for installing a joystick or flight yoke controller:

1. Double-click the My Computer icon on your desktop.

2. Open Control Panel by double-clicking on it.

3. Double-click on Game Controllers.

4. Click on the Add button.

5. The Add Game Controller window will appear. Scroll down the window and select your controller from the list.

6. If your controller is not listed in the Add Game Controller list box and you have a driver disk for your

Adding a controller begins at Control Panel, where you double-click Game Controllers.

controller, click on the Add Other button. If you don't have a driver disk for your controller, select Custom from the list box. Fill out the required controller information, and then click on OK when finished. From here you can proceed to the Joystick Calibration section below. Otherwise, continue with the next step.

Add Game Controller	? X

To add a game controller, select the controller below and click OK.

Controllers:

[Custom...]
2-axis, 2-button joystick
2-axis, 4-button joystick
2-button flight yoke
2-button flight yoke w/throttle
2-button gamepad
3-axis, 2-button joystick

If your game controller does not appear in the list above, click on Add Other.

Add Other...

OK   Cancel

If your desired controller isn't listed here, you'll need to click Add Other...

7. If you have a driver disk and you clicked on the Add Other button from the Add Game Controller window, the Select Device window should now be open. Click on Have Disk and follow the instructions.

8. You might receive the following error message; The specified location does not contain information about your hardware. If so, you'll need to consult your controller's documentation. Some controllers come with software that must be installed before you can install the controller as a device in Control Panel.

Once you have the proper controller drivers installed, you'll need to calibrate your joystick. To calibrate your joystick:

1. Double-click on My Computer.

2. Open Control Panel by double-clicking on it.

3. Double-click on Game Controllers.

4. Click on the Properties button.

5. The Game Controller Properties window will open. Click on the Settings Tab.

Select Device

Sound, video and game controllers: The following models are compatible with your hardware. Click the one you want to set up, and then click OK. If your model is not on the list, click Show All Devices. If you have an installation disk for this device, click Have Disk.

Mode**l**s:

Gameport Joystick
ThrustMaster ACM Game Card

○ Show **c**ompatible devices
○ Show **a**ll devices

[Have Disk...]

[OK] [Cancel]

The program will then ask you to supply a disk with the necessary drivers...

Game Controllers

General | Advanced

Game Controllers

Controller	Status
Thrustmaster Flight Control System	OK

[A**d**d...] [**R**emove...] [Properties...]

To configure or test a controller, select the controller and click Properties.

Use the Add or Remove buttons to update the game controller list.

[OK]

You'll know if the installation is a success by the OK listed beneath Status.

6. If you have a rudder controller, click on the Rudder/Pedals check box to enable them.

7. Click the Calibrate button to begin the calibration routines.

Joystick Troubleshooting

If you have problems getting Windows to recognize your joystick or if your joystick refuses to calibrate, here are a few solutions to common problems:

- There may be more than one game card or game port installed in the system. Only one should be enabled. See your game card or soundcard manual for details on how to disable any extra game cards/ports.

- If one or more of your game ports are Plug-and-Play types, Windows 95 sometimes has trouble figuring out which to keep activated. One solution is to power down the system and then remove all game cards. Install the one you want to use, and set it up in Win95. Next power down the system again, reinstall the remaining cards, and tell Win95 to disable/remove any new game port devices.

- The Windows 95 joystick driver is missing, or the Windows 95 joystick driver may be installed improperly. See your Windows 95 manual or joystick manufacturer's instructions for details on proper installation.

- The Windows 95 Game Controllers configuration may not be selected properly. Make sure the type of joystick you select has the required number of axes for your setup. The "4-button flight yoke w/throttle" configuration works with a four-button joystick and analog throttle. Selecting the check box enables rudder pedals.

- The calibration of the Windows 95 driver is incorrect. If you can't calibrate your controllers in the Windows 95 Game

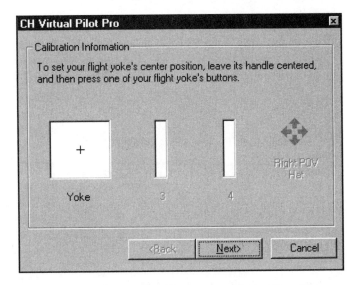

To begin the calibration process, open Settings within Game Controller Properties.

The key part of the calibration process is checking the center position of your flight yoke, the point of reference for your controller's field of movement.

Controller Properties Test tab, it won't be calibrated when you run Flight Simulator either. If you have the proper driver and joystick selected, any problems here may mean your joystick or game card could be malfunctioning. The only way to find out for sure is to swap both of them out for ones that are known to work properly.

Common Calibration Problems

Nearly every computer sold today has a game port either built into the motherboard, located on a multifunction card, or located on a soundcard. Unfortunately, some of these don't work correctly with some of the higher speed computers—which can cause calibration problems. So if you experience calibration problems, don't overlook the game card as a possible cause. A dedicated, speed-adjustable game card is by far the best to have, but they aren't always necessary. Make sure your game card is really the problem before considering replacing your current one.

Once your controllers are installed and calibrated, you'll need to enable them in Flight Simulator. The place where controllers are configured in Flight Simulator 98 is under the Options menu selection in the Customize Controls submenu.

To open Customize Controls:

1. Click on Options menu selection.

2. Select Customize Controls from the drop-down menu.

In the upper left corner of the Customize Controls Sensitivities tab is the Joystick Enable box. The first thing you need to do is click on the Enable Joystick check box to enable any controller other than the keyboard or mouse. (You can also

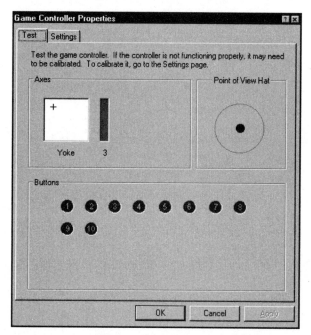

If you can't calibrate your controllers in the Windows 95 Game Controller Properties Test tab, it won't be calibrated in Flight Simulator either.

toggle the joystick on and off while in the cockpit by pressing the K key.) When the Joystick On check box is enabled, flight control capabilities for the mouse and keyboard are disabled.

If you've been following along, at this point your joystick should already be calibrated properly. But should you ever need to recalibrate it while you're in Flight Simulator, clicking the Calibrate button in this Customize Controls window will take you directly to the Game Controllers windows found in Control Panel.

Below the Joystick Enable Box is the Control Device list box that lists each installed controller. To the right is an Axis drop-down box. The controller/device that is selected in the Control Device list will determine which axes will be available in the Axis drop-down box.

Directly below the Axis drop-down box are two slide controls. There is one to adjust flight-control sensitivity and one for Null Zone. Just as the name suggests, sensitivity means how sensitive that control will be. Sliding this control toward High will make your airplane more sensitive to control movements, and sliding the sensitivity control towards Low will do just the opposite. Depending on which device you've chosen in the Control Device box, the Null Zone slide control may be grayed out. That's because Null Zones only apply to joystick axes. In any case, the slider controls below the Axis box reflect the controller options for the axis currently selected.

> **Tip:** *Many controller problems are not hardware related. In fact, most of the time, the controllers are just set up incorrectly. If you have a programmable joystick (a Thrustmaster FLCS, for example) and currently have the view hat or buttons programmed for digital operation (mimics keypresses), the calibration routines won't recognize these as joystick signals.*

Don't overlook the game card as a possible cause of calibration problems. A dedicated, speed-adjustable game card like this ACM from ThrustMaster will work correctly in a high-speed computer.

The sliding controls help you determine how sensitive your joystick will be and how much unresponsive ("dead") space will exist around the neutral position of your stick.

Tip: *You can enable the mouse for flight control and use it simultaneously with a joystick by clicking the right mouse button and selecting Mouse As Yoke. You'll be able to use the mouse for flight control, but once you move the joystick, it will override any mouse control inputs.*

Naturally, if you haven't been flying yet, there's no way to tell if your control sensitivities are right for you or not. So you may want to leave these settings as they are until you feel a need to change them. Although this is another one of those matters of personal preference, most people know when something isn't responsive enough or is totally uncontrollable. If you find that you can't turn or get off the ground, you'll want to increase the offending axis's sensitivities. Conversely, if you find the slightest movement of your joystick causes your airplane to overreact, turn the offending axis's sensitivities down.

Null Zone refers to the amount of *dead space* where nothing will happen around the neutral point of the controller. If you find that your aircraft will unintentionally maneuver with the slightest control movement while in the neutral position (centered), consider widening the Null Zone. Such problems are usually caused by joystick or game card problems, but this adjustment can help alleviate a hardware problem through software. Note that this Null Zone setting in the Preferences window will adjust the Null Zone for all controller axes and that all settings made here are global, so they'll affect all flights.

Below the slider controls is a Reverse Joystick check box. Enabling this option will reverse the operation of the selected axis. Not only will this help with nonstandard controller operation, it can let you easily alter the operation of

a throttle controller to work in the same direction as a helicopter collective lever. (The collective on a helicopter increases collective as you pull on it as opposed to an airplane throttle control that increases as you push it.) But because this option is a global setting, you'll have to remember to switch it back for airplane throttle use.

> **Note:** *The Reset Defaults button in the lower left-hand corner of the Customize Controls window will reset all of the sensitivity and Null Zone settings back to their default positions, but be aware that Enable Joystick will be disabled as well.*

Custom Assignments

One of the new features in Flight Simulator 98 is the ability to assign alternate keyboard and joystick inputs for Flight Simulator's commands. To give you an example of what this means, you can change the landing gear command from G to another key or even assign the landing gear to operate at the press of a joystick button—provided the new key or joystick button isn't already assigned to another command.

The Assignments feature can be especially handy:

- If you're used to the key commands from another game, you can program them into Flight Simulator 98. This will quickly make you feel right at home.
- If you don't have a programmable joystick, you can map joystick buttons and stick movements to commands as well.
- If you do have a programmable stick and some odd key combinations won't program properly.

To alter keyboard and joystick controls through Customize Control Assignments:

1. Click on the Options menu selection.

2. Select Customize Controls from the drop-down menu.

3. Click on the Assignments tab.

4. Select the category of commands you wish to alter by clicking the appropriate radio button. Your choices are Normal and Slew. Slew commands control aircraft positioning, direction, altitude,

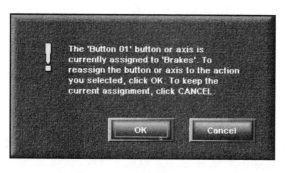

Customize Controls

To assign an action to a key combination or joystick button, click the action and then press the key combination or joystick button

○ **Normal**   ● **Slew**

Sensitivities

Assignments

Forces

Action	Keyboard	Game Device	Repeat
Pan View left and down		Button 38	☑
Pan View right and up		Button 34	☑
Pan View right and down		Button 36	☑
Pan View tilt left			
Pan View tilt right			
Pan View reset	CTRL + Space		
Look ahead	SHIFT + Num 8	Button 33	☐
Look ahead/right	SHIFT + Num 9		

Reset Defaults   Assign   Clear

OK   Cancel

Not only can you adjust your joystick's sensitivity on the Customize Controls screen; you can also assign functions to a programmable joystick.

and location without flying.

5. Find the function you wish to change and double-click on the corresponding Keyboard column (or Joystick column, if that's what you want to change).

6. When you are prompted, press the key on your keyboard or the button on your joystick you wish to assign to that function. Click on the Repeat box if you want the command to be repeated when the controller button is pressed. If the new key or button conflicts with another command, you'll be notified. Click on OK to reassign the control, or click Cancel to leave the current assignment as it is.

7. When you've made all your changes, click OK and your changes will be saved. If you click on Cancel, all changes will be lost.

Here are some final notes:

! The 'Button 01' button or axis is currently assigned to 'Brakes'. To reassign the button or axis to the action you selected, click OK. To keep the current assignment, click CANCEL.

OK   Cancel

Helpful warnings like this one will keep you from assigning two different functions to the same joystick button or control.

• Keyboard flight control commands will function only if the corresponding flight control is turned off. For example, the arrow keys will not control your airplane if joystick control is enabled.

• Reset Defaults only restores the currently selected command.

- Clicking the Assign button has the same effect as double-clicking a selection in the Keyboard or Joystick columns.

- The Clear button will clear the selected command. This will also disable the Reset Defaults button and keep it from restoring the last command.

> **Tip:** *If you accidentally click Clear when you didn't mean to and need to know what the old command was, click the Cancel button. You'll lose all of your changes, but at least you'll be able to start over.*

Use the Force (Feedback Joystick), Luke

Flight Simulator 98 supports force feedback joysticks through Direct 5.0, but the only driver currently available is for the Microsoft Sidewinder Force Feedback Pro. Regardless, a force feedback joystick is truly a pleasure to use with Flight Simulator 98. Of course, you need to get past the philosophical differences between flight yokes and joysticks for some of the aircraft, but regardless, the benefits of a force feedback joystick really add to the Flight Simulator 98 flight experience.

Through the force feedback feature, you'll be able to literally feel the shaking of oncoming stalls, the bumping of turbulence, appropriate control stiffening when airspeeds increase, and the contrasting loosening as airspeed decreases. Given the fact that you can't feel with your body what your Flight Simulator airplane is doing while you sit in front of your computer, force feedback can help remedy this deficiency.

See Chapter Nine for more information and a test flight of the Sidewinder Force Feedback Pro.

To access the Customize Control Forces window in Flight Simulator:

1. Click on the Options menu selection.

2. Select Customize Controls from the drop-down menu.

3. Click on the Forces tab.

Controller Positioning

One aspect of controller configuration that usually goes unaddressed when discussing flight simulators is physical controller placement. What we're talking about is the physical location of each controller in relation to where you sit and what you sit on. When you sit inside the cockpit of an airplane in flight,

because your aircraft is moving and possibly bouncing around quite a bit as well, the only way to maintain precise control of your aircraft is to have steady hands. The way you can help keep your hands steady under such conditions is by bracing your arms (or more precisely your elbows) on something. When your elbows are supported against something solid, it gives your hands the required stability for good aircraft control.

Naturally you don't need to worry about turbulence or other jarring movements while sitting in front of your computer, but the technique used in real airplanes can be beneficial to computer pilots just the same. Moving your controls to an exact precise position is really difficult to do without bracing yourself against something. What you can use to brace yourself with ranges from pressing your back into a sturdy chair to resting the edge of your palm or wrist against the base of your joystick as you move it.

In the cockpit you can generally rely on your body as being a fairly stable place to brace your elbow against because you're strapped in your seat pretty firmly. Pressing your elbow against your rib cage can give you the support you desire, but it can become tiresome after a while. Another popular bracing point is on the cockpit armrest. Of course, such decisions are a matter of personal preference, but the armrest works the best for many pilots. Now that you know what to look for, try anything you can think of and see what works best for you.

On the other hand, helicopter pilots develop what is known as *helicopter hunch*. Because the cyclic stick is positioned in between the pilot's legs, using the armrests for bracing would be impractical (unless you have some really, really long forearms). So what most pilots do is rest their forearms on the top of their legs for stability. This creates that helicopter hunch body positioning.

Although this is the way it's done in real life, computer joysticks are not designed to be used in a between-the-legs position. Rely on one of the airplane bracing methods mentioned earlier instead. Again, even though you aren't faced with outside forces that affect your controller stability, bracing your hands will increase the precision of your controller movements greatly. Try it; you'll like it.

Graphics and Hardware Issues

One of the oldest quandaries about computer games and simulations is what many call the *look-and-feel* dilemma. Unless you're at the peak of the bleeding edge of computer technology or in the "hardware of the week" upgrade club,

you're forced to make the decision to fly simulators that either look good and feel bad, or feel good and look bad.

Fortunately, Flight Simulator 98 has some middle ground for those of us who don't have the fastest machines on the planet. We'll discuss how that works and why you have to make such choices in a minute. But if you have some extra money burning a hole in your pocket, let's look at some of the hardware options available to you.

Just as there is no such thing as being too sexy, having too much money, or having too much hard disk space, you can't have a computer that's too fast for Flight Simulator 98 either. Any additional computing power you may have (or dream of having) can be turned into higher-resolution graphics. While most of you won't have to face such problems, Flight Simulator 98 supports two new hardware technologies that help minimize that look-and-feel dilemma we discussed earlier.

You may have heard the moniker MMX lately. MMX is a standard set of 57 CPU (Central Processing Unit—the brains of your PC) instructions that are specifically designed to manipulate and process video, audio, and graphical data efficiently. These instructions are oriented for the highly parallel, repetitive sequences often found in multimedia operations. Speeding up the processing of certain computer-intensive loops found in multimedia and communication applications enables the latest multimedia software—from audio to video to 3D graphics—to run faster on your PC.

Currently there are three CPU manufacturers that produce processors featuring the MMX instruction set: the Intel Pentium with MMX technology, the AMD-K6, and the Cyrix 6x86MX. All of these products feature Socket 7 compatibility, so you may be able to simply swap out your present Pentium or Pentium pin-compatible processor to an MMX version. But to find out for sure, you'll need to check with your system vendor or motherboard supplier.

The DirectX 5.0 specification includes Direct3D (D3D), and D3D is supported by all mainstream graphics board vendors. Therefore, Flight Simulator 98 will work with most 3D-accelerator cards out there through D3D. If this is all new to you, maybe we should back up a bit.

3D video accelerators are graphics cards or add-on daughter cards that work in conjunction with your existing video card to assist your CPU with displaying 3D graphics. To be more specific, to turn a mathematical model of 3D space into an image that your monitor can display (in 2D) is what is referred to as the 3D pipeline. The first stage of this 3D pipeline begins with the geometry engine.

The geometry engine performs three operations:

1. First it takes the mathematical model of the 3D scene and divides the descriptions of objects and surfaces into polygons. Most of the time the polygons of choice are triangles. This explains why this whole process is often called *triangularization*.

2. Next it performs various transformations on each polygon to reflect the user's viewpoint by rotating, sizing, and/or repositioning the triangles as necessary to make them appear correctly.

3. Finally, the geometry engine eliminates any polygons outside of the viewer's window of sight. This is known as clipping. (Rendering objects outside of the viewer's sight just wastes CPU processing power because the viewer wouldn't see it anyway.) Lighting effects are also applied at this stage as well. This processed information is now sent to the rendering engine.

The rendering engine is the second stage of the 3D pipeline. The information that's provided by the geometry engine is put through another series of operations so it can be drawn as a complete pixel-by-pixel 2D representation of the scene on your monitor.

What a 3D accelerator does takes place entirely in the rendering (or *rasterization*) stage of the pipeline. The 3D accelerators are designed to perform the millions of pixel-level calculations necessary to draw each frame, and offloading these tasks from the CPU frees it up to perform other tasks.

Some of the popular 3D video cards available today are based on the following 3D graphics chip sets:

Tip: *If you're installing a bunch of new hardware to fly Flight Simulator 98, do yourself a favor and install only one device at a time. Make sure it's working properly before installing the next piece of hardware. Adding too many things at once will just complicate troubleshooting if a device doesn't work properly.*

- 3Dfx Voodoo Graphics and Voodoo Rush
- ATI 3D Rage II+ DVD
- Cirrus Logic GD5464
- Matrox MGA 1164 SG
- Rendition's Verite V1000
- S3 ViRGE and ViRGE DX

3D capabilities (such as fog and haze effects), as well as overall D3D performance, vary from chip set to chip set and sometimes from manufacturer to manufacturer. So do a little shopping around before you put out your hard-earned cash for one of these cards. You absolutely must have D3D compatibility, but that's usually a given with most graphics cards. Regardless of what you buy, the performance gain over a 2D-only video card will be noticeable. You'll be able to run Flight Simulator 98 with more detail, while still enjoying the same or even better frame rates. As they say, your mileage may vary.

Setting Preferences

Preferences are, of course, almost always a matter of personal tastes. When it comes to Flight Simulator 98, what you want to get out of Flight Simulator can influence which preferences are preferable to your activities and hardware capabilities. Preference settings not only detail what you'll see and hear, but also how well they are seen and felt. Let's talk about exactly what that means.

Feel for Graphics

Everyone wants to run simulations at the highest resolution and at silky smooth frame rates, but the importance of graphics quantity and quality is dependent on what you plan to do in Flight Simulator 98. If you're into looking around (sightseeing), you'll probably be willing to accept a loss in frame rate for prettier scenery. On the other hand, if you're into flying instrument approaches, you'll probably do without the scenery and favor faster instrument updates instead.

OK, new terms. *Frame rate* is a phrase that refers to the amount of times your screen (frame) is redrawn within a second. The faster your screen is redrawn, the smoother the animation/flight/scenery or whatever will appear. But when it comes to simulations, a low frame rate will affect how the simulation feels as well. For example, if screen updates are too slow, everything will be too choppy to fly comfortably. So again, if you're just into checking out the Grand Canyon in all its glory, you probably won't care if your altitude fluctuates from 200–300 feet every few seconds.

Microsoft Flight Simulator 98

Flights Aircraft World Options Views He

FRAMES/SEC = 16.3 +1.0 Gs

Shift + Z will cycle through the coordinate display and frame-rate counter.

When you get down to it, this is another subjective area that can only be left to personal preferences. What's comfortable for one person may not be comfortable to another. So the best we can do is offer some guidelines.

Anything you do to the Flight Simulator display settings will affect your graphics performance. This includes the amount of detail set, screen resolution, traffic, weather, number of windows, and window sizes. If you're after flying instead of sightseeing, what you want is a detail and resolution setting that makes your airplane feel instantly responsive and is able to update your instruments smoothly and instantly. If your system isn't able to keep up with your current detail and resolution settings, you'll always be "playing catch up" and you'll never fly your aircraft well.

Although people have different opinions on the subject, and faster is better, most people find that frame rates under 15 frames per second are too choppy for serious flight. Flight Simulator has a frame-rate display that can help you determine what your tolerances are and can assist with your graphics detail balancing. Pressing Shift + Z on your keyboard will cycle through the coordinate display and frame-rate counter in the upper left corner of your current window. Now that you know what you want, let's take a look at what you can change to reach your goals.

Display Preferences

Display Preferences are global settings. Changes made here will affect all fight situations.

To access the Display Preferences window:

1. Click on Options menu selection.

2. Select Preferences from the drop-down menu.

3. Click on the Display tab.

As mentioned earlier, display options affect graphic performance. If you're not too keen about setting your own graphics options at this point, the drop-down box labeled Performance Mode at the top of the window lists some suggested configurations that can, at the very least, get you in the ball park. From there you can tweak your settings (cross-checked with the frame-rate display) to match your needs.

Basically, there are three criteria used in the suggested configurations: machine type, performance preference, and graphics resolution. Here are some

recommendations and suggestions to aid in your quest for graphics perfection:

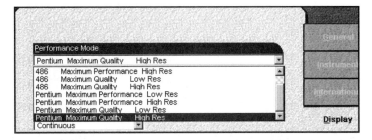

The Performance Mode drop-down box lists some suggested configurations based on machine type, performance preference, and graphics resolution.

- Begin your selections based on your machine type or lower.
- Select Maximum Performance for more serious flying and Maximum Quality for sightseeing.
- Choose between High Res and Low Res based on frame-rate preferences.

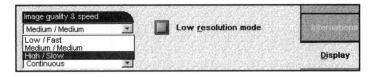

Image Quality & Speed controls the size of some terrain textures and the distance at which objects begin to blur.

If you decide after flying around a bit that the suggested configurations require the personal touch, the first place to start depends on what you think needs changing. The Image Quality & Speed drop-down box, located below the Performance Mode box, controls the size of some terrain textures and the distance at which objects begin to blur. (Textures are pictures that are laid over objects to give the illusion that they're actually made of that material or to add the appearance of architectural objects such as doors and windows. They are also used to provide markings on aircraft and other vehicles.) Naturally, the higher the image quality, the lower the speed.

The Low Res mode box is self-explanatory—check the box for Low Res mode, and un-check it for High Res mode. Low Res is more conducive to faster frame rates but produces much more jagged objects and blockier graphics.

Click on the Display Options button to view the display options you have available to you. There are four tabs in the Display Options sub window: Aircraft, Map, Scenery, and Hardware Acceleration. We'll leave the Map options until we talk about navigation, but in the meantime, we'll cover the Aircraft Scenery and Hardware Acceleration options because they all affect

The Las Vegas strip in Low Res mode.

The Las Vegas strip in High Res mode.

the level of your graphics performance.

Aircraft Display Options are as follows:

Aircraft Textures: If you have this option disabled, all aircraft will be devoid of any markings such as stripes or numbers, and while in Virtual Cockpit mode, you'll lose the cockpit interior as well.

See Aircraft Shadows: This only applies to your aircraft shadows. Other than looking a bit odd from external views, there's little reason to keep this on other than for aesthetics. But if you see a performance hit when shadows appear, just turn it off. You probably won't miss it because, unless you fly from external views near the ground or fly extreme banking maneuvers or dives near the ground, you'll hardly ever see your shadow.

See Own Aircraft From Cockpit: This option removes the interior and exterior of your airplane from all of your views in Cockpit view and Virtual Cockpit view. If you have this toggled off, you won't be able to see your propeller from inside the aircraft if you have the next option enabled.

See Propeller: This option makes your propeller invisible while in Virtual Cockpit view and in all external views. This option probably falls in the category of "eye candy," since it doesn't really add to the scenery and it doesn't help your performance as a pilot either. Then again, if you don't see a performance hit when your propeller is visible, there's little reason to turn this off.

The next set of Display Options we should talk about are found on the Scenery tab. It's a good assumption that the more of these options you enable, the more CPU power would be required to handle them. But in reality, just as we've seen with the other Display Options, if you don't see the subject of the option, enabled or not, you won't notice any performance change.

Tip: *Anytime you adjust any display options on the Display Preferences window or any of the Display Options sub-windows, the Performance Mode box will automatically switch to read User Defined.*

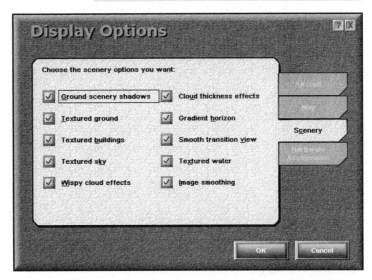

There's often a trade-off between complexity of the scenery and program performance. Here's where you determine the complexity of those backgrounds.

The Scenery tab contains the following options:

Ground Scenery Shadows: If you're sightseeing, this is a nice option to have enabled. But if you're flying for other reasons and need to gain some extra frames, turn this off.

Textured Ground: This option is a big CPU hog. On the other hand, the ground is really ugly without it.

Textured Buildings: Turning this option off makes buildings look like colored boxes. You'll lose all windows and doors. Unless you're flying near a city, you won't gain much with this option turned off.

Textured Sky: If you disable this option, you'll lose the ability to toggle the next two options on and off. Sky textures probably should have been named cloud textures. Turning this option off can gain you a lot of extra frames if there are clouds in the area to be seen, but the penalty is your clouds will now look like big blocks of color in the sky.

Wispy Cloud Effects: These are nice effects, but they don't add much more than a flashing effect as you fly through clouds. On the plus side, they don't require a lot of CPU power.

Cloud Thickness Effects: Without this option enabled, flying through thick clouds seems like someone turned down the lights. Enabling this option makes flying through clouds more realistic.

Gradient Horizon: This option adds the haze out on the horizon, but only if there is no cloud cover to block your view. In other words, unless you have a clear sky, you'll never see the gradient. The effect makes the view look less artificial, and the frame-rate penalty is pretty small. Unless you have a relatively low-powered computer, there's no reason to turn this off.

Smooth Transition View: This option affects the way you view the transition from Tower view to Spot view. When this option is disabled, you'll see a real cinematic style fly-by back to the exterior of your aircraft. When it's enabled, you'll just speed through the process; if you're far enough away, you'll only see some colors flash by. The Smooth Transition view setting doesn't really have anything to do with frame rate because you do your flying when you're actually in one of the views and not during the transition. But if it takes too long to cycle through Tower view to Spot view, turn it off. (To cycle between Cockpit view, Virtual Cockpit view, Tower view, and Spot view, press the S key.) Note that this option will be noticeable only if the distance between your aircraft and the tower is far enough to warrant a difference in transition speed.

Textured Water: As the option name suggests, this option enables water textures. By now you probably realize that unless there's water to be seen, this option will have no effect on your graphics performance.

Image Smoothing: This option smoothes out the terrain texture maps and makes them look less blocky.

The last set of Display Options we'll talk about in this chapter are found on the Hardware Acceleration tab. This tab contains the options pertinent to 2D and 3D graphics accelerators.

The Hardware Acceleration tab contains the following options:

Fullscreen Device: Flight Simulator 98 can be run inside Windows 95 as a regular Windows application or in Fullscreen mode. You can toggle between both modes using Alt + Enter. Because some 3D accelerators do their magic only in Fullscreen mode, this drop-down box allows you to choose the device you'll use while in Fullscreen mode. If you don't have a 3D accelerator, you won't need to change this option.

Fullscreen Mode: This drop-down box allows you to choose the screen resolution Flight Simulator 98 will use when you run in Fullscreen mode. Be aware that the higher the resolution you run, the slower your frame rate will be. Note that you don't need to have a 3D accelerator card to take advantage of this feature.

Enable Hardware Acceleration: Unless you have a 3D card, you won't be able to toggle this option on. This allows you to choose whether or not Flight Simulator 98 will use your 3D accelerator card for graphics rendering.

Reset: The Reset button restores all of the default settings for this configuration window.

Filter Texture Maps: This option smoothes out ground and building textures. Most 3D cards can handle this with minimal degradation, but only experimentation will tell for sure what will happen on your system.

MIP Mapping: MIP (multim in parvum) Mapping is a method of enhancing the illusion of depth by using several different resolutions of an object's texture to represent the distance of an object. Whether or not you'll want to enable this option depends on your 3D card's performance and capabilities. If performance degrades excessively when it's enabled, you'll probably want to turn it off.

Sound Preferences

Sound Preferences won't affect your graphics performance as much as the settings made in Display Preferences. Depending on the speed of your computer, you may need to tinker with Sound Preferences. Sound Preferences settings are also globally applied, but the choice of whether to hear any sounds

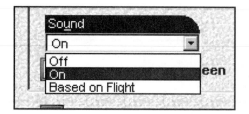

The three sound selections (Off, On, and Based on Flight) are configured on the General Preferences tab under Start Up options.

at all (that is, totally on or totally off) is situation-based. Because this overall sound setting is saved when you save a flight, you have the option of using, ignoring, or overriding this setting. Let's talk about that first before we get to Sound Preference specifics.

All sounds can be toggled on or off by pressing the Q key on your keyboard. On the General Preferences tab (click Options and then select Preferences), Start Up Options has a drop-down box in the middle of the window named Sound. From this drop-down box you can choose from three sound selections: Off, On, and Based on Flight.

The Off selection disables all sounds by default. This means any time you start Flight Simulator 98, you will not hear any sounds regardless of the sound state saved in the saved flight. Conversely, On enables all sounds regardless of whether sounds were enabled or not. The Based on Flight option sets overall sound to the saved flight settings. There are two points you should note:

An aviation mixing board? Flight Simulator 98 lets you shape the game sounds to your liking.

pressing the Q key will override any of these settings, and turning the sound Off in the Start Up options will not disable the sound in the opening introduction film.

OK, let's get back to Sound Preferences. To access the Sound Preferences tab, click No Options on the menu bar and then click on the Sound Tab. On the left side of the Sound Preferences window there are five categories of sounds that you have control over. Directly to the right of each is a volume slider control. To disable a particular group of sounds, just un-check the appropriate

box. To adjust the volume of each sound group, slide the corresponding volume control bar. High increases the sound volume, and low decreases it.

The five sound groups and what they encompass are:

Engine: This only affects the sound of your engine. It can come in handy for those really long cross-country trips.

Cockpit: Cockpit sounds include stall warnings and message beeps while in multiplayer mode. You'll probably want to keep this one enabled since both stall warnings and message beeps are pretty important. The only thing you may want to adjust here eventually is the volume.

Environment: The Environment group of sounds includes crashes, splashes, landing skids, and bumps. Although these sounds may not seem to serve any purpose other than to satisfy some warped, sadistic motives, they can help you. Well, maybe not the crash and splash stuff, but knowing when your wheels actually touch the ground during a landing through an audio cue can only help you with situational awareness.

Navigation: Sounds are limited to radio navigation such sounds as marker beacons for ILS landings. You definitely want to keep this enabled.

Adventures: If you disable these sounds, you'll really be missing a treat. This option enables the ATC (Air Traffic Control) radio instructions and co-pilot voices.

Windows, Windows, and More Windows

Although we've covered how the graphics and sound configurations affect system performance, there is still one aspect of the graphics picture we've yet to cover. By now we know that graphics performance is directly related to what is displayed, how much is displayed, and the quality of the image being displayed. (We'll cover Dynamic Scenery and Weather and how they affect graphics performance in later chapters.) The last three graphics performance qualifiers we should discuss are the size of the display, the number of displays, and the view itself. Let's begin with displays.

Maybe we should start at the beginning. The term *window* can be very easily confused with several things in Flight Simulator 98. You may have to read through this several times before it makes sense, but see if you can follow this.

Microsoft
Flight Simulator 98

Flight Simulator 98 is a Windows 95 (the operating system) program that runs either on the Windows desktop (operating system) in a window (a graphical bordered box—and in this instance with a title bar and menu bar) or Fullscreen. This is the same regardless of whether Flight Simulator 98 is run Fullscreen and windowed (same graphical box), Flight Simulator 98's views (cockpit, Virtual Cockpit, tower, and spot views) and instrument panels as windows (other graphical boxes) too. So in essence, when you run Flight Simulator 98 in a window (on the Win95 desktop), you are also running windows (instrument panels and views) inside the Flight Simulator 98 window.

> **Tip:** *The Flight Simulator 98 main window size and position is global, but view and map windows (docked or undocked) are situation based. On the other hand, instrument panel windows are neither global or situation based when they're undocked, but they'll remain wherever you put them throughout your session. But when they are docked, they behave like situation-based windows.*

Size Matters

Each of the windows we've discussed (other than the operating system itself) conforms to general Win95 conventions. You can move them to another position by dragging them with your mouse or resize them by dragging the corner or side of the window. OK, first concept: the size of every window will affect graphic performance. The larger the window, the lower your frame rate. This effects results from the resizing of the main Win95 window to the view and instrument panel windows. Unlike what we've seen before, it doesn't matter if the instrument window covers your view window. The size of the windows themselves dictates the performance penalty. Therefore, when you're setting up new views, it's best not to use a large view window if half of it

An improvement over the real thing: Flight Simulator 98 gives you access to multiple views, including how your plane looks from the closest tower.

is going to be covered by the instrument panel window.

Window-Mania

The next concept has to do with the number of windows being drawn. The physical number of windows will also decrease your frame rate. Naturally, the more windows you have to draw, the less computing power will be available for each individual window. So to keep graphic performance up, the rule of thumb is to

The toggle to disable the restoring of window positions when you load saved flights is located on the Flight Options Preferences tab.

use as few windows as possible for your requirements. Of course, different flying activities require different viewing strategies. (We'll talk more about that in a minute.)

A new feature in Flight Simulator 98 is multiple undockable windows. What this means is view and instrument windows (the windows inside the Flight Simulator window) can be *undocked* from the main Flight Simulator window and placed elsewhere on your desktop.

To Undock a window:

1. Right-click on the view or panel window you want to undock.

2. Select Undock Window from the pop-up menu that appears.

To Redock an undocked window:

1. Right-click on the undocked window you want to redock.

2. Re-select Undock Window from the pop-up menu to remove the check mark next to it.

To close an undocked window:

1. Right-click on the undocked window you want to close.

The Cockpit view of a Cessna Skylane 182S.

2. Select Close Window from the pop-up menu.

   or

1. Click on the Close box on the upper right corner of the window.

However, just as we were able to override saved sound settings in saved flights, we can do the same with window positions. The place to toggle off Load With All Flights Window Positions is found under the Options menu heading, Preferences selection, on the Flight Options tab.

You can save, view, and map window sizes and positions with saved flights. There is one catch, though. Full-screen views of view or map windows (obtained by pressing the W key) cannot be saved. The only way to save a full-screen window is to enlarge the window itself manually by dragging it open with your mouse. This is because the Save Flight option only saves window sizes.

Undockable windows are a neat feature, but don't get carried away, creating too many windows. Not only can it become confusing, but also frame rate can drop to unacceptable levels very quickly.

Window with a View

Now that we've got the window and view definitions out of the way, we can talk about how to set them up. You have several view choices in Flight Simulator: the Cockpit view, the Virtual Cockpit view, the Tower view, the Spot view, and the Map view. As mentioned earlier, views are the final graphics performance factor. Each view requires different levels of computing power, so the views you use will affect your frame rate.

View Descriptions and Recommendations

View	Benefits	Drawbacks	Good for	Not as good for
Cockpit—the standard cockpit views (front, left, right, and rear)	Quick switching between views	Not as impressive as Virtual Cockpit view	Everything	
Virtual Cockpit—seamless 360 degree rendering of the cockpit	Good sensation of flight	Instruments don't work, needs lots of CPU power, slow scrolling views	Thrillseeking and sightseeing	Instrument flying
Tower View—external fixed view of your aircraft from the nearest control tower	Unique view	Difficult to fly, can't fly far from tower	Simulated radio-control flying and viewing aerobatics	Instrument flying, cross country flying, or realism
Spot View	Great views of your aircraft for screen shots and sightseeing	No instruments and unrealistic point of view	Sightseeing, aerobatics, and arcade-like flying	Instrument flying, long distance cross-country flying, or realism
Map View	You can see great distances all around you	No instruments and nearly impossible to fly from	Navigation and sightseeing	Flying

Which views you should use really depends on the type of flying you intend to do. There are no hard and fast rules about this, but nevertheless, some recommendations are listed above in the View Description and Recommendations table.

To create and configure a view window:

1. Press the [key. This will open a new window.

2. Right-click on the new window and select Cockpit view, Virtual Cockpit view, Tower view, Spot view, or Map view from the pop-up menu.

3. Once the new view window is created, you can drag it where you want and resize it by dragging an appropriate window border or corner with your mouse.

Tip: *If you need a little more room in the main Flight Simulator 98 window, bring up the pop-up menu with a right mouse click, and select Hide Menu Bar. To temporarily access the menu bar while it is hidden, just press the Alt key.*

Control Commands

Action	Keystroke
View Front	Shift + keypad 8
View Rear	Shift + keypad 2
View Left	Shift + keypad 4
View Right	Shift + keypad 6
View Left Front	Shift + keypad 7
View Right Front	Shift + keypad 9
View Left Rear	Shift + keypad 1
View Right Rear	Shift + keypad 3
View Straight Down	Shift + keypad 5
Pan Up	Shift + Backspace
Pan Down	Shift + Enter

The Tower view is only clear near the airport, naturally.

You can alter the orientation of views by using the commands listed in the Control Commands Table.

View Configuration Recommendations

Just when you thought there couldn't possibly be anything else to say about view windows, there's one final aspect we should discuss—view placements. As always, everyone's got his or her own way of doing things, but if you don't know where to start, here are some suggestions. Start with one of these setups and fly around a bit with it. After a short time, you'll probably see something you'll want to change. Now that you're equipped with the knowledge of how things are done as well as the drawbacks, you shouldn't have any trouble making the *ultimate* viewing layout for your flying activities.

Sightseeing: Try the Virtual cockpit view without the instrument panel plus a smaller zoomed-out map window. If you run Flight Simulator in a window, try undocking the map window for maximum scenery viewing.

Instrument Training: Use the standard cockpit window plus the instrument panel. If graphics performance is a problem, try undocking the instrument panel and enlarging

it to your liking while
reducing the Flight
Simulator window
to as small a size
as comfortable.

Aerobatics: Use the
Cockpit view in a small
resized configuration with
two smaller additional
windows comprised of the
left cockpit view and the
right cockpit view.

Airplane Joyriding: Try
the Virtual Cockpit view
with See Own Aircraft
From Cockpit turned off.

Realistic Helicopter: Use
the Virtual Cockpit view
for maximum flight effect,
but keep the instrument
panel around. Just move it
into the position that you'd
see if you were really
sitting in the pilot's seat.
Use the non-functional
Virtual Cockpit instrument
panel as a reference. Don't
be afraid to pan the view
around if you need to.

Virtual Cockpit view.

Map view.

Aircraft Settings

The next (and final!) group
of preferences we need to cover before getting into any aircraft is Aircraft
Settings. Each of these settings are situation-based, so they are all retained with
saved flights. But just as there was an option for ignoring saved window
positions and sound when loading saved flights, you can set Flight Simulator to

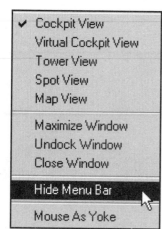

✔ Cockpit View
Virtual Cockpit View
Tower View
Spot View
Map View
Maximize Window
Undock Window
Close Window
Hide Menu Bar
Mouse As Yoke

Thanks to the Alt key, if you choose to hide the menu bar, it's out of sight but not out of reach.

Flight Simulator 98 presents you with much gorgeous scenery to enjoy. Here we're flying by France's most famous landmark: the Eiffel Tower.

ignore Aircraft Settings as well. The toggle for options is located on the same tab where we set Flight Simulator 98 to ignore saved window positions—the Flight Option Preferences tab under the Options menu heading.

We're not going to mess with all of the Aircraft Settings at this stage, but we should look at the main ones that'll help keep you in the air. Specifically, we want to look at the Realism tab, Reliability tab, Crash / Damage tab, and Instrument Displays tab. We can leave the rest for a more appropriate time.

To access the Aircraft Settings tabs:

1. Click on Aircraft menu selection.

2. Select Aircraft Settings from the drop-down menu.

Realism Settings

The first tab we want to look at is the Realism tab. At the top of the Realism window is a Flight Realism slider—one end is labeled Easy, and the other is labeled Real. As you may have surmised from the descriptions, Real is harder to fly. So where should you set this?

There are two schools of thought on this subject. One says, "In the real world there is no easy slider. When you learn to fly, you have to fly the real thing whether it's hard or easy. If you can do it in real life with your butt on the line, you should be able to do it on a computer."

On the other hand, there are those who say, "In real life you have an instructor sitting next to you who can take over if things go wrong, but more importantly, can teach you by showing you how to do things. Most of you don't have that luxury at home (or work! Ah,

lunch hours...), so starting at a less realistic (easier) level is perfectly acceptable even if it may let you be a little sloppy in the flying skills department."

Who's right? That's up to you to decide based on what you want to get out of Flight Simulator 98. Whatever realism setting you choose, just make sure it's not so hard that you get frustrated. If you don't enjoy flying Flight Simulator, you won't fly it, and if you don't fly, you'll never get any better at it. Let's move on.

There are four check boxes on the Realism tab and an Altimeter Calibration dialogue box on the right. We'll leave the altimeter for a later chapter. For now, let's just talk about the four check boxes and what they do.

Auto-coordination: This feature is sometimes referred to as rudder coupling. Basically what it does is coordinates your rudder to work with your

You'll want to enable multiple views if you decide to perform some daring aerobatics.

Painstaking visual detail helps Flight Simulator depict the Vegas Strip.

Tip: *If you ever forget a key command, open the Customize Controls window and scroll through the commands. Every command and its corresponding keypress or controller action is listed there.*

ailerons when you turn. We'll go over this again in more detail later, but as far as this setting is concerned, the only advice that's for sure is not to disable this if you don't have a rudder control device. If you have rudder pedals, try disabling this option. You'll be able to do things that would otherwise be impossible.

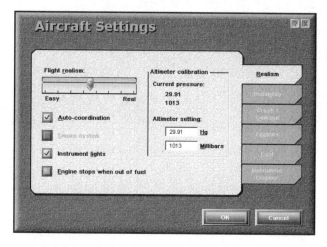

Joyride or educational tool? The flight Realism bar lets virtual pilots determine what they get out of Flight Simulator.

Smoke System: The Smoke System enables your aircraft to make smoke trails like the type seen in aerobatics exhibitions. You can toggle this on and off from the cockpit by pressing the I key.

Instrument Lights: You'll only need these at night, but you can toggle your lights on and off in the cockpit by pressing the L key for your navigation lights, Ctrl + L for your landing light, and the O key for your strobe lights. You can also toggle any of these lights on or off by clicking on the light switches on the cockpit instrument panel with your mouse.

Note: If you're flying the JetRanger helicopter, you have to accept no Auto-coordination.

Engine Stops When Out Of Fuel: It really doesn't matter how you set this option right now. If you're a new pilot, it's doubtful that you'll fly long enough to actually be in danger of running out of fuel.

Reliability Settings

The next tab down from the Realism tab is the Reliability tab. Because we're just starting, leave the slider all the way to the right for maximum reliability. You've got enough to worry about without having the extra strain of

mechanical failures. Lights
Burn Out and Gyro Drift are
both facts of aviation life, but
since we have the option, let's
leave these out of the loop until
you build up some flight time.

Crash/Damage Settings

Below the Reliability tab is the
Crash/Damage Aircraft Settings
tab. Although these options may
seem like another one of those
features designed to further
satisfy somebody's sadistic
inclinations, they're actually
quite handy. The top half of this
window is of particular interest

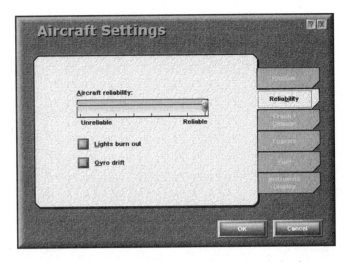

Newcomers would be well advised to make their planes
as reliable as possible.

for a new flyer. These three radio buttons allow you to choose how Flight
Simulator 98 will handle crashes.

The Crash options are:

Ignore Crashes: This setting allows you to continue flying no matter what you
hit. (You can still run out of fuel, for instance, if you've set that option.) If
you're a beginner and haven't earned your wings yet, consider using this
option—especially if your computer takes a long time to load or reset flights.
Sightseers and aerobatics thrillseekers will also find this setting useful.

Detect Crashes And Reset Situation: If you hit something with this setting,
you will crash. Then Flight Simulator will return you to the automatically saved
flight conditions and situation you were last flying in. This is a good crash
preference choice if you want to practice a maneuver over and over.

Detect Crash And Show Graph: This setting allows crashes just like the
Detect Crashes And Reset Situation option and will reset your situation in the
end, but it shows you a performance graph before it resets. This crash graph
illustrates the vertical velocities of your flight path just before your crash. Of
course you don't need this kind of information if you know you planted the
nose of your airplane in the ground, but if your airplane breaks apart on a hard

The Show Damage view gives a graphic representation of why an airplane should never try to tangle with a skyscraper.

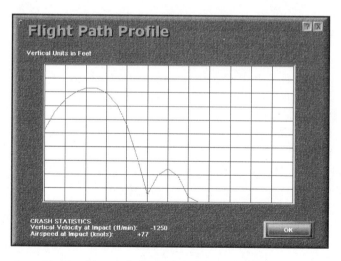

A graph like this can help you understand just what went wrong.

landing, looking at the information on a graph like this can help you determine where the landing went wrong.

Below the Crash options on the bottom of the Crash/Damage Aircraft Settings tab are the Damage options.

Aircraft Receives Damage From Stress: Enabling this option will allow you to overstress your aircraft by flying it outside of its design limitations. The most common way of doing that is by flying too fast or being too rough on the controls at high speeds. If you're flying Flight Simulator seriously, set this on. It will help you avoid learning bad habits. Otherwise, you can leave it off.

Show Aircraft Damage: OK, this option may seem like its just for perverse fun. Most believe there's little reason to watch a crash—you know when you crash, but this option does have some other value. By being able to view a crash from the outside, it can sometimes help you understand why you crashed or even what you hit. When you start pushing the envelope in some of the aircraft in Flight Simulator, there'll be times where you may hit something without ever seeing it coming.

Off-Runway Crash Realism: This option toggles the dectection of Off-Runway damage on and off. With it enabled, you'll no longer be able to taxi at high speeds anywhere other than on a runway or other suitable surface. If you don't like the fact that you won't be able to blaze new trails or go off-roading in your Learjet, leave this option disabled.

Crash When Hitting Dynamic Scenery: We mentioned Dynamic Scenery as another graphics performance factor a little earlier, but we didn't mention exactly what Dynamic Scenery is. Dynamic Scenery encompasses all of the mobile objects that you'll see in the Flight Simulator world. This includes ground traffic, boats, and other aircraft in the sky. Enabling this option will make Dynamic Scenery objects solid. This means they won't behave like ghosts and allow you to fly or taxi through them. Our suggestion is to enable this option. It's good for learning if you're a serious pilot, and it's more fun if you're not.

Engine Settings

Just as the name suggests, the Engine Settings tab controls your engine settings. In addition to the engine realism settings, this tab also controls engine functions as well. Let's talk about that first.

Across the top of the Engine Settings tab are four drop-down boxes labeled Engines 1 through 4. These are the magneto switch (mag switch) controls. You can set your magnetos (mags) in these drop boxes or while in the cockpit by pressing the M key followed by a plus sign or minus sign.

Just to give you a quick introduction, a magneto is a type of generator that operates

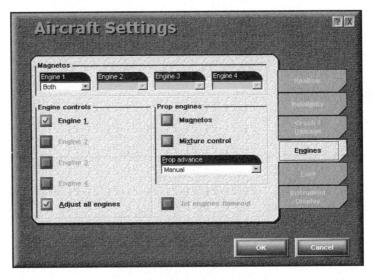

On this screen you can tweak any of your individual engines or all of them at once (via the Adjust All Engines button).

Note: *Only twin-engine aircraft are modeled in Flight Simulator 98.*

like the alternator on an automobile. When your engine is running, an alternator (and magneto in our case) generates electricity. The difference between the two is a magneto's job is to keep the engine's ignition system going (by powering the spark plugs), and an alternator is generally associated with charging systems to charge the vehicle's batteries. Batteries, in turn, power the vehicle's electrical systems.

An FAA-certified internal combustion aircraft is equipped with a double redundant magneto system and an alternator or generator as well. This way, if you have a battery and alternator failure, it will not affect your engine operation. We'll talk more about exactly what the mag switches do when we start flying, but for now just know:

- Where the magneto controls are.
- Magnetos only apply to internal combustion engines.
- Although there are four magneto boxes for four engines, there are only single-engine internal combustion aircraft modeled in Flight Simulator 98.

Below the Magneto controls on the left side of the Engine Settings window are the Engine Controls. Note that, according to the aircraft you're flying and the number of engines it possesses, anywhere from one to three of these engine-control check boxes may be grayed out.

To control an individual engine on a multi-engine aircraft, click on the corresponding engine box. To control an individual engine from within the cockpit, press the E key followed by the engine number you want to control. For example, to control engine 2, you'd press E + 2 on your keyboard.

At the bottom of the Engine Controls box is a check box labeled Adjust All Engines. If you enable this option, it will override any single-engine control setting you may already have, and this allows you to adjust all engines at once. To perform this same function from the cockpit, press E + 1 + 2 (in a twin engine aircraft) on your keyboard. Because we'll be flying a single-engine Cessna for training, the Adjust All Engines option is ineffectual.

To the right of the Engine Controls box is the Prop Engines settings box. Naturally, you'll only be able to access the options in this box if you're flying a prop airplane. Check boxes for Magnetos and Mixture Control are located here as well as a drop-down box for Prop Advance. Enabling the Magnetos and Mixture Control options will allow you to adjust them from inside the cockpit.

We'll be teaching you how to work these controls, so you'll probably want to enable these. There's no drawback to enabling these options even if you never fiddle with your mags or mixture controls.

As for the Prop Advance options, you have the ability to choose from Fixed Pitch, Manual, and Automatic. Although most trainers (training airplanes) have Fixed Pitch propellers, we'll be teaching you how to use the Manual selection. Which you choose to use is up to you, but in order to follow along with our flights, you'll need to set this to Manual. But the bottom line is that the difference between fixed and constant speed props (what the Manual setting is adjusting) is in performance. A constant speed prop is more efficient, but it requires more handling by the pilot. The Automatic setting gives you the best of both worlds.

Finally, at the very bottom right-hand corner of the Engines setting window is a check box labeled Jet Engines Flameout. Obviously this only applies to turbine-powered aircraft, but what it does is makes your turbine quit operation if you exceed 48,000 feet.

Fuel Settings

The Fuel Settings tab is where you can view your current fuel load and manage your fuel usage. At the top left corner is a check box labeled Manual Fuel Control, and directly to the right of it is a drop-down box labeled Fuel Selector. Now, depending on whether the Manual Fuel Control is checked or not will dictate whether you'll have access to the Fuel Selector control.

Manual Fuel Control allows you to manually switch your fuel supply

Aircraft Settings

Manual fuel control — Fuel selector

Fuel Weight Lbs/Gal: 6.6015

Fuel level

	%	Gallons	Pounds	Capacity
Left aux:	80	216	1429	269 Gal
Left:	98	176	1163	179 Gal
Center:	0	0	0	0 Gal
Right:	98	176	1163	179 Gal
Right aux:	80	216	1429	269 Gal

OK   Cancel

Having enough fuel (and knowing where to store it) is serious business. Through this screen, you can make whatever fuel allocations you like or choose to let the program handle then for you.

Off or to any fuel tanks available (whether they contain fuel or not). If you disable this Manual Fuel Control, Flight Simulator 98 will handle your fuel management duties.

The amount of fuel you can carry and the location and number of fuel tanks you have is dependent on the particular aircraft you fly. (The Schweizer sailplane carries no fuel.) Below the Fuel Control section of the Fuel Settings tab are gauges that list your current fuel situation. These readouts reflect the same exact numbers that your cockpit fuel gauges read, but these are easier to read than the small gauges on the instrument panel. In addition, they'll provide fuel remaining in total capacity percentages in gallons and by weight.

Regardless of how you measure the stuff, the amount of fuel you carry does not reflect all the fuel you can use. There are two numbers you should be aware of: total fuel capacity and total usable fuel. For example, the 182S has a 92 U.S. gallon total capacity, but it has a usable capacity of only 88 U.S. gallons. This stuff is good to know, lest you become a glider pilot unexpectedly!

Instrument Display Settings

There are actually two places where you can configure your instrument displays. One is the Instrument Display tab under the Aircraft Settings selection, and the other is back in the Preferences section. Since we're already here in the Aircraft Settings area, let's begin with that.

The check boxes and drop-down boxes in this window allow you to disable radios and instruments on a system-wide scale or on an individual indicator basis. The reason you'd want to willingly disable any of these would be for training purposes. Of course if you slid the Aircraft Reliability slide on the Reliability tab back to Unreliable, a random failure of one or more of your indicators or systems would happen eventually, but if training is your purpose, you can create your own failures. We'll talk about instrument and system failures in another chapter, but for now, just keep everything here enabled.

Instrument Preferences

Allow For Non-Rectangular Panel Windows: Some video cards don't display nonrectangular instrument panels efficiently. If you notice excessive degradation with this option enabled, disable it. All you'll lose is a corner or two of your external view when your instrument panel is displayed.

Allow Panel To Resize With Parent Window: When this option is enabled, your instrument panel will resize when you resize the Flight Simulator 98 main window, which isn't necessarily a bad thing. But if you don't resize the window in proportion to the original size, your instrument panel can end up looking pretty warped (literally!).

Indicated Airspeed: Absolutely keep this enabled. All performance numbers quoted in this book and in the Flight

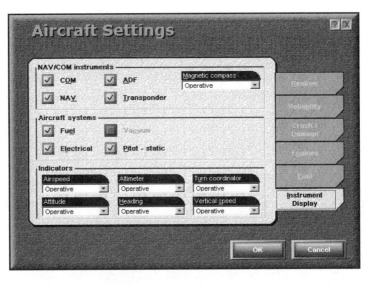

The Aircraft Settings screen serves as a mini-warehouse for a variety of plane functions.

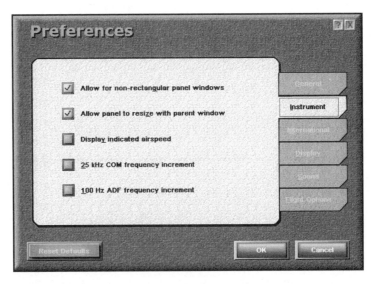

There's no end to the control that Flight Simulator 98 affords you—everything from customizing screen graphics to determining radio frequency increments.

Simulator 98 Pilot's Handbook and Help system are in Indicated Airspeed. We'll discuss why and when you may want to use true airspeed (what you'd get if you disabled this option) in subsequent chapters.

25 KHz COM Frequency Increment: COM is an abbreviation that refers to your COMmunications radio. Enabling this option will allow you to receive, send, and receive on 720 frequencies instead of 360 when this option is disabled. This is because you're dividing the frequencies within the band into smaller increments. Although the extra channels may sound like a boon, in practice the extra channels just require more keypresses to tune. That's because, if you fly in the U.S., you won't use the narrow frequency channels. If you fit into this category, do yourself a favor and leave this option disabled.

100 Hz ADF Frequency Increment: ADF is an acronym for Automatic Direction Finder. It's one of the radio navigation aids we'll talk about later, but the same effect we've discussed with COM frequency increments applies here as well. More channels equal more tuning. Unless you fly outside of the U.S., you won't need this option enabled.

Chapter Three

AVIATION CONVENTIONS

Simulators by nature are meant to mimic the real world. That's why many of the conventions used in the real world of aviation directly apply to the simulation world as well. We need to cover some of the basic conventions used in aviation so there's no question about what's being discussed. Flying is hard enough already without being confused about the terminology. While that's what this chapter is mostly about, we'll also discuss some aviation conventions that are good to know. We've got lots to cover, so let's get started.

Forces of Flight

There are four forces that act upon an airplane in flight: thrust, drag, lift, and weight. Here are some of the ways they interact:

- Thrust provided by the engine acts against drag.
- Drag decreases lift.
- Lift provided by the wings counteracts the weight of the aircraft.
- Gravity (weight) acts against lift.
- Lift creates drag.
- Drag counter-acts thrust.

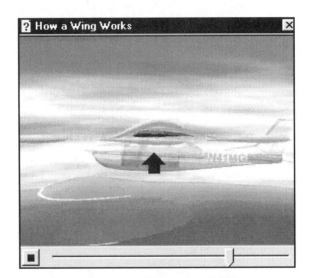

The Help files contain useful movie clips explaining forces such as lift.

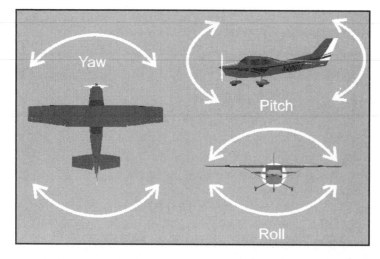

Yaw

Pitch

Roll

Aircraft maneuver along three axes—pitch, roll (bank), and yaw.

Flight Axes

All aircraft maneuver along three imaginary axes. These movements are known as *pitch* (turning about the lateral axis, with the front end rising and falling), *roll* (often referred to as *bank*, or rotating on the axis that extends from the nose of the aircraft through the tail), and *yaw* (turning about the vertical axis).

Spatial and Flight Relations

Spatial relations and flight relations are very important to understand for three reasons: collision avoidance, clarity, and efficiency. Although you have the option of whether you'll be flying alone in the skies of the Flight Simulator world (you have the choice of flying with other human Flight Simulator pilots over the Internet, LAN, and direct connect, or sharing airspace with computer-generated traffic), learning to recognize potential collisions is a valuable survival skill to develop. That's because colliding with the ground is every bit as dangerous as running into other aircraft.

With regard to our discussions, the other reason for understanding spatial and flight relations is so when you read or hear things like *8 o'clock low* or *off the port wing*, you'll understand exactly what they mean. Spatial relations are described in this manner because we don't have the luxury of saying "Hey, look over there!" and pointing a finger in that direction. It's just not precise enough. And from another practical standpoint, the "shout-and-point" method doesn't work in radio communications or while manually controlling instruments. Also, aviation lingo also sounds cool, so be prepared to learn some aviation-speak. We'll have you walkin' and talkin' like genuine pilots in no time!

Airplane or Boat?

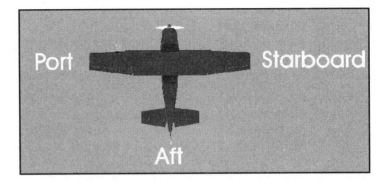

The left is known as port, right is starboard, and the rear is aft.

Although there's much speculation about why airplanes and boats have so much in common, the one theory that seems to make the most sense is that back during the early development of the airplane, the only form of relatively reliable navigation for relatively long ranges was the nautical system. (Another strong argument assures that many early aircraft were flying boats that sailed on water as well as in the air.) Whatever the reason, aviation is chock-full of nautical terminology.

Unless otherwise specified, relative positions are determined from one reference point: the pilot's sitting-in-the-cockpit position. Your left side is known as *port*, your right side is termed *starboard*, and the rear is called *aft*. An easy way to remember this is by recalling that the word *right* has more letters in it than the word *left*, and that the word *starboard* also has more letters in it than the word *port*. As for *aft*, just remember that "aft" comes *aft*-ter you.

The front of your aircraft is known as the *nose* (purely an aviation term), and anything in front of the aircraft is termed *forward*. Other nautical terms, such as *bow*, *stem*, and *stern* are not used in aviation.

Military and general aviation conventions describe external spatial relations using the metaphor of a clock.

Around the Clock

In military aviation, the convention for external spatial relations is to describe them using the metaphor of a clock. While there are no military aircraft in Flight Simulator, this convention has

made its way into general aviation. The way this works is to imagine yourself sitting in your airplane directly in the center of a giant imaginary clock, with the nose of your aircraft facing the 12 o'clock position. Directly to your right (off your starboard wing) would be 3 o'clock; directly aft is 6 o'clock; and directly off your port wing, 9 o'clock.

Determine the relative altitude of an aircraft by its relation to the horizon.

High-Low Do You Go?

We live in a 3D world and Flight Simulator is a 3D environment, so in addition to directional orientation, we need to consider *altitude*. The terms *low*, *high*, and *level* are simple enough to understand, but figuring out which is which is not nearly as obvious to the untrained eye. The way to tell the difference is by comparing the position of the object in relation to the horizon. To give you an example: if an airplane appears above the horizon, it is above you. If an airplane appears below the horizon, it's below you. But if an airplane appears level with the horizon—watch out! It's at the same altitude you are, and you may be in danger of colliding with it.

Range Rover

Whether or not an aircraft at your altitude is really a problem depends on the third dimension we've yet to discuss: range (or distance). If the distance between two aircraft at the same altitude is large enough, it makes the situation less urgent, but any aircraft within visual range should always remain high on your list of potential problems, regardless of its distance.

Unfortunately, unless ATC (Air Traffic Control) can advise you, the pilot-in-command (as we'll discuss later) of the other aircraft's distance, or unless your aircraft is equipped with collision-avoidance detection equipment (none of the aircraft featured in Flight Simulator are so equipped), you can only estimate the range of other aircraft. The rule of thumb for this is obvious (the bigger it is, the closer it probably is), but accuracy is something that only

> **Tip:** *Keep the nose of your airplane above the horizon or any object in front of you, and you won't hit it. That is, provided your airplane can supply sufficient power and lift to maintain its new course.*

experience can develop. In any case, the best advice is to remain alert and keep track of any aircraft within your visual range, regardless of its direction, altitude, or proximity.

Relative Flight Paths

What changes a *potential* collision situation into an *impending* collision situation is whether the aircraft in question increases its ability to collide with you. This can happen only if your relative flight paths converge. Airplanes move pretty fast, and the closer your two aircraft are to each other, the less time either of you will have to react. So how can you determine your relative flight paths?

The way that most people can tell which way an airplane is heading is by watching its path in the sky. The other way you can tell is if you can visually make out the shape of the airplane. You know that airplanes fly forward (unless the airplane in question is an AV-8B Harrier JumpJet—but you're unlikely to see many of those in Flight Simulator), so if you can distinguish where the nose of the other plane is, you can pretty much figure out that airplane's direction of travel.

You know what your present course is, but if the other aircraft only looks like a dot in the sky, it's difficult to tell its flight path by its orientation. The way you can tell whether another aircraft is heading directly for you is by its relative motion. If you can see it moving in relation to your cockpit window, you're not in immediate danger of collision. But if the other aircraft remains in the same relative position, it's headed either directly toward you or directly away from you. When faced with such a situation, it's always best to assume the worst.

The way to handle this type of situation is to change your heading and see whether the other aircraft starts moving in your window. The usual rule of

You can tell whether another aircraft is heading directly for you by its relative motion.

thumb is to turn away from other aircraft. This accomplishes two things: the maneuver will put some more distance (or reduce the closure rate) between your two aircraft and you'll show the other aircraft a larger section of your aircraft (of course, this only applies when you're sharing the sky with a human pilot, not a computer-generated one that's part of the Flight Simulator program). By turning away from the other aircraft, you'll show them the underside of your wing as you turn. Many collisions and near misses are the result of one pilot simply not seeing the other aircraft. By showing the other aircraft your wing, you actively work to get the attention of the other pilot.

Navigation Lights

Because of the darkness, most people believe that collision avoidance becomes a little more difficult at night. Well, actually it isn't all that clear. If you're new to flying, the collision benefits or hazards of night flying won't become an issue for a while because you'll probably want to stick to flying in the daylight until you perfect some of your flying skills. Nevertheless, we should discuss navigation lighting so when you do make your first night flights you'll know what to watch for.

The conventions governing aircraft lighting are another one of those carry-overs from the nautical world. The term *navigation lights* refers to any of the marker lights found on an airplane or ship. Airplanes have a single red light on the port wing and a single green light on the starboard wing, as well as one white light mounted on the top of the tail. Finally, there are also anticollision lights. Those are the super-bright flashing strobe lights that you see in the sky at

night when airplanes fly by.

Anyway, even though you can't determine the orientation of another aircraft from its shape in the sky, navigation lighting can help. You can tell which way an aircraft is heading based on the relation of its navigation lights to each other. For instance, if you see a red light on the left, a white light in the middle, and a green light on the right, you know that the airplane in question is flying away from you. But on the other hand, if you see a red light on the right and a green light on the left with little or no white light (generally, the white light should be visible only from the rear), the airplane is heading toward you. This isn't to say it's coming directly at you, but it *is* headed in your general direction...so you should remain alert.

The relation to each other of its three visible navigation lights can determine which way an aircraft is heading.

Tip: *A good way to remember what to look for at night is to remember the phrase, "Red, right-returning." This means that if you see a red light on the right, the aircraft is returning toward you.*

Numbers and Letters

If we're going to learn to fly by the numbers, we should talk about some aviation numbers. OK, that probably sounds a bit odd, since numbers are numbers. Read ahead, though, and you'll understand.

Navigation and Runway Numbering

There are three methods of navigation used in general aviation: (1) *pilotage*, or flying by reference to landmarks; (2) *dead* (or *deduced*) *reckoning*, which relies upon calculations based on maps, headings, ground speed, wind, and time; and (3) *radio navigation*, which makes use of radio aids. (There is a fourth type of

navigation called *celestial navigation,* but it isn't used much, if at all, anymore.) All three methods use directional headings based roughly on the magnetic compass. Note the word *roughly.* Without going into any details about deviation error, turning errors, and acceleration/deceleration errors, it should suffice to say that magnetic north (the N at which your compass needle points) and true north in most places around the world are not one and the same. This phenomenon is known as magnetic variation.

Regardless of its quirks, there are 360 degrees on a compass, just as there are in a circle. When it comes to aviation navigation, north corresponds to 360 degrees, east is 090, south is 180, and west is 270. Notice that three digits are used to represent compass directions (or *headings,* as they're more commonly referred to). When headings are pronounced, they are recited as three separate digits rather than as a whole number. For instance, 360 would be voiced as *three-six-zero* rather than *three hundred and sixty,* and 090 would be pronounced *zero-niner-zero* instead of just *ninety.* (We'll get to the *niner* bit shortly.)

Runways are numbered based on the direction used for takeoff and landing. For instance, if a runway runs north and south, this means when we're taking off and landing facing northbound, we'd call it runway 36 and when we're taking off and landing facing southbound we would call it runway 18. It's the same runway, of course, but the change in designation indicates your direction of travel. The runway number designations correspond with the compass headings minus the last digit. In other words, runway 18 would correspond to heading 180 (south). By the way, although 36 and 00 technically both mean north, 00 is not used for runway designations.

Next, if more than one runway were oriented in the same direction, the runway would be labeled as runway 16 Left and runway 16 Right (the 16 being an arbitrary example, of course). One final point of interest is that if you add the two digits of a runway designation, the total will add up to the total of the two-digit designation from the other end of the runway. For example, runway 09 (eastbound) and runway 27 (westbound) each add up to 9. What value is there to this bit of trivia? It's just one of many ways to help you figure out reciprocal headings, which we'll get to later.

Walk a Mile

The next sets of numbers we need to consider are speed and distance numbers. A statute mile is 5,280 feet. A nautical mile, on the other hand, is 6,080 feet, which corresponds to one geographical minute of latitude (or longitude at the equator). Although people in the U.S. use statute miles for ground navigation, in the air and on the sea, nautical miles are used.

Airspeeds in Flight Simulator (and for all aircraft manufactured after 1976) are reported in KIAS (Knots Indicated Airspeed). Flight Simulator, however, has a feature that displays your aircraft's speed in KTAS (Knots True Airspeed) or just TAS (True Airspeed in MPH). We'll discuss the difference between these three measurements in the next chapter. What's important to understand now is that one knot equals one nautical mile. It's a common misconception that the "K" in KIAS stands for kilometers. It does not; one kilometer equals 3,280.84 feet. Feeling thoroughly confused? Don't be—just remember that everything in aviation is in knots/nautical miles. The only practical exception in Flight Simulator is the Airspeed Indicator of the Schweizer 2-32 sailplane. It was manufactured in 1962 and displays MPH.

Altitude

Just as with anything else, a measurement of something must be in relation to something else. You're probably aware that altitude refers to an airplane's height in the air, understanding that in terms of "ground" altitudes—that is mountains, buildings, and so on.—can mean the difference between crossing over a mountain ridge safely or creating a smoking hole in the ground.

Aviation uses two forms of altitude measurements: absolute altitude and true altitude. Absolute altitude is the height above the surface or AGL (Above Ground Level), and true altitude is your height above mean sea level (MSL). We'll talk about this again a little later, but you should note that although the altimeter readings in Flight Simulator's airplanes are supposed to be based on MSL, their *indicated* altitudes are not correct unless your altimeter has been adjusted to reflect current atmospheric conditions.

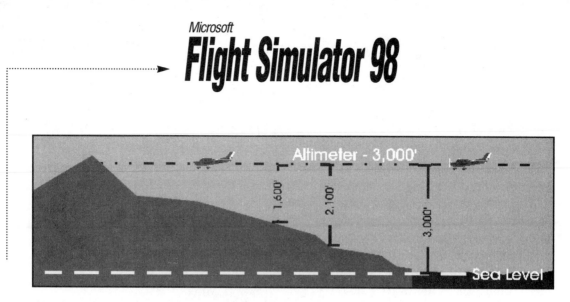

Absolute altitude is the height above the surface of the earth or AGL (Above Ground Level), and true altitude is your height above mean sea level (MSL).

Cruising Altitudes

FARs (Federal Aviation Regulations) on VFR (Visual Flight Rules) cruising altitudes require that aircraft flying 3,000 feet or higher above the surface must fly at odd-numbered thousands-of-feet plus 500 feet, if their magnetic course is between 0 and 179 degrees. Conversely, planes whose course falls between 180 and 359 degrees are required to maintain altitudes at even-numbered thousands-of-feet plus 500 feet. What this means is if you're flying on a heading of 265 degrees and you want to cruise above 3,000 feet, the first cruise altitude available for you to fly at is 4,500 feet.

IFR (Instrument Flight Rules) cruising altitudes require that aircraft flying below 18,000 feet MSL must fly at odd-numbered thousands-of-feet if their magnetic course is 0 to 179 degrees and even thousands-of-feet if their magnetic course is 180 to 359 degrees. This means under IFR, if you're flying on a heading of 265 degrees, and you want to cruise above 3,000 feet, the first cruise altitude you can fly at is 4,000 feet.

Flight Levels

Altitudes 19,000 feet and above are called flight levels. This convention removes the last two zeros from the altitude and adds *flight level* to the beginning of the description. In other words, 19,000 feet would be listed as FL190 or spoken as "flight level one-niner-zero". Cruising altitudes 18,000 feet and above are handled as follows:

- VFR cruising altitudes that are above 18,000 feet MSL but below FL290 must fly at odd thousands-of-feet plus 500 feet if their magnetic course is 0 to 179 degrees. For headings between 180 and 359 degrees, flights must be maintained at altitudes of even-numbered thousands-of-feet plus 500 feet.
- IFR cruising altitudes above 18,000 feet MSL (Mean Sea Level) but at or below FL290 must fly at odd-numbered thousands-of-feet if their magnetic course is 0 to 179 degrees and even-numbered thousands-of-feet plus 500 feet if their course is 180 to 359 degrees.
- VFR cruising altitudes above FL290 and on a magnetic course from 0 to 179 degrees require flying at odd-numbered thousands-of-feet at 4,000 foot intervals beginning at FL300, and even-numbered thousands-of-feet at 4,000 foot intervals for 180 to 359 degrees, beginning at

Note: *When flying above 18,000 feet MSL (transition altitude), the Federal Aviation Regulations (FARs) require that your altimeter be set to 29.92". This is to minimize altitude variations due to barometric change over the course of a flight. The lowest usable flight level is determined by the atmospheric pressure in that area of operation, as shown in the Atmospheric Pressure's Effects on Flight Levels table.*

Atmospheric Pressure's Effects on Flight Levels

Current Altimeter Setting	Lowest Usable Flight Level
29.92 /or higher)	180
29.91 through 29.42	185
29.41 through 28.92	190
28.91 through 28.42	195
28.41 through 27.92	200
27.91 through 27.42	205
27.41 through 26.92	210

To convert minimum altitude prescribed under Sections 91.119 and 91.177 to the minimum flight level, the pilot shall take the flight level equivalent of the minimum altitude in feet and add the appropriate number of feet specified below, according to the current reported altimeter setting:

Current Altimeter Setting	Adjustment Factor
29.92 (or higher)	None
29.91 through 29.42	500
29.41 through 28.92	1,000
28.91 through 28.42	1,500
28.41 through 27.92	2,000
27.91 through 27.42	2,500
27.41 through 26.92	3,000

intervals beginning at FL300, and even-numbered thousands-of-feet at 4,000 foot intervals for 180 to 359 degrees, beginning at

FL320. This means when flying eastbound, you can fly at FL300, 340, or 380. When flying westbound, you can fly at FL320, FL360, or FL400.

- IFR cruising altitudes above FL290 and on a magnetic course from 0 to 179 degrees must be flown at odd-numbered thousands-of-feet at 4,000 foot intervals beginning at FL290, and even-numbered thousands-of-feet at 4,000 foot intervals for 180 to 359 degrees beginning at FL310. This means when flying eastbound, you can fly at FL290, 330, or 370. When flying westbound, you can fly at FL310, FL350, or FL390.

Airport Traffic Patterns

Airport traffic patterns are covered in detail in Flight Simulator's tutorials and Help system. But here are a couple of points that may not be so obvious:

- All turns within traffic patterns are always made to the left unless visual markings or light signals specify otherwise.
- Pattern altitudes are generally 1,000 feet AGL unless otherwise specified. For large or turbine-powered aircraft over Class D, airspace pattern altitude is 1,500 feet AGL (except to meet cloud avoidance criteria).

> **Tip:** *To figure out pattern altitude, add the AGL height to the airport's elevation.*

- The term *abeam* (another nautical term) describes the relation of an object at right angles to your airplane. For example, the phrase "downwind abeam the tower" usually refers to being on the downwind leg of the airport traffic pattern with the control tower directly off your port wing (assuming a left-hand traffic pattern).

Time Flies

Like the military, the aviation world uses a 24-hour clock. Instead of the 12-hour clock times of a.m. and p.m. that we use in everyday life, the 24-hour clock is expressed in four digits. For example 7:15 a.m. is 0715 hours. The p.m. times on a 24-hour clock are the 12-hour clock time increased by 12 hours (that is, 3:15 p.m. is 3:15 + 1200, or 1515 hours).

Zulu Bugaboo

For navigational purposes, aviation time is also standardized to Greenwich Mean Time (GMT). This convention is also commonly referred to as *Universal Time* or *Zulu Time* (Z). The world includes many time zones, and a single time standard is supposed to eliminate confusion as you pass through them. In aviation, Zulu time is used for weather reports and forecasts. If you think about it, you may find this practice kind of silly. After all, the weather forecasts you listen to are local, so why shouldn't time be given as local time as well? Good question.

Zulu time requires a calculation to convert it into something you can use. Fortunately, the only situation where you'll see Zulu times in Flight Simulator is during weather reports given by ATIS. To convert local time to GMT, add the appropriate number of conversion hours to your local time. To convert GMT to local time, subtract the appropriate hours. GMT conversions for the United States are shown in the table below.

United States GMT Conversion Table

To Convert From:	To Greenwich Mean Time:
Eastern Standard Time	Add 5 hours
Eastern Daylight Time	Add 4 hours
Central Standard Time	Add 6 hours
Central Daylight Time	Add 5 hours
Mountain Standard Time	Add 7 hours
Mountain Daylight Time	Add 6 hours
Pacific Standard Time	Add 8 hours
Pacific Daylight Time	Add 7 hours

Phonetic Alphabet Soup

As the story goes, back in the early days of aviation when engines were really loud and the pilot sat exposed to the rushing, open air (and also when radios seemed like they broadcast as much static as they did signal), the phonetic alphabet was created. It was designed to help pilots understand what was being said while under the barrage of all that noise. Sometime between then

and now, the International Civil Aviation Organization (ICAO) endorsed the use of the phonetic alphabet to avoid confusion during radio communications.

Although you won't have those kinds of problems in Flight Simulator and you won't need to send any verbal messages, ATIS (Automated Terminal Information Service) broadcasts will use letters from the phonetic alphabet as weather report designations. Besides, if you're still wondering about that *niner* business from earlier in this chapter, this is where it came from.

ICAO Phonetic Alphabet

Character	Pronunciation	Character	Pronunciation
A	Alpha	S	Sierra
B	Bravo	T	Tango
C	Charlie	U	Uniform
D	Delta	V	Victor
E	Echo	W	Whiskey
F	Foxtrot	X	X-Ray
G	Golf	Y	Yankee
H	Hotel	Z	Zulu
I	India	0	Zero
J	Juliet	1	One
K	Kilo	2	Two
L	Lima	3	Three
M	Mike	4	Fo-wer
N	November	5	Five
O	Oscar	6	Six
P	Papa	7	Seven
Q	Quebec	8	Ait
R	Romeo	9	Niner

Chapter Four

On the Flightline

To quote General Chuck Yeager (Ret.), "There is no such thing as a natural pilot. Training is everything." Granted, we're not flying military prototype aircraft or fighters, but the general's sentiments remain valid. As some of you may have discovered already, if you have no previous aviation experience (real or simulated), you can't just hop into a Microsoft Flight Simulator 98 aircraft and expect to be Captain Perfection your first time up. It doesn't work like that.

Although there is no question that you can build flying skills through practice (and there is no substitute for practice), practice can only get you so far. Truly great piloting skills require a foundation of aviation knowledge. The Flight Simulator Pilot's Handbook and Pilot's Help system both do an excellent job of outlining what you need to know about the physics of flight. But you must bridge the gap between the physics of flight and how those concepts affect you as a pilot.

This chapter is about basic piloting concepts and skills. It's better to get these basic concepts out of the way now rather than overload yourself while you're in the air (when we should be talking about procedures instead).

Any way you look at it, you need to study *and* practice. You're the only one who can do anything about practicing, but you've already taken the first step—studying—by reading this book. Whether you practice flying or not, this chapter will improve your flying skills.

Situational Awareness

Situational awareness (SA) is a term that you hear many desktop fighter pilots refer to. For Flight Simulator rookies, the loss of SA is just as deadly as a bandit (enemy plane) shooting missiles or bullets. When experienced fighter simulatorjocks talk about SA, they are often referring to knowing where the bandits are around them. It is usually just taken for granted that the pilot knows his present flying attitude and where the ground is. Just because civilian pilots

By the Seat of the Pants

I've lost count of how many times I've heard some newbie flight simulator pilot complain that he or she loses SA because the simulation "doesn't actually move." This is a misconception. In the real world, new pilots tend to fly based on what they feel. One of the first lessons any good flight instructor will teach a student is how unreliable "seat-of-the-pants" flying really is.

From level flight, the instructor will have the student close his or her eyes while making some turns. The instructor will then fly the airplane in an attitude different from the one they were just flying in. He'll then ask the student to keep his or her eyes closed and bring the airplane back to level flight. I've yet to hear of a student who can do this.

Most people experience vertigo and will put the airplane into a slow, turning, shallow dive. Needless to say, if you continued to fly like this, you'd eventually crash into the ground. From this little exercise, you quickly learn rule number one—do not trust what you feel; trust your instruments. So, in actuality, not having a full motion simulator may be an advantage for simulator pilots. You learn to fly by instruments and overcoming the natural tendency to follow your seat.

I guess a saying that one of my flight instructors used to say really applies—"Fly with your head, not with your butt!"

The best way to learn SA is to thoroughly familiarize yourself with your instruments. The most in-depth way to learn your instruments is to practice flying while refering to instruments only. Learning to fly Instrument Flight Rules (IFR) is tough. The rules have a very steep learning curve, but the reward is a degree of situational awareness that most simulator fighter pilots only dream about. Even if you're not interested in seriously flying IFR, learning these skills will make you a better Visual Flight Rules (VFR) pilot.

don't have to worry about bandits doesn't mean they aren't any less true pilots than fighter pilots.

When compared to Flight Simulator pilots, fighter simulator pilots naturally enjoy some advantages that allow them to ignore the ground for longer periods of time than their unarmed cousins. Fighters usually fly at higher altitudes, they rarely fly in bad weather, and their aircraft usually boast an excess of power and maneuverability. If a fighter simulator jock gets into trouble, he can usually maneuver quickly enough and get back to worrying about those bogies.

In Flight Simulator you fly closer to the ground, you have to contend with bad weather, and you have to fly in aircraft that are notoriously (albeit realistically) underpowered, and not very maneuverable. If that doesn't sound challenging enough, consider that general aviation (GA) simulations generally focus on the most statistically dangerous aspects of flying—takeoffs and landings. As any real world or simulator pilot will tell you, SA is *everything*. No matter what type of simulator or aircraft you happen to be flying, the ground is a very worthy adversary—one that you don't want to run into!

Attitude Flying

Let's get this straight: attitude flying is not the same thing as flying around with a chip on your shoulder (i.e., flying with an *attitude*). It's not a reference to your emotional state while in the air. Attitude flying refers to the instrument known as the attitude indicator or artificial horizon.

Whether you're flying VFR or IFR, you should get into the habit of using the attitude indicator (AI) as the reference for every conscience movement of the flight controls (i.e., changing pitch or bank). This is exactly what *attitude flying*—or more descriptively "flying by the attitude indicator"—means.

Without getting into the natural reservations about trusting flight instruments right now, the primary reason for attitude flying is because the AI is the only instrument that gives direct information about the aircraft's attitude. The key word here is *direct*. You can interpolate your aircraft's attitude through the indications from other instruments, but the attitude indicator does not require any additional thought: what you see is what you get.

Attitude Indicator

The attitude indicator is one of the six basic flight instruments that comprise what is known as the standard instrument cluster. A standard instrument cluster is arranged in two rows of three instruments across and is comprised of:

- Attitude Indicator (AI)
- Airspeed Indicator (ASI)
- Altimeter (ALT)
- Vertical Speed Indicator (VSI)
- Turn Instrument (either Turn Indicator or Turn Coordinator)
- Directional Gyro (DG)

The AI is located in the center position of the upper row. This is perhaps the most prominent position of all your instruments, so that should serve as some indication of the AI's importance. Recall that the AI provides pitch and bank information. But it's important to note that a bank doesn't necessarily

Attitude Towards Flying

Although an airplane is a complex machine, each of its individual systems is really quite simple to operate. It's when you put them all together that you can easily reach pilot overload. The best advice is to take things at your own pace. If some options make flying too tough, then turn them off. Granted, you can't do that in real life, but in real life you have an instructor sitting next to you to help as you go along.

I suppose the bottom line is this: don't be stubborn about "realism." It's very difficult to progress if you're in over your head. You can turn off options in Flight Simulator, so take advantage of it. If your settings are beyond your skill level, you won't enjoy flying Flight Simulator, and if you don't fly, you'll never build your skills enough to advance to the level of full realism.

Being able to handle in-flight emergencies is also part of real world flight training, but even though your life isn't in danger in Flight Simulator, you'll still sometimes get sweaty palms. Handling in-flight emergencies is all part of the fun. (That probably sounds pretty warped, but if you've ever experienced it, you know what I mean.)

In any case, when you find yourself in an emergency, the number one rule is: don't panic! What you're after can be summed up by the phrase "cockpit cool." Getting through a bad situation is a satisfying reward in itself, but if you can do it while maintaining your cool on the outside, it just makes it that much sweeter.

indicate a turn, and a nose-high attitude doesn't necessarily mean that you're climbing. For example, during slow flight or landing descents, you can have a nose-high attitude even though you are not climbing.

Flight Simulator 98 models four different AIs. However different they may appear, they all work on the same principle and they all present the same information. First, every AI works on a property known as gyroscopic inertia, which is sometime referred to as "rigidity in space." AI readings are based upon the inertial frame of reference provided by a spinning gyroscope.

Understanding the AI

The first type of AI we'll talk about is known as a non-caging AI. The AI gyros used in most small aircraft *tumble* if the pitch attitude exceeds +/-70 degrees or if the angle of bank exceeds 100 degrees. This causes them to become useless for controlling the airplane. If you spin an airplane with a non-caging attitude indicator, it ends up spinning uselessly like a pinwheel. (This is one reason partial-panel unusual attitude recovery is a part of pilot training.)

Although Flight Simulator has no such problem with any of the modeled AIs (the Cessna 182RG, 182S, and the Bell 206B JetRanger all have non-caging AIs), the Extra 300 displays a caging AI. Even though the caging features of the 300's AI are non-functional (hence the word *displays*), basically a caging AI allows you to lock its position so you can perform your aerobatic maneuvers without causing your AI to go crazy.

The third and fourth AIs modeled in Flight Simulator are found on the Boeing 737-400 and the Learjet 45. Let's discuss some of the differences between these two AIs and the caging and non-caging AIs we just covered. First, these AIs feature electronic displays instead of the mechanical displays most GA pilots are used to seeing. The other thing they have in common is that instead of being run by an engine-driven vacuum pump like their caging and non-caging cousins, the gyros in the AIs of these two commercial aircraft are electric. It isn't really important to remember that now, but it will come in handy later when we talk about systems failures.

These electronic AIs also differ from each other in name. The 737's AI is referred to as Attitude Direction Indicator (ADI), while the AI in the model 45 is just an AI. Why the 737's AI is called an ADI is a bit baffling because it does not provide any directional information. Hence, we'll refer to it as an AI throughout the rest of this book.

Just as the name *artificial horizon* suggests, what's depicted in the AI corresponds with the horizon outside your cockpit windshield. An AI's *ground* is generally depicted as a dark color (black in the caging type, brown in the non-caging type, orange in the 737, and dark gray in the 45), and the sky is generally a lighter color (light gray, blue or green).

Across the top of the AI is an arc made of index lines pointing towards the center of the AI. This is known as the bank index. Each line represents a certain amount of bank attitude. The index mark in the 12 o'clock position (clock position—not spatial positioning, as described in Chapter Three) represents zero degrees of bank. Directly below it is the bank index pointer or *bank bar*, as it's sometimes called.

The two shorter index lines of the bank index to the left and right of the zero degree mark represent 10 degrees of bank each. The longer bank index lines represent 30-degree increments of bank. Naturally, if your bank index pointer points to the horizon line, it would indicate a 90-degree bank.

This is the non-caging AI found in the Cessna 182RG, 182S, and the Bell JetRanger.

The Extra 300 is equipped with this caging AI.

The Boeing 737-400's AI is called an Attitude Direction Indicator.

Note: *The Schweizer 2-32 and the Sopwith Camel are not equipped with AIs.*

The 737 and model 45 both have additional bank index marks representing 45 degrees of bank. On the 737, the 45-degree index is a medium length index line, and on the model 45 the same degree index is a small inverted triangle.

The electronic AI in the Learjet 45.

Pitch information on the AI is provided via the pitch index or pitch ladder. These are the horizontal lines that appear above and below the artificial horizon line (where the two colors of the artificial sky meet artificial ground—which is sometimes separated by a white line). Since the pitch pointers and indexes vary from AI to AI, let's talk about each of them individually.

The AI pitch pointer on the 737 is the small square dot in the center of the AI, combined with what can be described as two downward-facing capital letter "L's." When these lines and the dot rest on top of the orange AI ground, you are level. The shorter pitch bars (also referred to as pitch lines or *rungs*) represent 7.5 degrees of pitch. The longer rungs represent 15 degrees of pitch. Naturally, the pitch lines above the AI horizon indicate a pitch-up attitude (i.e. nose above the horizon) and pitch lines below the AI horizon indicate a pitch-down attitude (nose below the horizon).

In the model 45 AI, the pitch index pointers are the short yellow bars on the right and left center of the display and the wide arrow at the center. Each short pitch line represents 5 degrees of pitch and the longer lines represent 10 degrees of pitch. The way to use these pointers is to rely on the outside pointer bars for level flight, and line up the cut-out in the bottom of the arrow with a pitch line to establish the next higher line of pitch. In other words, to establish a 10-degree pitch climb, you'd line up the 5-degree pitch-up bar with the center cut-out of the arrow.

Both the caging and non-caging AIs have similar pitch index pointer and pitch bar layouts. The pitch index is a dot in the center of the AI and the two bars on either side of them. The color of the caging AI pointer is orange, and the non-caging version is white.

Pitch bars on either of these AIs are just reference marks and they are not meant to represent any specific degree of pitch. You're probably wondering why. It's rather difficult to explain at this point without first covering all of the other instruments first, but the short answer is: it's because GA aircraft climbs are made with reference to airspeed rather than reference to pitch or rate-of-

climb. This is because GA aircraft generally do have not enough power to maintain a climb solely by reference to pitch or rate, without causing concern that airspeed might become a problem.

Note: *The AI will not show level in the Extra 300 when sitting on the ground because that plane is a tail dragger and it sits nose up.*

Airspeed Indicator

We should consider the airspeed indicator (ASI) next. In a standard instrument cluster, the ASI is always located directly to the left of the AI. (There are some variances in Flight Simulator that we'll cover in a minute.) As we discussed in Chapter Two, when it comes to flying Flight Simulator we're mostly interested in IAS (Indicated Airspeed). That's because all of the performance specs are given in indicated airspeed. Another reason is that performance based on the IAS indicator doesn't vary as much numerically as when using the TAS indicator.

Many desktop pilots try to explain the difference between IAS and TAS this way: "TAS shows your plane's speed in relation to the ground." Well, this statement is a little misleading. The air pressure exerted on the airspeed indicator, which is channeled from a pickup or sensor called a *pitot tube*, measures IAS. This mechanism doesn't know that the atmosphere gets thinner the higher you fly, or as temperature increases. It only knows how much air pressure it receives.

TAS is, just as its name suggests, true airspeed. Specifically airspeed corrected for pressure, altitude, and temperature. Even though Flight Simulator models weather, TAS is automatically calculated for you and the results are the same as ground speed in level flight. But the thing to bear in mind is that this conversion can't always be absolutely relied upon as ground speed. That's because they really aren't the same things.

To illustrate this point, let's say you dive straight down toward the ground. Your TAS indicator will increase, *but your ground speed will drop to nearly zero*. The truth is that TAS is just another way to measure the air flowing around an aircraft. These are just different scales or references used to do the same thing.

Note: *Although the abbreviations IAS and TAS normally refer to airspeed in statute (ground) miles, the airspeed indicators in Flight Simulator represent both indicated and true airspeeds in nautical miles (knots) except for the Schweizer 2-32. A statute mile is 5,280 feet; a knot is 6,080 feet.*

Tip: *If you want or need to measure ground speed, the DME (Distance Measuring Equipment) is superior to TAS. That's because TAS requires wind corrections to establish ground speed. We'll discuss DME further when we discuss navigation later on.*

None of the aircraft in Flight Simulator will care whether you use IAS or TAS. All they know is how much airflow they need to make the maneuvers you want them to perform.

Understanding the ASI

Flight Simulator models three types of ASIs—analog, digital, and a combination analog/digital. Furthermore, the analog and analog/digital combo ASIs come in two versions—with ASI limitation markings and without ASI limitation markings.

The Sopwith Camel's ASI does not display limitation markings.

Airspeed Indicator Limitation Markings are color-coded marks on the ASI that indicate the performance limitations of the particular aircraft. The ASI in the oldest aircraft in Flight Simulator, the Sopwith Camel, does not contain airspeed limitation markings. Then again, this probably shouldn't come as too much of a surprise because the Camel's ASI isn't located on the left side of the instrument panel where the AI should be (if it had one, that is). But this was a true "early bird," so some non-standard features are to be expected.

The ASIs of the 182RG and 182S do display limitation markings.

ASI limitation markings provide quick visual reference to potentially dangerous airspeed situations. Flight Simulator aircraft with ASI limitation markings are the Cessna 182RG/182S, and the Bell 206B JetRanger. The significance of each marking is explained in the Airspeed Indicator Limitation Markings table.

On the other end of the spectrum are the fully digital ASIs. The Learjet 45 is the only aircraft in Flight Simulator that has a fully digital ASI. It's located on the left side of the AI and it displays airspeed in KIAS, and across the top of the AI, it displays airspeed in Mach numbers. (A Mach number is the relation of airspeed to the speed of sound.) There are, however, no limitation markings on the display. Overspeed warnings are made known by an audio cue (this is realistic) and a visual message on the right side of your current view window (unrealistic—but handy).

Airspeed Indicator Limitation Markings

Marking	Significance
White Arc	Flaps Extension Range
Green Arc	Normal Operating Range
Yellow Arc	Caution Range (Operations conducted only in smooth air)
Radial Red Line	Never Exceed (Maximum speed all operations)
Radial Blue Line	1. Engine Out Maximum Speed - JetRanger Only
	2. Best Rate Of Climb Single Engine - Multi-engine Airplane Only (not used by any Flight Simulator aircraft)

The ASIs on the Extra 300 and the Schweizer 2-32 are a bit of a hybrid between the fully analog and fully digital displays. They have the usual needle going around the clock display of the traditional analog units, and at the center of the dial are digital displays as well. The digital portions of these ASIs correspond with the analog readouts.

These hybrid displays are useful for two reasons. One is that most people interpret the meaning of digital numbers faster than looking at needles. The other is an analog ASI can display only a limited airspeed. For instance, the Schweizer 2-32's ASI only goes up to 160MPH IAS. If you went above 160MPH IAS (not recommended by the manufacturer!), the digital portion continues to display your correct IAS.

The Bell 206B JetRanger's ASI displays limitation markings.

Finally, the Boeing 737-400 has a digital ASI on the left side of the AI (with Mach airspeed numbers across the top of the AI), and an analog/digital hybrid ASI (with the Mach number displayed in the upper digital windows) positioned to the left of the AI/digital ASI. While the analog/digital ASI does not have any of the traditional ASI limitation markings, it does have a maximum airspeed indicator (a red and white striped pointer).

Note: *The JetRanger's ASI has scales for the knots-per-hour (outer scale) and a scale for miles-per-hour (inner scale). Also, there is no flaps extension range (white) arc (because the JetRanger does not have any flaps), no caution (yellow) arc, and there is blue radial line at 100KIAS (Engine-Out Maximum Speed).*

The Altimeter

The altimeter (ALT) is arguably the most important instrument for flying. In the simplest terms, your height above the

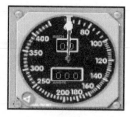

The fully digital ASI display of the Learjet 45 does not display any limitation markings.

The analog/ digital ASI in the Extra 300 also displays limitation markings.

The Schweizer 2-32's analog/ digital ASI uses MPH and does not display any limitation markings.

The Boeing 737-400 is equipped with a digital ASI on the left side of the AI, and an analog/digital hybrid ASI positioned to the left of the AI/digital ASI. Maximum airspeed limitation is indicated on the analog/digital ASI.

ground determines whether you're flying or not. The way an altimeter works is pretty simple. It's basically a barometer that's calibrated in feet instead of inches of mercury. The ALT accesses the atmosphere through the pitot system static source. This is in contrast to the pitot tube *ram air* source that powers the ASI. The ALT is usually located directly to the right of the AI on the standard instrument cluster. But once again, the ALT on the Camel and the sailplane are in non-standard positions. The Camel's ALT is located in the lower center of the instrument panel, and the sailplane's ALT is located on the far left side of the cockpit.

Understanding the ALT

Like the ASIs, Flight Simulator models three types of ALTs—analog, digital, and analog/digital. Furthermore, there are two versions of analog ALTs modeled as well: a modern standard type and a non-standard type. We'll begin with analog ALTs.

Standard analog ALTs are found in the 182 series airplanes, the sailplane, the 300, and the JetRanger. The face of the standard ALT looks like the face of a clock, but if you look closely, it only has 10 main divisions. Each small index line between each main division represents 20 units. There are three pointers or hands on a standard ALT. The longest indicates hundreds of feet; the medium-sized hand, thousands of feet; and the skinny white hand, tens of thousands of feet.

The Camel's ALT is the only non-standard ALT in Flight Simulator. The first thing you may notice about the Camel's ALT is that its pointer rotates counter clockwise. Each main numerical division corresponds to thousands of feet, and each small index corresponds to approximately 166 feet. (The designers used 12 divisions, for some reason. Perhaps they were thinking of a clock.) Also, the Camel's ALT numerical provisions only go up to 15. That means above 15,000 feet, you're on your own.

Just as we've seen before when we discussed ASIs, the model 45 has a digital ALT, and the 737 has both digital and analog/digital ALTs. Let's talk about the digital ALTs first. Digital ALTs are very easy to read—what you read is exactly how high you are. There's none of that searching for hand positions. Below the digital ALT readout is the ALT calibration setting. You'll recognize it by the "in" next to the number. This stands for inches of mercury. The 737 has an additional calibration readout at the top of its digital ALT listed in "MB" or millibars.

The analog/digital ALT of the 737 is a true hybrid. Like a standard ALT, there are 10 main divisions with each small index line representing 20 units. The single hand indicates hundreds of feet. The upper digital readout on the face indicates altitude and the lower digital readout indicates the current ALT calibration setting in inches of mercury.

This standard analog ALT is found in the 182 series airplanes, the sailplane, the 300, and the JetRanger.

The Camel's non-standard analog ALT rotates counter clockwise, and only registers altitudes up to 15,000'.

Note: *The little window on the right side of the ALT face is the Kollsman window. In real life, when you calibrate your ALT, the current ALT setting is entered in this window. We'll discuss this ALT calibration in the next chapter.*

Vertical Speed Indicator

The final static, air-source fed, pitot-static instrument is the vertical speed indicator (VSI). In a standard instrument group, the VSI is located directly below the ALT on the right side of the instrument panel. Like the ALT, the VSI is also a barometer, but this barometer has what is often called a "calibrated leak."

Tip: *Because the VSI reacts to your airplane's behavior, many new pilots make the mistake of trying to fly by the VSI instead of using it as a reference to what your control inputs have done. In other words, if you try to match the movements on the VSI with your controls, you'll never catch up because what you see on the VSI actually lags behind your control movements.*

During level flight, the pressure inside and outside the VSI is equal, so your VSI will read zero. When you climb or descend, a pressure differential is created, causing the VSI hand to indicate the trend. (Note the word *trend*. We'll come back to this again later.) The pressure differential exists only as long as your airplane climbs or descends because the air cannot move through the calibrated leak as fast as it can through its static air source.

Understanding the VSI

There are two types of VSIs modeled in Flight Simulator—mechanical and electronic. The mechanical VSIs come in three scales: 0-1,000 fpm (feet-per-minute), 0-2,000 fpm, and 0-6,000 fpm. The 0-1,000 fpm unit is found on the sailplane, the Cessnas are equipped to read 0-2,000 fpm units, and the 0-6,000 fpm units are in the 300, 737, and JetRanger.

Note: *Although the Learjet 45's VSI display is electronic, the VSI sensing unit depends on the pitot-static system to gather its information.*

On all of the mechanical VSI's, each of the smallest index lines represents 100 foot increments. The medium length index lines on the 0-1,000 fpm and 0-6,000 fpm VSI's represent 500 foot increments. Likewise on these same VSI's, the longest index lines represent 1,000 foot increments. The major index lines on the 0-2,000 fpm VSI's on the Cessnas are marked.

The only electronic display VSI modeled in Flight Simulator is found on the Learjet 45. This VSI indicates a range from 0-3,000 fpm. The short index lines represent 500 foot increments and the long index lines represent 1,000 foot increments.

The 0-1,000 fpm VSI is only found on the Schweizer sailplane.

Both the Cessna 182RG and the Cessna 182S are equipped with 0-2,000 fpm VSI's.

0-6,000 fpm VSI's are found on the 737 (pictured), Extra 300, and Bell JetRanger.

The only electronic display VSI modeled in Flight Simulator is found on the Learjet 45. Its indication range is from 0-3,000 fpm.

Power Management

While energy management (the process of maintaining airspeed and altitude through the use of gravity and momentum) is critical for success in aerobatics and sailplane flying, the management of power is critical for flying all powered aircraft. That's because powered aircraft's first design goal is to fly with power.

Three power sources—reciprocating piston engines, turbine engines, and wind/thermal—power the aircraft in Flight Simulator. We'll leave wind/thermal power for later on because there's not much we can do to control it, so that leaves us with piston engines and turbines. Descriptions of each are provided in Pilot's Help, so we won't go into the basics of how they produce power here.

What you do need to be aware of is that piston engines use propellers to produce thrust and turbojets utilize high-speed exhaust gases. A variation on the turbojet is called a turboprop. A turboprop is a turbine engine that uses a propeller to product thrust. Although there aren't any true turbopropped aircraft modeled in Flight Simulator, the Bell 206B JetRanger really qualifies as one—it's turbine-powered, and the main rotor is essentially a giant propeller. We'll discuss why shortly.

Throttle Control

The throttle controls engine power. You push the throttle forward (or what looks like up on your screen) to increase power, and pull it back to decrease power. Now that you know what the throttle does, let's talk about how to use it.

Depending on which aircraft you're flying and which view you are using to fly in, there are up to three ways to control the throttle in Flight Simulator:

- To control the throttle by keyboard, press F3 or 9 on the keypad to increase throttle, and F2 or 3 on the keypad to decrease throttle.
- To quickly add full power press F1, and to instantly cut power press F4.

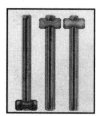

Engine controls on the 182RG and the 182S are adjusted by these control knobs.

- To control the throttle with a throttle controller, push the throttle controller (or slider) forward to increase throttle, and pull it back to decrease throttle.
- To control the throttle by mouse, click and hold the throttle control on the instrument panel, then move your mouse upward to increase throttle or downward to decrease throttle.
- To control the throttle by mouse, you must be in a view where the instrument panel is visible. Furthermore, not all of Flight Simulator's aircraft have instrument panels with throttle controls on them: in particular, the Camel, Learjet 45, and the JetRanger. (The JetRanger is a special case which we'll discuss shortly.)

The Extra 300's engine is controlled by this throttle quadrant.

The engine controls in the 182 series of airplanes are control knobs that must be pushed into the instrument panel. On the Extra 300, the engine control levers are arranged in what is known as a throttle quadrant. In either engine control setup, the control on the far left is the throttle, the middle control is the propeller control, and the control on the right adjusts fuel mixture.

The other type of throttle quadrants modeled in Flight Simulator belong to the 737 and Learjet 45. Because these airplanes are multi-engine turbojets, their throttle quadrants don't have prop controls or mixture controls.

Note: *The JetRanger's throttle control works by the same keyboard commands as the airplane's prop control.*

Furthermore, there are two throttle controls—one for each engine.

Flight Simulator allows you to control individual engines on a multi-engine aircraft. The way to do this from the keyboard (or a throttle controller) is to first select the engine(s) to control, then use the same throttle mentioned earlier to control the selected engine(s).

Note: *Engine 1 on all Flight Simulator multi-engine aircraft is the port engine. Engine 2 is on the starboard side.*

- To select an individual engine to control, press E + 1 to control Engine 1 or press E + 2 to control Engine 2.
- To control both engines on a twin engine aircraft, press E + 1 + 2.

To control an individual engine on a multi-engine aircraft with a mouse, click and hold the engine control of the engine you want, then move your mouse upward to increase throttle or downward to decrease throttle. To control both engines simultaneously with a mouse, click and hold a position between both engine controls, then move your mouse upward to increase throttle or downward to decrease throttle.

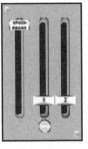

The throttle quadrant in the 737 does not have a prop control nor mixture control, but there are two throttle controls.

Clicking on Thrust Levers from the Instrument Panels selection from the Views menu will call up the Learjet 45's throttle quadrant.

Manifold Pressure

Manifold pressure gauges are only found on piston aircraft, and Flight Simulator only provides manifold pressure gauges for the 182S and the Extra 300. They both display fuel flow rates in GPH (gallons per hour) as well. We'll discuss fuel flow when we talk about fuel mixture controls, so let's limit this discussion to manifold pressure.

A manifold pressure gauge reports the vacuum pressure inside the engine's manifold. In simple terms, the manifold is the *plumbing* that guides the air/fuel mixture into the engine. The amount of vacuum pressure in this area is a direct indication of how hard the engine is working.

The manifold pressure/fuel flow gauge of the Cessna 182S.

The size of the Extra 300's manifold pressure/fuel flow gauge should be an indication of how important engine performance is to an aerobatics pilot.

Understanding the Manifold Pressure Gauge

In the most basics terms, when you increase throttle, you increase the fuel flow into the engine. With more fuel to burn, the engine's RPM (Revolutions Per Minute) increase and with it, its hunger for air to maintain the RPM. Manifold pressure is measured in inches of mercury below atmospheric pressure.

The 182S's manifold pressure gauge is located at the 8 o'clock position from the ASI, and the 300's is the second-to-last gauge on the right side of its instrument panel. Both the 182S and the 300's manifold pressure gauge read from 10-35 inches of mercury. Note that there is no redline (maximum limit) on either of them, and the 182S has a green arc (normal operation range) between 15-23 inches of mercury.

OK, you probably have a couple of questions about these things. First, although some engines do have manifold pressure redlines (usually only turbocharged or supercharged engines), the reason why there aren't any such limitations for these aircraft is because they can't produce enough power for the engines to self-destruct. The atmosphere thins as you increase altitude, so your maximum obtainable manifold pressure decreases the higher you fly. Supercharged and turbo-charged engines suffer from the same thin air problem, but they're able to make gains on the thinning atmosphere by pressurizing their engine's air intake. (That's what superchargers and turbochargers do.)

This explains why the green arc exists on the 182S's manifold pressure gauge. When you fly at a higher altitude, the poor little Cessna's engine can't produce a whole lot of power/manifold pressure. So to keep pilots from panicking, the green arc shows you "Oh, the engine is only supposed to be making this much power."

Fixed Pitch vs. Constant Speed Propellers

The term *constant speed propeller*, while descriptive about the way it does its job, doesn't really explain *what* it does. The other term this device goes by may be a little more descriptive: Constant speed propellers are also known as *variable pitch propellers*. At the most basic level (compared to fixed pitch propellers), variable pitch propellers can change their blade pitch (angle) in relation to the oncoming airflow. Fixed pitch propellers cannot change their pitch. The pitch is fixed at one angle.

The reason why you'd even want to mess with a propeller's pitch has to do with efficiency on two levels—aerodynamic and power. If you were to cut a section of propeller off and look at it, the cross-section shape of the blade would look just like an airfoil. That's because a propeller *is* an airfoil. It just generates lift in the direction you want to go be going. This is aerodynamic efficiency.

Airfoils, whether they're wings on an airplane or prop blades, generate more lift when there are more air molecules to create lift. If there aren't enough air molecules around, you can compensate by either increasing airspeed (which brings more air molecules around) or increasing the airfoil's angle of attack (AOA). Angle of attack is the angle of the wing chord line in relation to the oncoming airflow.

So how does this relate to your prop? When you start climbing high into thinning air, there are fewer air molecules for a prop to bite into. You can increase your prop's airspeed by increasing power (which in turn would increase prop RPM), or you can increase the pitch (which would increase the prop's AOA).

You're probably now wondering, "Why go through all the trouble with a variable speed prop if all you need to do is increase engine RPM to maintain thrust?"

This leads us to the engine efficiency part of the puzzle. Recall that engines produce less and less power as they climb higher and higher due to thinning air. If you're already at maximum manifold pressure and at a high altitude, there's no more power to provide additional RPM. But if you're flying at a lower altitude and still have power to spare, a variable-speed prop has its benefits.

Engines produce power in a way that, if mapped out on graph paper, more or less looks like a curve. If you're no stranger to auto sports or high performance sports cars, this is known as a power curve. Engines produce more power or are more efficient at a certain RPM. A variable pitch prop allows you to adjust your propeller RPM to take advantage of an engine's power curve.

The next question lingering in your head is probably something like this: Why not design airplanes that match engine power curves with propellers? It goes back to propeller efficiency again. To use the car analogy again, you can

gear a car so you have good power or good highway mileage. Well, you can try to gear things so you have a little of each, but one or the other (or both, most likely) will suffer from reduced maximum performance.

Airplane props and engines work the same way. Think of a variable pitch propeller as a way to "shift gears" and you'll begin to see some of the advantages.

Why is a variable pitch prop also called a constant speed prop? The simple answer is because it's the way that the device functions: a propeller governor keeps the prop's RPM at a constant speed. The governor will adjust the prop's pitch to maintain RPM. If the engine produces more power, the governor will increase prop pitch to make use of that power. If the engine produces less power, the governor will decrease prop pitch to decrease its load on the engine and to maintain RPM.

Desired prop RPM speeds generally work out according to the following rules. For maximum power during takeoff or maximum rate climbs, high RPM is desirable. For high-speed cruising and high altitude flying, a lower RPM is desirable. We'll cover exact RPM numbers a little later on, but the benefits of being able to fly at lower RPM, in addition to efficiency, include lower noise and lower vibration.

Although the JetRanger helicopter doesn't have a propeller, its rotor blades function the same way—they're constant-speed, variable-pitch devices. As mentioned earlier, a turbine engine also powers the JetRanger. That's why, technically, one could consider the JetRanger to be a kind of turboprop. The only difference as far as engine controls go is the corresponding system for prop control on an airplane is called the collective on the helicopter.

Prop Control

The prop control knob (or lever) is located between the throttle and mixture controls. There's only one fixed-pitch propeller aircraft in Flight Simulator—the Sopwith Camel. All of the other prop planes are of the constant speed variety.

- To adjust the pitch on a constant speed prop by keyboard, press CTL + F2 on the keyboard to increase prop pitch/lower RPM, and CTL + F3 on the keyboard to decrease prop pitch/raise RPM. To quickly increase prop pitch to maximum RPM press XL + F4, and to instantly feather the prop (full pitch) press CTL1 + F1.

- To control the props by mouse, click and hold the prop control on the instrument panel, then move your mouse upward to increase prop RPM or downward to decrease prop RPM.

Note: *The JetRanger's throttle control works by the same keyboard commands as the airplanes' prop controls. This just applies to Flight Simulator's commands. They are not similar systems.*

Collective Control

Because a helicopter can be considered a turboprop of sorts, the helicopter's collective would be considered the counterpart of the prop airplane's prop control. There are only two ways to control the JetRanger's collective—by keyboard, and by a game controller.

- To control the JetRanger's collective by keyboard, press F3 or 9 on the keypad to increase collective, and F2 or 3 on the keypad to decrease collective. To quickly add full collective press F1, and to instantly decrease collective press F4.
- To control the JetRanger's collective by a throttle controller, push the throttle controller (or slider) forward to increase collective, and pull it back to decrease collective.

Tachometer

Now that you know how to increase and decrease throttle and prop RPM, we should talk about the tachometer (tach). A tachometer shows you how many RPM your engine is turning at. Because your prop is directly connected to your engine in a piston-powered airplane, tach RPM shows you your prop RPM as well.

On the other hand, turbine-powered engine tachs show two RPM readings per engine. The N1 speed is the turbine fan speed, and the N2 speed is the speed of the turbine itself. The reason there are two tach speeds is because a turbine fan does not rotate at the same speed as the turbine.

The simplest analog tachometer is found on the Camel and there are no limitation markings on it.

Regardless of engine type, there are three types of tachometers modeled in Flight Simulator—analog, digital, and electronic. The simplest analog tach is found on the left side of the Camel's instrument panel. It can read from 0 to slightly over 2,600 RPM and there are no

Another analog tach is found on the 182 series airplanes. It has a green normal operating range arc, and red line maximum speed limitation mark.

limitation markings on it. Each long radial line represents 100 RPM and each of the smaller lines represents 25 RPM.

Another analog tach is found on the 182 series airplanes. It's located on the right side of the bottom row of instruments on the Cessna 182RG and 182S, and it does have limitation marks on it. The meaning of the green arc and red line should be familiar to you by now. This tach can read from 0–3,500. Its normal operation range is 2,000–2,400 RPM and it has a maximum RPM of 2,400. Each short index line represents 100 RPM and each long index line represents increments of 500 RPM each.

The last analog tach is found on the Bell JetRanger helicopter, and it's really two tachs in one. This two-tach wonder is located directly below the ASI. Although you won't notice it when the turbine and rotor head are all spooled up, there are two hands on this display. The long hand has a letter T marked on it, and the shorter hand has the letter R marked on it. The T hand indicates turbine speed, or what is also commonly referred to as N2 speed, and the R hand indicates rotor speed or NR speed.

Note: *The little box on the bottom of the 182S's tach is the tachometer Hobbs meter window. This meter logs hours of engine operation based on tach movement. These meters are used to keep track of engine time for overhauls, and in the aircraft rental business this is how you are charged. This meter is inoperative in Flight Simulator—which is a good thing...you can't be charged for flying Flight Simulator by the hour!*

Note that the term *RPM* has not appeared in the previous paragraph. That's because turbine engines operate at a truly phenomenal RPM, so rather than try to provide the pilot with huge numbers, RPM on turbine aircraft is only reported in percentages of maximum operation speed. This also explains why it's possible to achieve over 100 percent RPM. Limitation markings indicate normal operating range, and maximum and minimum RPM. The inner scale is for the NR hand, and the outer scale is for N2.

The only solely digital tachometer in Flight Simulator is found on the Extra 300, as shown in the accompanying figure. It's located on the far right side of the 300's instrument panel, and displays exact RPM numbers. The number you read is the number of RPM. No conversion is necessary.

Both of the 737's tachs, and the Learjet 45's tachs are located to the right of their respective standard instrument clusters in what is called the engine gauge

cluster, or just engine cluster. Because the 737 and model 45 are also turbine aircraft, their tachs also display two sets of RPM per engine. The two upper indicators of the engine cluster display are the N1 or fan speed tachs. There is one N1 tach for each engine. The left tach is for the port engine (Engine 1), and the right tach is for the starboard engine (Engine 2).

Two rows below the N1 tachs are the N2 tachs. (N2 speeds are turbine speeds—the same as in the JetRanger.) These are also arranged one per engine. Just as with the JetRanger, N1 and N2 tachs display speeds in percentages rather than actual RPM. Electronic dials and digital numbers display these percentages. The tach dials on the 737 display operating limitations with green arcs, yellow arcs, and red lines. Digital percentage readouts for each tach are displayed in the 12 o'clock position of each electronic dial. The tachs on the 45 are very similar to the 737's in the way they're read, but the only limitation markings these feature are maximum operating speed.

Torque Indicator

Back to helicopters again. OK, we have turbine speed and we have rotor speed, which roughly correspond to turbine and prop speed on a turboprop. We also have throttle control and collective, which roughly correspond to the throttle and prop control also on a turboprop. Where a helicopter's instruments differ from a turboprop is that the former has a torque indicator.

The torque indicator is located directly to the left of the ASI, and this is the instrument that is used as for setting collective. Although it doesn't measure RPM like the tach on an airplane, it is used roughly the same way. If you want more thrust (lift) you add collective, and as you add collective the torque indicator rises. What's different about a

The tachs on the Learjet 45 only bear maximum operating speed limitations.

The analog tachometer on the Bell 206B JetRanger is really two tachs in one. One hand indicates turbine speed, and the other indicates rotor speed.

The only solely digital tachometer in Flight Simulator is in the Extra 300, and it displays exact RPM numbers.

The 737's engine gauge cluster is located to the right of the standard instrument cluster on the instrument panel.

The JetRanger's torque indicator is an instrument only found on helicopters.

helicopter is that as you add collective and increase rotor blade pitch, the rotor does not slow down like a variable pitch prop would when you add pitch. (Well, it does a little, but only for a short period of time.) That's why a tachometer isn't as useful for the application of collective in a helicopter as it is for the application of power in an airplane.

Instead of RPM, what the torque indicator is showing you is the amount of resistance the rotor system (air plus drivetrain) is placing on the engine. As with our other turbine instruments, the torque indicator displays percentages. There are also normal, caution, and maximum-operation limit markings on it.

Mixture Control

Fuel requires a certain amount of air to combust inside an engine. If fuel exceeds the optimum air/fuel combustion mixture ratio, the excess fuel goes unburned or only partially burned. This is known as a rich condition. A good way to remember this is that fuel costs money and air is free. The consequences of a rich mixture are poor power and poor fuel economy.

Conversely, when air exceeds the optimum air/fuel combustion mixture ratio (what's known as a lean condition), there are more serious consequences to worry about. A lean air/fuel mixture causes the mixture to burn hotter and consequently raises engine temperatures overall—specifically, cylinder head and exhaust gas temperatures. Without getting too technical, basically the reason why a lean mixture will burn hotter, compared to an optimum air/fuel mixture, is because the physical density of a lean mixture is too thin for optimum combustion. The relatively higher density of an optimum air/fuel mixture will control the combustion explosion inside the piston cylinder.

To put the matter simply: a lean mixture ratio burns too quickly. A light bulb that burns twice as bright will only burn half as long. The big problem with lean mixtures is the increased heat they produce from burning "twice as bright." If the combustion chamber gets too hot, the incoming air/fuel mixture will ignite prematurely (before the spark plug is supposed to ignite the mixture). This condition, pre-ignition, is very bad for an engine because it can severely reduce power output or even physically damage the engine.

So what does this have to do with mixture controls? With piston-driven aircraft, the mixture control allows you to adjust the air/fuel mixture. You want to be able to adjust your mixture because air thins as you increase altitude. The higher you fly, the richer your mixture will become without any intervention on your behalf. Alternatively, if you have an optimized mixture ratio at high altitude, when you descend into the thicker air below, you end up with a lean condition.

Remember that only piston aircraft can have mixture controls (turbines work differently, and they also compress incoming air, reducing the effects of thin air), and the only piston aircraft in Flight Simulator without a mixture control is the Camel. On planes with one, the mixture control knob or lever is located on the right side of the throttle controls or throttle quadrant.

- To operate mixture control by keyboard, press Ctrl + Shift + F3 on the keyboard to enrich the air/fuel mixture, and Ctrl + Shift + F2 on the keyboard to lean the air/fuel mixture. To quickly move the mixture control to full rich press Ctrl + Shift + F4, and to instantly cut off fuel to your engine press Ctrl + Shift + F1.
- To operate mixture control by mouse, click and hold the mixture control on the instrument panel, then move your mouse upward to enrich the mixture or downward to lean the mixture.

Engine Gauges

Every aircraft in Flight Simulator that has an engine (aside from the Camel) has a number of engine-monitoring gauges. You already know about limitation markings from the other instruments we've discussed, so I'll refrain from repeating myself here.

Basically engine-monitoring gauges report temperatures, pressures, capacities, and anything else critical to performance and to maintaining operational status. There isn't much to say about their operation other than this: if they display *green* you're okay. You don't control gauges—they're only used for reference, indicating performance and helping you troubleshoot any problems.

Engine gauges can be categorized into three groups—performance monitoring, fluid monitoring, and system monitoring. Let's take a quick look at them.

The Extra 300's EGT gauge is located just right of center at the bottom of its instrument panel.

The 206 JetRanger's turbine temp gauge is located in the 8 o'clock position of the ASI.

A combination EGT/CHT gauge is located at the 8 o'clock position of the 182S's ASI.

Performance Gauges

EGT (Exhaust Gas Temperature) gauge: The EGT is only found on the Extra 300 and the 182S. This gauge monitors the temperature of exhaust gases in Celsius, and it's the primary reference used for air/fuel mixture setting.

Although EGTs are associated with mixture controls, and EGT is essentially a subset of engine temperature monitoring (you can't have a hot EGT and cold engine, or vice versa), the equivalents of EGTs on turbine aircraft are the turbine temperature gauges. As the name suggests, turbine temperature gauges monitor the temperature of the turbine. The 206 JetRanger's turbine temp gauge is located in the 8 o'clock position of the ASI. Both the Learjet 45 and 737 turbine temperature/EGT gauges are located between the N1 and N2 tachs. The reason why turbine temperature is monitored is because if a turbine is allowed to get too hot, fires can start or parts such as bearings can fail.

CHT (Cylinder Head Temperature) gauge: Only the 182S is equipped with a CHT gauge and it's located on the right half of the EGT gauge. The CHT is useful for cross checking with the EGT for lean mixtures, ensuring that the engine is at operating temperature (not running cold for the first flight of the day), and to help the pilot guard against *shock cooling* the engine. (Shock cooling is allowing a hot engine to cool too quickly. This can warp cylinder heads).

Fluid Gauges

Fuel gauges monitor fuel quantity and fuel flow. Fuel capacity is how much fuel the aircraft can carry. Note that fuel capacity and useable fuel are two different quantities: fuel quantity is the amount of fuel the aircraft is carrying. AVGAS is monitored in gallons, and Jet-A is monitored in pounds on the model 45 and on the 737, but it's monitored in gallons on the JetRanger. The reason for measuring a fluid in pounds is because it is more convenient for determining aircraft performance (performance is affected by weight).

Fuel flow gauges the amount of fuel being consumed per hour. Just as with fuel quantity gauges, AVGAS is measured in gallons, and the model 45 and 737 are measured in pounds. Fuel flow allows you to calculate flight range based on current and projected fuel usage. The only fuel flow monitoring gauge that doesn't use a flow gauge is the one on the JetRanger. It uses a fuel pressure gauge instead because its turbine basically operates at a single RPM (wide open) the whole time it's flying.

Although the Camel's fuel gauge reads AIR on it's face, it *is* the fuel gauge and it's located just below the ASI on the right side of the instrument panel. There is only one tank on the Camel, so one gauge is all you need. But one physical gauge doesn't necessarily mean there is only one fuel tank on an airplane.

The 182S is an aircraft with two fuel tanks but it has only one physical gauge. It's located to the left of the EGT/CHT gauge. This fuel capacity gauge monitors the fuel levels for both the left and right tanks in gallons with two needles—one for each tank. Fuel flow is displayed on the same physical gauge as the manifold pressure gauge.

The Extra 300 also has two fuel tanks, but it's equipped with two fuel gauges. They're located at the bottom left side of the Extra 300's instrument panel. The left and right gauges monitor the fuel levels (also in gallons) of its left and right tanks respectively. Fuel flow is displayed in two places. The first place is on the bottom half of the manifold pressure gauge, and the other is a digital version located right center of the bottom of the instrument panel.

Directly below the VSI on the 737's instrument panel are its two digital fuel capacity gauges. Even though there are physically four tanks on the 737, these two gauges report the total fuel onboard for each wing. Pounds of fuel numbers are reported in 1,000-pound increments. The middle image shows the two larger number 17s followed by smaller number 2s. This translates into 17,200 pounds of fuel per wing. (To

The JetRanger uses a fuel pressure gauge instead of a fuel flow gauge, and it's located below the fuel quantity gauge on the left side of the instrument panel.

Although its face says AIR, the gauge located just below the ASI is the Camel's fuel gauge.

The 182S's fuel gauge monitors fuel for two tanks.

The Extra 300's two fuel gauges monitor the fuel for each of its two tanks.

The Extra 300 is equipped with a digital fuel flow gauge in addition to the one found on the manifold pressure gauge.

The quantity of fuel on board the 737's four fuel tanks is reported by two fuel gauges in pounds. Fuel flow is also reported in pounds to the right and slightly below the fuel quantity gauges.

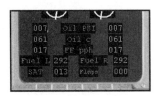

Digital displays report fuel capacity and fuel flow on the Learjet 45.

view individual fuel levels look in the Aircraft menu under the Aircraft Settings: Fuel selections.)

To the right and slightly below the 737's fuel quantity gauges are its fuel flow gauges. These display in increments of 10 pounds per hour flow. In other words, if the numbers in one of the fuel flow gauges of the 737 report 103, add a zero and you'll get your answer.

The Learjet 45 has perhaps the easiest to read fuel quantity and fuel flow gauges These completely digital displays are located near the bottom of the engine gauge cluster, and they report fuel capacity and flow in increments of 10.

Oil gauges monitor oil pressure, temperature, and on some aircraft oil capacity as well. Oil lubricates the moving parts of an engine and it also helps cool it. That's why it's so important to monitor. A loss of oil pressure will warn you of an oil leak or pump failure—either of which cause less oil to reach the engine. High oil temperatures can indicate a loss of lubrication or may lead to the breakdown of the lubricating properties of the oil. Finally, monitoring oil capacity can warn you of leaks or potential oil usage problems.

Every oil pressure indicator in Flight Simulator displays oil pressure in pounds per square inch (PSI) except for the one found in the Camel. Believe it or not, the Camel's oil pressure gauge (located to the right of its magneto switches) is nothing more than a glass tube that's connected to the engine's oil system. When you have oil pressure, the oil will visibly rise inside this glass tube. Simple, but effective? More likely only a little bit better than nothing at all.

Oil temperature is measured in both Fahrenheit and Celsius depending on the particular airplane you're flying. The scale that's used doesn't matter. As long as you stay in the green arc or normal operating range, you'll be okay.

Both of the 182S's and the Extra 300's oil pressure and oil temperature readouts are housed within one physical gauge. They also both read in Fahrenheit and PSI. The 182S's oil gauge is mounted to the left of the manifold pressure/fuel flow gauge. The Extra 300's oil gauge is mounted below its ALT.

Oil pressure in the Camel is monitored through this glass tube that's connected to the engine's oil system.

The 182S's oil pressure and oil temperature readouts are housed within one physical gauge.

The Extra 300's oil pressure and oil temperature readouts are also housed within one physical gauge mounted below the altimeter.

The JetRanger has two oil monitoring gauges. One for the engine, and the other for the transmission.

The 737 has all of its oil gauges grouped together in a fashion similar to the engine gauge cluster.

The JetRanger's oil pressure and oil temperature gauges are also housed in one physical gauge, but there are two of these gauges. Yes, the JetRanger is a single-engine aircraft. The other dual-display oil gauge belongs to the helicopter's transmission. And no, there aren't any gears to shift on a helicopter; it's not that kind of transmission. A helicopter's transmission converts the turbine's shaft output into main rotor and tail rotor movement. Both the engine oil and transmission oil gauges are located on the top left side of the JetRanger instrument panel. The left needles display pressure in PSI, and the right needles display temperature in Celsius.

Once again the Learjet 45 has the display that's easiest to read. The fully digital oil pressure and temperature readouts are located above the fuel readouts, and they are scaled in PSI and Celsius. The 737 on the other hand, has all of its oil gauges grouped together in a fashion similar to the engine-gauge cluster.

The top two gauges are oil pressures in PSI (one for each engine). The next two below it are the oil temperatures in Celsius. The oil capacity readouts make

Tip: *Monitoring the oil temperature on the Camel is a bit problematic. A real world pilot would have probably put his bare hand on the pressure monitoring tube and worked with that. You have no such luxury on a desktop simulator, so the minute you even believe your engine is in trouble, you should start looking for a place to land.*

up the digital display directly below the oil temps. It's displayed as a percentage of oil capacity—100 percent is perfect. Finally, the bottom gauges are turbine vibration indicators. They have nothing to do with engine fluids, but since they're located there and are unique, we'll discuss them here.

Hydraulic pressure gauges monitor the hydraulic systems of the 737. Although hydraulic fluid is not engine oil, it is a fluid that's monitored by a gauge. Hydraulic fluid is used in systems that require a power assist such as the landing gear extension system, so the status of this fluid is very important. Hydraulic fluid is monitored like oil, but only by pressure and capacity. The hydraulic readouts are located below the turbine vibration indicators. The digital readout at the very bottom indicates total hydraulic fluid capacity in percentages the same way that engine oil capacity is reported.

Systems gauges

There are two systems that are related to engine power. They don't affect engine power, but the engine affects them. They are the vacuum system and the charging system.

Suction gauge: The vacuum system powers gyroscopic instruments. The gyroscopic instruments, in a standard instrument cluster, are the AI, the directional gyro, and in some cases the turn-and-slip indicator. (You know about the AI already. We'll get to the others soon.) Although there are electric-powered versions of these gyroscopic instruments, if your airplane is equipped with the vacuum-powered versions, any problems with the vacuum system will cause gyroscopic instrument problems.

Although other aircraft have vacuum systems, the only suction gauges that are visible to you are on the 182RG and the 182S and they are located in the upper left corner of the instrument panels.

The vacuum system is monitored by a suction gauge. Any drop in suction will indicate either a leak, or a problem with the engine-driven pump. Although the Extra 300 and the JetRanger both have vacuum systems, the only suction gauges that are visible to you are on the 182RG and the 182S. The 182's suction gauges are the small circular gauges located in the upper left corner of the instrument panels.

Ammeter: An aircraft ammeter measures electrical Amperage loads placed on its electrical system. There are many electrical devices on an airplane and they are powered either by an electrical system made up of batteries alone (as is the case with the sailplane), or by

batteries and either an alternator or generator. Generally, alternators are found on smaller engines, and generators on turbines. That's why the ammeter on the JetRanger is labeled *Generator Load*.

The difference between the two approaches is that an alternator provides more electrical power output at a lower engine RPM than a generator. Because the JetRanger's turbine operates at a higher and more or less constant RPM, it works best with a generator.

There are only three ammeters visible to you in Flight Simulator. One is on the JetRanger and is located on the right half of the fuel pressure gauge. The other is on the Extra 300 right next to the EGT. The third is on the sailplane, but it's non-functional. (It's just above the master avionics switch.)

The only other visible and working ammeter in Flight Simulator is on the Extra 300.

Throttle vs. Airspeed vs. Lift

Okay, now that we know all about power management, let's talk about how power affects flight. Lift increases with airspeed because more air molecules pass under (and over) the wing, thereby producing more lift. So when you add power, you'll increase airspeed, which in turn increases lift, and the end result is that you climb. Essentially what we're saying here is that throttle controls altitude. Or does the throttle control airspeed? Read on.

Elevator Trim

The use of elevator trim is a very simple process, but inexperienced desktop pilots invariably have a hard time using it. Part of the problem is, unless you have a Microsoft Force Feedback joystick, it's kind of difficult to know when elevator pressure is easing off. But there's a much bigger problem: no one has ever told new pilots that a trim tab setting only works for the particular airspeed that it was set at. What does this mean?

Back to our wing and airspeed example. An airplane's horizontal stabilizer (the little wing in back of the airplane that the elevator is attached to) helps maintain the airplane's pitch by either producing positive lift (raising the tail), or more commonly, producing negative lift (downward force pushing the tail downward) to counteract the lift being generated from the main wing. As airspeed increases or decreases, the amount of lift generated by the main wing and the horizontal stabilizer (which, remember, is also a wing) does not

increase or decrease at the same rate. This causes the pitch changes that require elevator control input.

An elevator trim tab acts like (and sometime literally *is*) a small version of the main wing flaps. They increase or decrease the amount of lift on the elevator control surface. This helps the elevator maintain its position, which is in turn providing the right amount of lift to counteract the lift from the main wing. So here's the bottom line: you can trim an airplane for any attitude, airspeed, or altitude as long as your airspeed remains constant.

Here's how to use elevator trim:

1. To trim your airplane to fly level, hold the joystick exactly where it has to be to remain flying level.

2. Wait a few seconds until the airplane has finished accelerating or de-accelerating (reached equilibrium).

3. Now press the 7 key on the keypad or 1 on the keypad to trim the elevator. Use the 7 key if your controller is pushed forward to fly level or use the 1 key if your controller is pulled backwards for level flight. With each consecutive trim key press you should be able to return the controller back to neutral. If not, you're pressing the wrong trim key.

Eventually, after following this process, you'll be flying level with your controller in the neutral position. Your trim will remain steady until you change your power setting, flight attitude or bank—all of which will affect your airspeed. See how that works? Now you're gettin' it!

Elevator vs. Airspeed vs. Lift

You know that elevator controls airplane pitch. You pull back on the elevator and the nose of the airplane pitches upward causing you to gain altitude. Push forward on the elevator and the nose pitches downward causing you to lose altitude. (As some pilots put it, "pull back on the yoke and the houses get smaller, push forward and the houses get bigger.") This makes it very easy to conclude (incorrectly) that the elevator controls altitude. (Pitch controls AOA, and AOA controls lift.) But wait a second! Didn't we just say that *throttle* controls altitude?

Here's a way to prove what's what. You can try this after you get some flight time in and feel comfortable trimming your airplane for level flight. First trim your airplane for level flight. Next, pull back on the elevator and watch your ASI. Your airspeed will drop. Level out and trim up your airplane again. This time push forward on the elevator and watch the ASI. You airspeed will increase. But so will your altitude, so you're probably still not convinced. Fair enough. Try this next. Trim your airplane for level flight again, but this time at less than full throttle. Once you're all set up, go ahead and give it full throttle. Watch the ASI and ALT. You'll notice that your altitude will increase, but your airspeed will remain more or less constant. OK, bring the airplane back to level flight and trim it up at less than full throttle again. This time decrease throttle and watch what happens. You'll find that you are descending (losing altitude) but your airspeed will again remain more or less at a constant speed.

So there you have it. Elevator controls airspeed under constant power, and throttle controls altitude, or, more precisely, rate of climb and rate of descent. Remember these principles because we'll rely on them later on.

Stalls

With all of this talk about climbing and descending, a few words should be said about stalls. Stalls are categorized as either elementary or advanced stalls. Elementary stalls consist of power-on stalls (also known as *takeoff* or *departure stalls*); power-off stalls (or *approach to landing stalls*); and turning stalls (power-on or power-off stalls while turning). Advanced stalls include cross-control, accelerated, and top-and-bottom rudder stalls.

Contrary to what most people believe, stalls are not caused by flying too slowly. Stalls occur when your wings exceed the critical angle of attack. This means you can stall your airplane at any airspeed, any pitch attitude, any altitude, and any power setting.

People believe that stalls are caused by flying too slow because slower airspeeds create less lift. What usually happens is this: when a pilot realizes that he or she is losing altitude, instead of applying power, the pilot simply pushes the elevator up to make up for the lost lift. The idea is that increasing angle of attack (AOA) will increase lift. This is, in fact, true, but the problem is that slow airspeeds require higher AOA's to generate the same lift that can be produced at a higher airspeed. This makes it very easy to exceed the critical AOA, because you're at a higher AOA to begin with, when you fly at a very slow airspeed. If the pilot left the airplane alone, it would compensate for flying too slowly by lowering its nose all by itself. To be blunt: the pilot's adjustment of the elevator caused the stall, not the lack of airspeed.

Regardless of what type of stall you're in or what caused it, the way to recover from all stalls is the same. When you *feel* the stall buffet or hear the stall warning (which comes first), reduce elevator backpressure. If you're in a bank, neutralize your ailerons as well. If your power setting is less than full power, smoothly increase power in addition to the other steps.

Spins

In order for an airplane to spin, it must first stall. What causes an airplane to spin is one wing is creating lift while the other is stalled. So if you never stall your airplane, you'll never have to worry about getting into spins.

Recovering from spins is very similar to stall recovery. (Which shouldn't really be a surprise because one causes the other.) First neutralize your ailerons, then instead of relaxing elevator backpressure, apply full-down elevator. Next apply full rudder in the opposite direction of the spin. In other words, if you're in a counter-clockwise spin, apply full-right rudder to counteract the spin. Keep correcting with your rudder to keep the nose steady.

Even though you may be tempted to apply opposite aileron to counteract the spin, resist the urge. It'll only delay the recovery. Hold full-down elevator

until the spin stops, and then slowly ease the elevator back to neutral. Your airplane will raise its nose by itself as your airspeed rises again. Hopefully you'll have enough altitude to recover.

The only aspect of spin recovery that isn't an exact science is the application of power. Sometimes the application of power helps spin

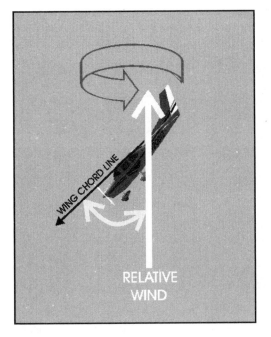

In order for an airplane to spin, it must first (and always) be stalled.

A spin rotation is caused by one wing creating lift while the other wing is stalled.

recovery, sometimes it doesn't. The benefits of pulling back the throttle when attempting spin recovery is that you'll tend to lose less altitude with the power off because of your slower airspeed. On the other hand, if you don't recover, the altitude you saved can only help you when you try applying power for spin recovery.

So in that light, the recommendation is to first pull power off. However, if you don't recover within one or two turns max, hit the power. You've got nothing to lose and everything to gain at that point.

Turns

Now that we've got the *up and down* stuff all figured out, let's take a look at turning. The first thing to understand is that lift is very important when it comes to turning an airplane. Rudder turns are possible, but unless you're flying a vectored thrust airplane like an F-22 (which isn't modeled in Flight Simulator),

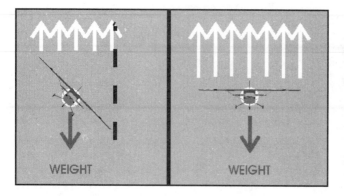

A banked airplane only has a smaller percentage of its wing able to generate the lift in the right direction required to offset its weight.

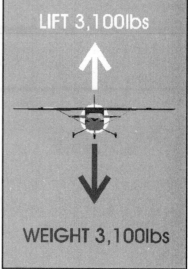

The wings of an airplane in level flight must generate the same amount of lift as the weight of the airplane.

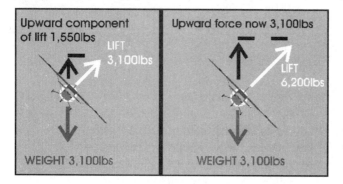

An airplane with its wings banked at 60 degrees requires twice the lift to maintain altitude because the upward component of lift is not being used to counteract gravity. (Shown on the left.) This is why it's necessary to add up elevator in a turn to maintain altitude.

the airplane must bank in order to turn, regardless of the control surface that created the bank.

When your airplane is banked, only a smaller percentage of the wing is able to generate the lift in the right direction required to offset the weight of the airplane. This causes a loss in altitude. To counter this altitude loss you must increase lift. The easiest way to do that is to increase AOA by pulling back on the elevator.

Let's take a look at what's happening here. In order for an airplane to fly in level flight, the wings must generate the same amount of lift as the weight of the airplane. But when an airplane turns with its wings banked at 60 degrees, it requires twice the lift to maintain altitude. (The cosine of 60 degrees is 0.500, or 50 percent.) This is because your upward component of lift is not being used to counteract gravity. Therefore, it's necessary to add up elevator in a turn to maintain altitude.

Turn Coordination

Turn coordination is something you need to concern yourself about only if you have auto-coordination turned off in Aircraft Preferences. (This is located in the Aircraft menu under Aircraft Settings. Please refer to Chapter Two for more information on how to do this.)

Turn rate is the number of degrees the nose of an airplane can move within a certain amount of time. The more degrees it can move, the higher the turn rate. Generally, the faster you fly, the faster you can move the nose of your airplane. (This is only limited by the point where centrifugal force exceeds the lift being generated to keep the airplane in the turn.)

A coordinated turn is a turn that neither slips nor skids. An airplane slips in a turn when its turn rate is less than the amount of bank it can bear. Conversely, an airplane skids in a turn when the turn rate is too high for the amount of bank being used. What this basically boils down to is that a coordinated turn is one in which the combined force of gravity and centrifugal force is directed straight through the floor of the airplane.

One analogy that's used to illustrate slipping and skidding errors is to think of your airplane as a racecar racing down a banked turn. If your speed is very high (which corresponds with a high turn rate), you car will skid towards the outside of the track. If you drove this same turn very slowly (which makes for a slow turn rate), your car would slide towards the inside of the track.

Okay, slide, skid, what's the big deal? If you were flying a real airplane it would be a *big* deal to any passengers you may have flying with you. Uncoordinated turns are pretty uncomfortable. But uncoordinated turns at low airspeeds can also lead to stalls and spins. So you should know how to recognize and deal with uncoordinated turns. There are three turn instruments used in Flight Simulator to help you recognize an uncoordinated turn. They are:

Slip indicator: The slip indicator is a liquid-filled, curved glass tube with an agate or steel ball inside of it. The liquid inside the slip indicator acts as a shock dampener. (A slip indicator looks very similar to the bubble level indicators found on a carpenter's level.)

The Sopwith Camel's slip indicator is located just below the ASI.

Looking like a carpenter's bubble level indicator, the 737's slip indicator is just below the AI.

The turn and slip indicator is often referred to as the "old ball and needle."

In a coordinated turn, the ball will remain in the center of the indicator because centrifugal force offsets the pull of gravity. This unpowered device is found in one form or another on all the aircraft in Flight Simulator except for the sailplane. But the slip indicator in its stand-alone form is only found on the Camel (just below the ASI). The 737's slip indicator is just below the AI, and the Learjet 45's is at the very bottom of the instrument panel below the AI.

Turn-and-slip indicator: One of the two gyro-operated turn instruments (turn-and-slip indicator and turn coordinator), the turn-and-slip indicator (T/S) shown here is the older of the two. This *ball and needle* turn instrument has a slip indicator at the bottom, and a needle at the top. You should be familiar with the slip indicator because it functions the exact same way as the stand-alone version.

The needle on the T/S indicates the direction and rate of your turn. The needle points to the L when you make a left turn and to the R when you make a right turn. The amount of needle deflection indicates the rate of turn. A larger deflection indicates a higher turn rate. The JetRanger and Extra 300 are the only two aircraft in Flight Simulator with a T/S. The T/S is located below the VSI on the JetRanger and on the 300, but remember that the VSI on the 300 is on the left side of the instrument panel.

Turn coordinator: The turn coordinator (TC) shown for the 182 uses a miniature airplane in place of the needle found on a T/S. But more significantly, unlike the T/S, the TC responds to roll. The wings on the little airplane dip in response to aircraft roll. As you'd expect, the left wing dips when your airplane banks to the left and the right wing dips when your airplane banks to the right. But it's important to note that although the TC indicates a bank, that doesn't necessarily mean that the airplane is really banked.

What the TC really displays is rate of yaw. The only instrument that relates true bank is the AI. Regardless, the only aircraft in Flight Simulator with TC's are the Cessnas, and they are both located on the same place on the instrument panels—below the VSIs.

Now that you know what the turn instruments do, we need to talk a bit about how to use them. There are two ways to correct for slips and skids. One way is to increase or decrease bank. But in the real world this isn't done. It's much easier and safer to use the second method—apply the appropriate amount of rudder correction.

Adding rudder will yaw the airplane to line up, a result of the combination of centrifugal force and gravity. In a slipping turn, you'd add inside rudder (rudder in the direction of the turn). In a skidding turn, you'd add outside rudder (rudder in the opposite direction of the turn). The easiest way to remember this is to remember the phrase *step on the ball*. Step on the ball means to *step* on the rudder (apply rudder) on the side where the ball is riding. The amount of rudder you need to apply depends on how far the ball has deviated from center. You only need apply enough rudder to re-center the ball.

The turn coordinators in Flight Simulator are only found on the Cessna 182RG and 182S, and they respond to roll instead of turn rate.

Standard Rate Turn

If you've taken a close look at the T/S and TC, you probably noticed the "2 MIN" reference made on their faces. What this means is those turn instruments are calibrated for two minute turns. In instrument flight, all turns are made at 3 degrees per second or less. A 3 degree turn is called a standard rate turn or two minute turn. This means a 360 degree turn can be completed in two minutes. The amount of bank needed to turn your airplane at this rate is dependent on your airspeed. Use the turn coordinator to help you figure this out.

Turns made at a rate steeper than standard are considered dangerous. However, it's fine to make turns at less than the standard rate (heading changes of less than 5 or 10 degrees). Whether or not you're interested in learning to fly IFR, you should try to always limit yourself to standard rate turns. One of the first mistakes that new pilots tend to

Note: *In modern aircraft, all gyroscopic turn instruments are electric powered instead of vacuum powered. This is so the pilot will still be able to receive bank information even if there is a vacuum failure.*

Tip: *The reaction of the T/S and TC to a turn is exaggerated until you reach a steady angle of bank. As we saw with the VSI, if you try to "chase" these instruments you'll lose.*

Note: *Aircraft flying at over 200KIAS make turns at 30 degrees of bank maximum even if it results in 360 degree turns of more than 2 minutes.*

make is to over-control the airplane. To avoid this, you need to use slow, steady, controlled movements. Training yourself to fly standard rate turns can only increase your control over the aircraft.

Use the T/S or TC as your guide to make standard rate turns in an aircraft flying less than 200KIAS. When the needle matches the *doghouse* pointer on the T/S, you are turning at standard rate. On a TC, you'll be turning at standard rate if the lower (dipping) wing lines up with the lower index. Note that your airspeed will affect the required amount of bank, but the turn instruments will still guide you.

Directional Gyro

The directional gyro (DG) is essentially a better version of the old magnetic compass. While it can't find North by itself, it can remember where you set it better than a magnetic compass can, under certain conditions.

A magnetic compass can suffer from an instrument error called *deviation*. This error is caused by the ferrous metal parts of the aircraft. Magnetic compasses are also subject to what is known as magnetic dip errors. These are errors that occur during turning and acceleration/deceleration maneuvers. Because of these inherent problems, the only time a properly calibrated (calibrated for deviation) magnetic compass is accurate is during straight and level, unaccelerated flight.

So in addition to not being subject to magnetic dip and deviation errors, the main advantage that a DG has over a compass is that it doesn't bounce around in rough conditions. The DG also will not fluctuate its heading as wildly during a turn, either.

Understanding the DG

Essentially there are several versions of the DG. Some are simple, like the one shown here (modeled on the Cessnas and on the Extra 300 in Flight Simulator), and others are combined with a radio navigation instrument called a Horizontal Situation Indicator (HSI). (See JetRanger's HISI.) In either case, the operation of the DG part of the instrument is the same, and its location within the standard instrument cluster remains the same on all of the aircraft in Flight Simulator—directly below the AI.

The numbers on the DG and the outside of the HSI correspond to the directions on a compass, but the last digit is removed. In other words, 36 is 360 degrees, and 19 is 190 degrees. The DG number in the top (12 o'clock) position under the pointer indicates your current heading.

Stand-alone directional gyros are only modeled on the 182RG, 182S, and Extra 300 in Flight Simulator.

There are two display versions of the HSI modeled in Flight Simulator— mechanical and electronic. This mechanical HSI is from the JetRanger.

The Instrument Scan

A fundamental skill, and the key to good situational awareness and instrument flying, is learning a good instrument scan pattern. This is because when you're flying IFR with nothing outside to look at except clouds, you should only need to scan your instruments to fly the aircraft well. There is no ideal scan pattern for all pilots or all situations. There are recommended patterns, but most pilots develop their own habits to maximize their efficiency. We'll describe a typical basic scan pattern, but keep in mind that you'll probably want to discover your own.

The idea behind an instrument scan is to keep your eyes moving so that they can continuously read every gauge on your instrument panel. A common mistake is fixating on one gauge. Another is omitting or skipping some instruments. You have to constantly read, compare and analyze what you see.

A typical basic scan pattern is based around the AI. This is because most pilots feel they can learn the most about their

Developing an instrument scan pattern will greatly increase your situational awareness skills.

present situation from this device. In most cases, the AI is almost as good as looking out the window (or better, some claim). You can tell if your wings are level and your nose is pointed at the horizon.

Next, scan down to the DG to see if you're flying your intended heading. Then scan back to the AI for a quick glimpse, finishing with the VSI to see if you're climbing or descending. Once you've completed the entire scan, start over again back at the AI.

That's one basic scan pattern. Between the basic pattern, you should also mix in what, lacking a better term, we'll call "sub scans." These sub scans involve quick scans to the VOR displays (we'll get to them), the ALT, the ASI, and the TC. When you maneuver, your scan pattern should alter a bit. For example during a turn, you should scan the TC more often. Other gauges get scanned occasionally, but *every* gauge gets scanned regularly.

The instrument scan is a tough skill to learn and you won't grasp what each instrument is displaying the first time you scan them. Just keep scanning and the blind spots will become apparent after a couple of cycles. Keep practicing and don't give up. It's really pretty awkward at first, but if you stick with it and get the hang of it, the rewards will be well worth your efforts.

Visualize!

The word *visualize* probably sounds like the mantra of a self-help seminar or something, but if you try to visualize in your mind where you are, and where you're going, it can help tremendously. Obviously, you won't "see" everything, especially if you're flying in a new area, but visualizing the situation can help you keep up on what needs to be done. Flying (especially IFR flying) requires you to think ahead. This is so you don't get caught off-guard, and also because the workload becomes so heavy during certain maneuvers like landing. If you get as much done before you're in the thick of things, it'll just make everything that much easier.

Chapter Five

NORMAL PROCEDURES

This chapter is all about flying. At the beginning of this book we spoke a little about "flying by the numbers," meaning that if you configure your aircraft at specific settings for pitch, power, and bank, its performance will be repeatable.

This concept is summarized by an expression used in aviation that looks like this: ATTITUDE + POWER = PERFORMANCE.

Although this phrase sounds like a slogan chanted at some kind of motivational seminar, what it means is that given a certain pitch attitude and power setting, you can more or less expect the same airspeed, climb, or descent. As you might imagine, knowing exactly how your airplane will perform goes a long way toward helping you maintain precise control over that aircraft.

This chapter will walk you though the procedures associated with a normal flight in two of the new aircraft in Microsoft Flight Simulator 98—the Cessna 182S Skylane and the Bell 206B JetRanger. We'll cover the exact configuration settings you'll need to fly by the numbers. We'll do it by running through checklists. Our checklists are a little more detailed than the ones you'll find in Flight Simulator (hence the term *amplified*), so as we go through them, you may want to pause the simulation by pressing the P key between steps.

These are the six normal flight configurations used in an airplane:

- Climb
- Cruise
- Descent
- Approach
- Approach Descent
- Non-precision Approach Descent

We're only going to worry about the first four configurations. They're enough to get you off the ground and back again safely. The other two configurations are generally used for IFR flight only. While it wouldn't hurt to

Note: *Although what we're about to cover may seem like a true flight, it's only presented as an example to illustrate procedures. A true simulated flight would have some sort of navigation plan.*

learn to fly with IFR precision in a VFR environment, you don't need to be bogged down with too much at once. New pilots in the real world don't instantly jump into flying IFR, so you shouldn't really expect to be able to, either.

Starting Out

We're going to take off from Chicago's Meigs Field in the 182S during the daytime. When you first start up Flight Simulator 98 and click Fly Now! from the opening screen, you'll see the default Meigs Field flight (assuming that you haven't already selected a custom flight as the startup default using the Save Flight option on the Flights menu).

The time of day will be based on your computer system's clock time. So unless you work at night (or are lucky enough to fly Flight Simulator at work during the day), you'll probably have to adjust the Flight Simulator world to daytime. Because the Meigs default flight is a day flight, the fastest way to do

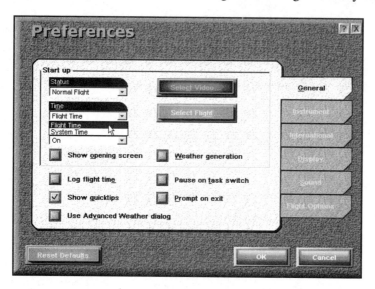

that is to reset the Flight itself by pressing Ctrl + semicolon (;) on the keyboard, and the Flight will reset itself to its saved time.

If you get tired of resetting your first flight of the day every time you run Flight Simulator, you can change the Start Up options to load the saved flight time instead of the system time. The Start Up options are configured in the General Preferences screen under the Options menu selection. By

Selecting Flight Time on the General Preferences screen tells Flight Simulator to use the saved flight time when it loads its default flight.

selecting Flight Time from the drop-down box, you tell Flight Simulator to use
the saved flight time when it loads the default flight (when Flight Simulator first
runs). When you enter the Meigs flight, you'll find yourself on the runway with
your engine already started, so we won't bother with engine starting procedures.

All of the procedures listed in this book are made with the assumption that
certain aircraft realism settings are enabled.

Here are some of the specific configuration settings we'll be using:

- Realism Slider—Real
- Auto Coordination—Disabled
- Manual Fuel Control—Enabled
- Magnetos—Enabled
- Mixture Controls—Enabled
- Prop Advance—Manual

Remember that all of the settings listed above are situation-based and are
only saved with a flight. If you don't re-save the default flight with these
settings (it's best to do this under another flight name,
so you can leave the original intact), when you restart
or reset this flight, you'll have to reconfigure all of
the options every time as well.

Lists, and More Lists

The Pilot's Help Aircraft Handbooks contain aircraft
flight checklists, and simplified checklists that are
available on your cockpit screen by default. These
cockpit checklists offer tips for basic situations such
as takeoff and landing.

For our procedural flights you won't need these,
so you can close them and gain back some instrument
panel "real estate."

To close the simplified checklists, click the Close
button at the bottom right hand corner of the list. You
can display and toggle through these lists by pressing
Shift + C at any time or by clicking Checklists on the
Aircraft menu and then selecting the specific
checklist you want to see.

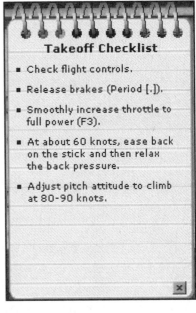

Simplified checklists are available
on your cockpit screen by default.

Pre-Takeoff/Ground Check

Just as an "aircraft preflight" is a safety inspection, aircraft pre-takeoff or *ground check* procedures are more of the same thing...with a few reminders added. The main difference between the two inspections is that during the ground check you're sitting inside the airplane and the engine is running. Basically, this is your last chance to make sure everything is A-OK before committing yourself to takeoff.

Ground check procedures are usually performed before taxiing out onto the runway. But since we're already out on the runway, we'll perform them here. Normally, if you have your aircraft reliability settings set to Reliable, there really isn't much point in performing the ground check—you *know* everything is going to work. But if you've got that reliability setting set to anything other than Reliable, it'd be wise to take the time and do as many checks as possible while you're still on the ground.

1. Brakes (SET)

Your parking brakes should be set by default when you first enter the Meigs Flight. However, if they aren't set in advance, brakes are applied by pressing the . (period) key on the keyboard or by pulling the trigger on your joystick. The 182S has two brakes, one for each wheel. Pressing the period key applies both brakes evenly. To operate each brake individually, which is useful for turning while taxiing, press F11 to apply the left brake, and F12 for the right brake.

In any case, this first step is intended to prevent your aircraft from rolling away and getting into trouble while you're busy performing the rest of the ground check. To set your brakes in the locked position (parking brakes) press Shift + . (period).

2. Seats, belts, and harnesses (SECURE)

Okay, this one's a little silly for desktop piloting. Unless you have seat belts on your computer chair—and don't laugh, I know guys that do—you can skip this one. Just say "secure" and move on to the next step.

3. Doors (CLOSED and LOCKED)

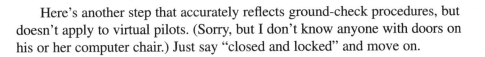

Here's another step that accurately reflects ground-check procedures, but doesn't apply to virtual pilots. (Sorry, but I don't know anyone with doors on his or her computer chair.) Just say "closed and locked" and move on.

4. Flight controls (FREE and CORRECT)

In a real airplane, checking your flight controls entails moving each of them to their limit. (This usually isn't possible with the rudder because the nose wheel is stationary.) You're basically making sure that your ailerons and elevator controls aren't sticking and that the control surfaces are moving in the right directions. As a desktop pilot, you may believe that you're immune to such problems, but the truth is, that if you're using a joystick, rudder pedals, or flight yoke, you might want to pay attention to this.

On the 182S (just to the left of the throttle control knob) are the control position indicators. The real 182Ss (and non-fly-by-wire aircraft) don't have anything like this because they just don't need them. Your flight controls are physically tied to the control surfaces. However, on a computer, your control movements correspond to virtual aircraft control movements, which are not physically connected. In other words, your virtual aircraft is controlled through software, and depending on how that software is set up, the result will be proper or improper control of your virtual aircraft. So let's talk about what to look for.

> **Note:** *Control reversing is very rare, but I've been told it has happened on cable-controlled aircraft after major servicing and similar activities.*

Just as the name suggests, the control position indicators are graphical representations of where your control surfaces are located within their range of movement. The center vertical index represents your elevator, the horizontal index on the top represents your ailerons, and the horizontal index on the bottom represents your rudder.

Back in Chapter Two, we covered the details on how Flight Simulator adjustments are made, so if you need help with those adjustments, refer to that chapter for step-by-step instructions.

The first thing you should look for is whether the pointers are centered when your stick is centered. If they aren't, you may need to adjust your joystick trim wheels, if it has them, or you may need to recalibrate the offending controller(s).

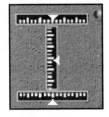

These control position indicators are located just to the left of the throttle control knob.

The next thing to check for is proper movement in both axes and directions. Move your controllers around and watch the control movement indexes. Make sure that the aileron control moves the aileron index and so on. Furthermore, you want to make sure that control movement moves the corresponding index in the correct direction. For the ailerons and rudder, left control index movement corresponds with left controller input and vice versa. The elevator index should move up for up elevator controller input and vice versa. If you have a problem here, you may have the Reverse Joystick option enabled in Custom Controls within the Options menu.

Control travel should be checked next. The entire length of a control position indicator box represents 100 percent control deflection in both directions. The middle represents the neutral position. Slowly move one control axis as you watch the corresponding index on your instrument panel. If the index never reaches the ends of the position indicator box, you need to increase that particular axis's sensitivity (unless you've already adjusted this axis down to suit your preferences).

On the other hand, if the controller index reaches the end of the indicator box long before your controller reaches the end of its physical travel, the sensitivity on this axis is too sensitive. If an axis's sensitivity is too high, your aircraft will be over-responsive and hard to control. On the other hand, if the sensitivity is too low, it'll be tough to maneuver. You'll get the feeling that you're flying through molasses.

Naturally, controller sensitivities are a matter of preference, and everyone is different. Nevertheless, a good starting point for most people is a setup where the sensitivity setting moves the index to meet the end of the control position at the same time that your controller physically meets its travel limit. This will give you 100 percent control movement without any *dead spots*, areas where no additional control surface movement is possible. The only exception to this approach, that you may want to consider, is rudder travel. Most pilots feel more comfortable with a rudder sensitivity setting that nets less than 100 percent indicator travel.

As for Null Zone adjustments, that's really something you have to adjust in the air. But gross problems can be identified and corrected during the ground check. What you're looking for here are *spikes* when your controller is in its centered position. Spikes are erratic, non-intentional control inputs and are generally hardware-related, such as dirty potentiometers in your controller or

game card problems. Nevertheless, adjusting Null Zones can help. It's worth a try. Besides, it's free!

After all of that you should have each of your controllers set up properly, and that's a very good thing. A crack pilot may be able to fly with a poorly adjusted controller, but he or she will know something is wrong. On the other hand, new pilots usually won't be able to tell if there is anything wrong and may just blame their poor performance on their general lack of piloting skills. But perhaps the best benefit of properly setting up your controller is once it's been adjusted, you shouldn't have to do it again until you change controllers or reinstall Flight Simulator 98. (And if you've saved your FLTSIM98.CFG file from the Flight Simulator folder, you won't have to repeat setting up your controller even if you do reinstall. Just copy the saved FLTSIM98.CFG file back into your Flight Simulator folder after Flight Simulator 98 has been re-installed.)

5. Flight instruments (CHECKED and SET)

After reading Chapter Four, you should be well versed on what the flight instruments are, where they're located, and how to read them. The ground check is the time to check and calibrate them.

First, visually check all of your instruments. Start on one side of the standard instrument cluster and work your way to the other side. Don't skip around. This will help you avoid missing an instrument. What you are looking for is proper operation. The gyros on the AI, TC, and DG should be spinning (if one isn't, the display will be all cockeyed), and the ASI and VSI should both read 0 (zero).

Before taxiing off the ramp on a real flight, we'd listen to ATIS (Automatic Terminal Information Service) on our COM (Communications) radio for an altimeter setting, among other things. If you recall, the ALT is a fancy barometer, and an altimeter setting is the current barometer reading. We'll talk about using the radio in another chapter, so for now let's consider how to calibrate your instruments.

There are only two instruments in Flight Simulator that can be calibrated during the ground check—the altimeter and the directional gyro. Although a pilot usually takes this time to tune radios and NAV instruments as well, we'll leave those activities for later. Let's begin by calibrating the ALT (which is already calibrated for you when you start the default flight).

There are three ways to calibrate the ALT in Flight Simulator. One of them isn't absolutely realistic because of simulation limitations, and another isn't realistic because Flight Simulator allows you to cheat a bit. You'll see why in a minute.

- The first method requires that you listen to ATIS and get an ALT setting. Then you enter the Aircraft Settings window Realism tab (in the Aircraft menu) and type in the setting in the proper box. In real-world aviation, the ALT settings are entered in the Kollsman window by twisting the calibration knob on the front of the instrument. Although typing in an ALT setting isn't realistic, there isn't much choice because the Kollsman window is too small to be legible on a computer monitor.
- The second method doesn't require listening to ATIS. Again, in the real world, if you're at an airport where there is no altimeter setting available, you can just set your altimeter to the airport's altitude and that'll do just fine. The FAA allows you to use this method, and in case you're wondering, you can have up to a 75-foot maximum allowable error and still be legal to fly. So if you know the airport's altitude (if you don't, you can use Flight Simulator's airport directory), you can use your mouse to adjust the ALT to read the proper altitude. To do this, you click the ALT calibration when the mouse cursor turns into a hand. When the hand has a plus sign on it, it will increase the setting, and vice versa.
- The third method is the simplest. All you need to do is press B on the keyboard. Flight Simulator will automatically set the correct ALT setting whether or not you actually listened to ATIS.

So which of these three is the most realistic way to go about setting the ALT? You'll find that many of the procedures in Flight Simulator are simulated. (Well, *of course* they're simulated.) However, what I mean is that sometimes you have to choose to follow procedures even though there are no adverse consequences if you don't. Setting the ALT is just one example. For realism, listen to ATIS and memorize the ALT setting even though you won't need to use it. In the real world that's what you have to do. Then go ahead and press the B key. Granted, you couldn't do that in real life, but setting an ALT isn't much more complicated than that.

Next we're going to set the DG. As you know, the DG is a *brainless* instrument that doesn't know north from south until you tell it where north is. You do this by setting the DG heading to correspond with the magnetic compass heading. As when setting the ALT, there's more than one way to do it.

The magnetic compass is not located on the instrument panel.

The magnetic compass in the real 182S is not located on the instrument panel. In order to view the compass in Flight Simulator, you have to call it up from the Views section of the Instrument Panel menu. Set the DG's correct heading by either clicking the left DG adjustment knob or simply by pressing the D key. (You can just press D without looking at the compass. It will set the correct heading even if your compass is out of operation.)

6. Fuel quantity (CHECKED)

You have two full tanks of AVGAS by default. If you're manually managing your fuel, go to the Aircraft menu, Aircraft Settings, Fuel Tab and put the Fuel Selector to ALL (also known as *both*). Generally, when you're taxiing around, many pilots set their tanks to the fullest tank to try to even out the load. In any case, use the All Tanks selection for takeoff.

7. Mixture RICH

The default mixture setting is full rich, so you won't have to do anything here. But to double-check, move the mixture control (red knob) full forward with your mouse or by pressing Ctrl + Shift + F4.

8. Propeller (FULL INCREASE—HIGH RPM)

The default prop setting is also full forward. But if it isn't, you can move the prop control (the blue knob) full forward with your mouse or by pressing Ctrl + F4. You do this because you're going to be increasing power in Step

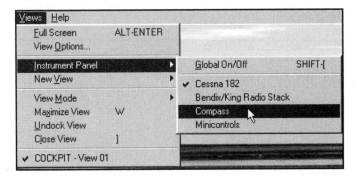

To view the 182S's compass, you have to call it up from the Views section of the Instrument Panel menu.

10 and if the prop pitch is set to a lower RPM, it'll produce unnecessary strain on the engine.

9. Elevator Trim and Rudder Trim (SET for takeoff)

Because there's no rudder trim in Flight Simulator, you only have elevator trim to deal with. The elevator trim position indicator is located to the left of the control position indicators. Takeoff trim setting is slightly aft of neutral. That translates into slightly higher than the middle location on Flight Simulator's elevator trim indicator.

The elevator trim position indicator is located to the left of the control position indicators.

10. Magneto check

THROTTLE 1800 RPM

CHECK L-B-R-B

MAX DROP 175 RPM

MAX DIFF 50 RPM

The magneto check requires several steps. First advance the throttle to 1,800 RPM by pressing F3 a couple of times. (Using the mouse for this isn't recommended because it's harder to be accurate.) Check your progress by watching the tachometer located at the lower right of the instrument panel.

Next you should systematically turn the magnetos on and off. The magneto switch is located at the bottom of the instrument panel at the far left. It looks like an ignition switch found in a car, and, in fact, it's very similar. The biggest difference between the two types is that instead of having only four positions (Off, Accessory, Run, and Start), the magneto switch has five (Off, Right, Left, Both, and Start).

The magneto switch looks like an ignition switch found in a car and is located at the bottom of the instrument panel at the far left.

The Start and Off positions are self-explanatory, and you can think of Right, Left, and Both as three different run positions. Right and Left refer to the two magnetos found on the engine. They are redundant systems which are there for safety purposes. You'll normally fly with both magnetos enabled so, if one mag goes out, the other will still be connected and will therefore keep the engine running.

During the ground check you examine the condition of each magneto by systematically turning one mag off at a time. To do this, press M on the

keyboard. Then press the - (minus sign) key to turn the mag switch counter-clockwise or the + (plus sign) key to turn the mag switch in a clockwise direction. The letters written on the ground-check list *L-B-R-B* stand for Left-Both-Right-Both. That means you should first move the mag position and switch to the Left position and then move it back to Both, followed by Right, and finally back to Both again.

Each time you switch from Both to one of the other mags and back, you should be watching the tach for RPM changes. See if there are RPM drops from the Both position to a single mag of less than 175 RPM. You're also looking for a drop of no more than 50 RPM between the right and left mags. Any RPM drops that are higher than the specifications call for indicate a worn magneto or other problem. Needless to say, you probably shouldn't fly if you find a problem here—unless you're interested in finding out how well your airplane works as a glider.

11. Propeller (CYCLE from HIGH-LOW-HIGH)

This step is intended to place a load on the engine and prop pitch control system. Prop pitch movement is handled by a high-pressure hydraulic system fed off the engine oil system. Cycling prop pitch accomplishes two things. First, it warms up the prop pitch control system by cycling oil through it. Second, by stressing the prop pitch system, you can force a weakness like a system leak to show itself. Although the checklist displays this step as one cycle, it isn't a bad idea to perform two cycles to make sure the oil in the prop governor is warm.

To cycle the prop, press Ctrl + F1 on the keyboard or pull the prop control (the blue knob) all the way back with your mouse. Leave it for a second or two and take a quick look at the oil pressure gauge located just above the mag switch. You want to make sure there are no sudden losses in oil pressure. Once this is checked, return the prop control back to the full forward position by pressing Ctrl + F4 or by using your mouse.

12. Suction gauge (CHECK)

With this step you're just checking to see that the suction gauge is in the green. In case you forgot, the suction gauge is located in the upper left corner of the instrument panel. You're checking suction because the 182S's DG and AI are vacuum-operated.

13. Engine instruments /Ammeter (CHECK)

This step is similar to step 12—you're just checking to make sure every gauge is in the green zone. If there were a functional ammeter to check, you'd turn on an electric device to see whether the gauge itself is stuck or whether the electrical system can handle a load. For example, turn on your landing lights to see whether the ammeter needle moves. If it does, that means the gauge is not stuck. If the needle moves too weakly, then you have either a charging system problem or an electrical short somewhere along the line.

14. Throttle (800—1000 RPM)

At this point, your engine should be thoroughly warmed up and you've concluded the stress tests, so you can return the throttle back to idle. To do this, use your mouse, or press F2 a couple of times. Watch the tach and set the engine to 800-1,000 RPM.

15. Lights and strobes (AS REQUIRED)

Unless you're going to take this flight at night, aircraft lighting isn't required. But if you do fly at night, you must have your navigation lights (NAV) and anticollision—or strobe—light(s) running. Something that may surprise you is that a landing light isn't required during either day or night unless you're flying for hire.

Regardless of whether you're flying in the day or night, turning on your anticollision lights is just good sense. NAV lights, on the other hand, are worthless during the daytime.

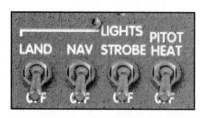

Instrument lights, navigation lights, strobe (anticollision) lights, and landing lights are all operable from the lighting control panel.

The FAA defines night as those hours between sunset and sunrise. In Alaska, however, night is defined as the period during which a prominent, unlit object cannot be seen from a distance of three statute miles or when the sun is more than 6 degrees below the horizon.

There are four kinds of aircraft lighting modeled in Flight Simulator—instrument lights, navigation lights, strobe (anticollision) lights, and landing lights. Each is operable from the lighting control panel directly to the right of the mag switch. Let's talk a little more about

each type of lighting and how it works.

Instrument Lights: What are called instrument lights in Flight Simulator are really a combination of instrument lighting and interior lighting. Interior lights are the red lights that illuminate the interior of the cockpit. Red is used during night flight because it allows you to see without causing the pupils in your eyes to contract. When your pupils contract, less light can enter, which makes it even

Red interior lights are used in planes so pilots will be able to see as much of the airspace outside the plane as possible.

harder to see. With red lighting you can look back and forth between the inside of the cockpit and the outside world with minimal eye adjustments.

Instrument/Interior lighting is toggled on and off by pressing the L key on the keyboard or by clicking the NAV lights switch on the lighting control panel. Note that instrument lighting is only operational during the nighttime and the default is set to On during any night flights. This toggle also controls the NAV lights as well, so let's talk about those next.

Navigation Lights: NAV lights are the position marker lights discussed in Chapter Three. These are required for night flight but are basically useless during day flights. NAV lighting is controlled by pressing the L key on the keyboard or by clicking the NAV lights switch on the lighting control panel. NAV lighting defaults to Off whether in day or night flight.

Strobe Lights: Strobe lights are often referred to as anticollision lights, but anticollision lighting usually refers to the extremely bright white flashing lights, while strobe lights can also refer to a rotating red beacon like the one modeled in the 182S. Either type of strobe light is difficult to see during day flights in real life, but either can get your attention, nevertheless. That's why most pilots fly day and night with them on.

Note: *Some pilots consider it courteous to keep strobe lights and landing lights turned off while performing a ground check at night. Having a brightly lit flashing airplane on the side of the runway while a plane is landing is understandably thought to be a distraction. On the other hand, if keeping the lights off causes you to forget to turn them on again just before takeoff, it's better to leave them on.*

Tip: *The landing light in the JetRanger can be moved around to point in different directions. This is a great feature for pilots looking for something to see on the runways at night or for those who just want to play "Los Angeles Sheriff's Department Air Patrol."*

The strobe light(s) are controlled by pressing the O key on the keyboard or by clicking the STROBE light switch on the lighting control panel. Strobe lighting also defaults to Off whether in day or night flight.

Landing Lights: The landing light is the big, bright headlight-style light on the front of the airplane. The jets in Flight Simulator have multiple landing lights, but our little Cessna is only equipped with one. A landing light is not required for night flight, so you don't need to turn it on. However, most new pilots like to use it because they feel it helps them see better. In reality there's nothing out on the runway that needs to be seen that you can't already see without the headlight turned on. Nevertheless, if you've got one, use it— if not to help you see better, at least to make it easier for you to be seen by other aircraft. Most commercial carriers have policies requiring the use of landing lights during the daytime when you're near airports for that very same reason.

To toggle the landing light on and off, press Ctrl + L on the keyboard or click the LAND light switch on the lighting control panel with your mouse. The default Landing light setting is Off whether in day or night flight.

Landing Light Control Commands

Action	Keystroke
Move Light Up	Ctrl + Keypad 8
Move Light Down	Ctrl + Keypad 2
Move Light Left	Ctrl + Keypad 4
Move Light Right	Ctrl + Keypad 6
Re-center Landing Light	Ctrl + Keypad 5

16. Radios and avionics (SET)

In this step you normally set your COM and NAV radio frequencies and headings. You won't need either of these for this flight, so we'll talk about them a little later.

17. Autopilot (OFF)

The autopilot module is located at the bottom of the radio stack. To access the radio stack, click the Master Avionics switch that's located just to the right of the lighting control panel. You can also access the radio stack by selecting Instrument Panel, and then Bendix/King Radio Stack from the Views menu, although clicking the Avionics switch is much faster.

We'll discuss specifics about autopilot a little later, but for the ground check procedure you just want to make sure that autopilot is turned off. You don't want autopilot causing the aircraft to fight you during takeoff.

To turn off autopilot, press the Z key or click the button labeled AP on the far left of the autopilot module. The red LED display will disappear when autopilot is switched off. To hide the radio stack,

The Master Avionics switch is located just to the right of the lighting control panel.

The autopilot is the bottom module of the radio stack.

The radio stack can be accessed by selecting Instrument Panel, Bendix/King Radio Stack from the Views menu.

Right-click the radio stack and select Close Window from the pop-up menu to close the radio stack.

The flap setting control is located to the right of the mixture control.

click the Master Avionics switch again, or right-click the radio stack and select Close Window from the pop-up menu.

18. Flaps (SET 0–20 degrees. 10 degrees recommended)

Flaps increase your lift, thereby lowering your stall speed. These are both good conditions when you're taking off and landing (when you're so close to the ground). The 182S's flaps have four position settings: 0 degrees, 10 degrees, 20 degrees, and Full. The recommended flap setting depends on your situation. Note the word *recommended*. Flaps are not *required* for takeoff, but they will reduce the takeoff roll required. For instance, using the 20-degree flap setting will reduce your takeoff roll by about 20 percent. Note that the Full flap setting is not authorized for takeoff.

We'll talk more about performance settings in the next chapter, but for a normal takeoff, the recommended flap setting is 10 degrees. To lower your flaps one increment at a time, press the F6 key. To raise them one increment at a time, press the F7 key. You can also adjust your flap setting by clicking the flap setting control, located to the right of the mixture control.

19. Clearance (VERIFY)

This step is just a reminder not to wander out onto the runway before receiving clearance to take off or clearance to proceed out onto the runway. But since we're already out here on the runway, we can move on.

20. Brakes (RELEASE)

This last step is another reminder. You won't get very far with your parking brake engaged on Flight Simulator's 182S, but if your brakes are worn or maladjusted, this reminder is to prevent you from attempting to take off with your brakes on. To release the parking break, press the . (period) key or pull and then release the trigger on your joystick.

21. Takeoff!

Ready to Roll

After reading through this next checklist, you'll probably think that it isn't humanly possible to do so many things simultaneously. So you'll probably feel better knowing up front that it takes some time for the airplane to start rolling and that you get most of the job accomplished within the first few seconds. It just seems like a lot of stuff to do when it's explained in detail. All right, now it's time to get you into the air.

    1. Throttle (FULL OPEN—FULL THROTTLE/2400 RPM)

Now that your brakes are released, smoothly apply full power with the F3 key, mouse, or your throttle controller. Take a quick look at the tach, manifold pressure gauge, and oil pressure gauge. Your RPM reading should be between 2,350–2,400 RPM. If it isn't, you'd better shut down your engine unless you want to see if your airplane floats.

The manifold pressure gauge should be registering pressure and should be in the green arc or higher. If there was a red line on the manifold pressure gauge and you were above it, you'd have to reduce power to keep below the line, or you'd risk overstressing the engine. Next, take a look at the tach to make sure it's not above the red line. Finally, take a glimpse at the oil pressure gauge to make sure it's reading higher than the lower red line.

If you've got the Realism slider (the Aircraft Settings option on the Aircraft menu) set all the way towards Real and Auto-coordination disabled, adding power too abruptly will cause the airplane to turn and bank slightly to the left due to engine torque and slipstream effect. That's why you're urged to smoothly apply power.

If you've turned the Auto-coordination option off, you'll be using the rudder to control the airplane on the ground. Moving the ailerons won't do a thing for you to change direction. If you're using rudder pedals, just add a little right rudder to compensate for the left-turning tendency and hold it there. I'm not exaggerating: a little means a *little*. Make small corrections to stay on the centerline. Unless there's a strong

> **Note:** *Slipstream (or propwash) results from the swirling airflow generated from the propeller pushing against the port side of the vertical stabilizer. The propeller rotates clockwise (when viewed from the cockpit) and produces a flow pattern that moves from forward port toward aft starboard.*

Follow Your Feet

At best, steering with your feet feels very awkward—especially after years and years of driving automobiles and steering with your hands. I can recall the odd feeling of not knowing what to do with my hands while taxiing around the airport during my flight training days. But don't get discouraged; it's possible, and it's done every day.

The biggest problem new pilots tend to have is that they use too much rudder and overcorrect. These overcorrections lead to what's known in the test pilot biz as PIOs (pilot induced oscillations). The secret to success is to add a little bit of corrective rudder and hold it there until you see its effect. From there you can set a new course of action. Granted, this is easier said than done, but here are a few more tips:

- *Try to relate your rudder movements to a place on the airplane. The most common spot is the nose. If you want to move the nose to the right, press the right pedal. If you want to move the nose to the left, press the left pedal. (This simple tip will come in very handy when you fly the JetRanger.)*
- *Remember that it's better to apply less rudder than you need than to apply too much and have to correct.*
- *If you're having a lot of trouble with this, your rudder controller sensitivity may be set too high, or your Null Zone needs to be increased.*

If none of the above helps and you're still having problems, take some time and practice high-speed taxiing down the runway. Keep your speed below 50 KIAS and don't use any flaps (so you don't take off). If you think rudder control is tough with tricycle gear setup, wait until you try a taildragger! Many a pilot has used this high-speed taxi training method to learn to handle a taildragger, so don't be shy. Get out there and practice.

crosswind (and there isn't with this flight), you won't need to do much to keep rolling straight down the runway.

2. Mixture (RICH)

You set the fuel mixture to rich during ground check Step 7, but there are a couple of reasons for this second check. First, you never want to attempt takeoff with an overly lean engine. You won't get the power you're expecting and the engine can stall.

What some experienced pilots do while awaiting takeoff clearance at a busy airport is to lean the engine while holding short of the runway (staying behind the white line on the runway border). The idea is that if you idle for too long at a rich setting, you'll foul the spark plugs and really be in a bind. Without this second check, you might attempt to take off at the lean setting you chose during idle.

In a real airplane, you don't need to look down at the mixture control. It's placed close enough to the throttle

and prop controls so that if you open your hand a little wider than the way you'd casually push on the throttle, you can feel that all three knobs are in the full forward position. Pilots keep one hand on the throttle all through takeoff just in case it backs out while they're not looking. That's a matter of procedure, but you won't have to worry about anything like that happening to you if you use the keyboard or mouse.

3. Raise nose (50-60 KIAS)

As the airspeed indicator reaches 50 knots, gently apply the up elevator to raise the nose wheel off the ground. This 50–60 KIAS speed is known as Vr or rotation speed. (V stands for velocity.) Rotation refers to the rotation of the airplane on the pitch axis. You won't have to use very much elevator at all. The airplane will pretty much take off by itself.

4. Climb speed (80 KIAS)

At this point, the airplane will lift off the ground and start to climb. This is when you'll begin to get your first taste of instrument scanning. There are several things you should look at. Take a look at the AI, ASI, VSI, and TC. You want to adjust the aircraft's pitch attitude to maintain about an 80 KIAS climb. This speed is the 182S's best rate-of-climb speed. That means if you climb at this speed, you'll climb to the highest altitude in the shortest time.

When you first take off, you have to accelerate to reach 80 KIAS. If your pitch is too high, you may even lose airspeed. A good pitch to use can be found by placing the dot in the center of the AI about halfway between the AI's horizon and first pitch line. Next scan over to the ASI and make sure you're still accelerating. Then, look at the VSI to make sure you have a positive rate of climb and that it isn't too high. Anything over 500 FPM is excessive right now (not to mention uncomfortable for passengers), so adjust your pitch accordingly by lowering the nose.

You're interested in altitude, but you can't get up safely without some airspeed. Under no circumstances should you let the airspeed drop below 70 KIAS after you've reached 70 KIAS—even if it means losing altitude. Finally, take a look at the TC and give it right rudder until the ball centers on the slip indicator.

During the climb out, pitch adjustments need to be made only at about the width of the pitch pointer. In other words, if you need a little more or less pitch,

Note: *If you are flying an airplane with retractable landing gear (like the 182 RG), you'd retract the landing gear after confirming through the VSI that you're climbing and that there's no more runway ahead of you to land on if the engine fails. At Meigs it's pretty easy to figure out when that is! (Can you say "splash")?*

Tip: *Busy enough yet? Normally, at this point you'd also be scanning the skies for traffic. You're near an airport, and (naturally) aircraft congregate around airports. So you would normally need to be extra alert during takeoffs and landings. If you think you can handle it, go ahead and quickly switch views (Shift + 4, Shift + 6, back to Shift + 8 on the keypad) to take a look around. Don't forget to lower the nose a bit to check in front of you as well.*

On the other hand, if you're new to all of this, you probably have enough to do as it is, so we'll just say that as your copilot of sorts, I'm doing the traffic scanning for you. That way you'll—Wait! Look out! (Just kidding...)

you need to move the AI pitch index only the distance equal to about the width of the pitch index itself. You can do this because you know what the takeoff configuration is. (Remember: attitude + power = performance.)

Finally, don't neglect to watch your heading and bank angle on the AI. Keep the wings level and continue the climb. Any time you adjust your bank, check back with the TC and step on the ball.

5. Flaps (UP)

By now you probably realize that the elevator trim setting gives you too much up elevator. Adjust the trim to maintain your pitch attitude. When your airspeed reaches 75 KIAS, retract the flaps. Be prepared for another pitch change and adjust the trim as necessary. Continue to let the airplane accelerate to 80 KIAS. Once it gets there, adjust your pitch to maintain that speed. (That'll be about three-fourths the distance between the horizon and the first pitch bar on the AI.)

Climb

The climb, or what's sometimes more descriptively called the *cruise climb*, is different than takeoff climb. It's configured differently, and it's intended to achieve something different. The takeoff climb (where you should be now—climbing at 80 KIAS) is designed to get you off the ground to the highest altitude in the shortest period of time. This is for safety reasons: if you lose your engine during takeoff, the more altitude you have when it happens, the longer you can glide—which in turn dramatically increases your landing options.

On the other hand, a cruise climb trades off altitude gain for more ground distance traveled. If you were taking a trip somewhere (as opposed to making an altitude record attempt in your

Cruise climb instrument readings of the 182S.

182S), there'd come a point where you wouldn't want to climb any higher and you'd be more interested in making good time to your destination. That portion of the trip is known as the cruise. A cruise climb is a compromise between a takeoff climb and a cruise—which neatly explains where the term *cruise climb* came from.

As a general rule of thumb, you transition from the takeoff climb to a cruise climb at about 1,000 AGL (Above Ground Level). Meigs airport's elevation is 593 feet—we'll call it 600 feet. So at 1,600 we transition to cruise climb—one of the normal flight configurations I mentioned at the beginning of this chapter. What this means to you is that you need to include the ALT in your instrument scan, in addition to everything else.

1. Airspeed 85-95 KIAS (cruise climb)

Lower the aircraft's nose to halfway between the horizon and the first bar on the AI, so you accelerate to 90 KIAS. Remember to use pitch to control your airspeed. If the airspeed gets a little fast, ease the nose up slightly. If speed starts to drop, lower the nose slightly. It takes only a small pitch change to create big changes in airspeed and rate-of-climb.

Also, remember to use the rudder to maintain coordinated flight. After lowering the nose, you won't require as much right rudder anymore. It's when the airplane is traveling at low speed with a high power setting (like the takeoff climb) that the most right rudder is required to compensate for the airplane's left-turning tendency.

2. Prop/Throttle (CLIMB POWER)

The next thing you should do is reduce the power. Although the engine can run at full power all day long, leaving it at full throttle does burn up a lot of fuel. One of the goals of cruising is to strike a good balance between performance and fuel economy. The cruise climb more or less aims for the same goal.

- Reduce the throttle to 23 inches of manifold pressure. (If you were taking off from a high-altitude airport, you'd reduce the throttle to 23 inches as well, but if you couldn't achieve that pressure due to the thin air, you'd use full throttle instead.)

3. Mixture (ADJUST)

Next reduce the mixture setting to 15 GPH or Full Rich (whichever is less). At this low altitude, you can leave it at Full Rich. But if you were taking off from a high-altitude airport, you'd be able to use a leaner mixture due to the thin air.

Cruise

The second normal flight configuration is the cruise. The cruise is the part of the flight where you're interested in making good time to reach your destination rather than climbing any higher. The exact altitude is known as (what else?) cruising altitude.

Cruise configuration instrument readings in the 182S.

Your magnetic heading determines what your cruising altitude should be. (The magnetic heading is a heading that's not corrected for magnetic variation; that is, true north and magnetic north are not the same place). See Chapter Three for more details on this.

Although it isn't listed as a step in our

checklist, the first thing you need to do is level off at your cruising altitude. (When the wings of the AI rest on the top of the AI's horizon line, you'll be at a flying pitch attitude.) Don't worry about letting the airplane accelerate. Whatever airspeed the airplane will give you is what you want.

> **Tip:** *One handy rule of thumb that can help you level off at the right altitude with minimal correction is known as the 10 percent rule. Begin to level the airplane at an altitude that's 10 percent of your vertical speed below your intended altitude.*
>
> *For example, our cruise climb configuration should net you a climb rate of 600 FPM vertical velocity. So, to level off at a cruise altitude of 5,500 feet, you should begin to level off at 5,440 feet (60 feet below the final altitude).*

    1. Power (15-23 IN Hg, 2100-2400 RPM)

Because performance and fuel economy rely so heavily on atmospheric conditions (air is the working "fluid" for an engine—the more you can get inside, the more power you can produce), cruise power needs to be determined by a chart. Cruise performance charts for the 182S are listed in Chapter Seven. But here are some numbers and suggestions:

Cruise power is configured with throttle and props. Economy is a function of fuel mixture based on the throttle and prop settings. Cruise charts provide you with specific prop and throttle settings and specify what those settings achieve in airspeed (usually KTAS—Knots True Airspeed) at a specific altitude. Without going into detail, for a flight in the 182S cruising at 5,500 feet using the Meigs default weather, one throttle setting and one prop setting for 6,000 feet altitude would be 23 inches and 2,000 RPM. This will net you 123 KTAS at 10.3 GPH fuel burn.

    2. Elevator trim (ADJUST)

With the increase in airspeed, you'll need to re-trim the airplane. Just make sure you do this after the airplane has finished accelerating (has reached its equilibrium) or you'll have to do it again. That's not a big deal, but *flying the elevator trim* is like chasing the VSI. If your trim adjustment changes your airspeed, the new trim setting won't be correct any longer. Generally, you'll only have to wait about half a minute to reach equilibrium once you've leveled off.

3. Mixture (LEAN)

You've got your performance all set up, so the next step is to look for economy. At this altitude you can lean the mixture. The way that mixtures are normally leaned is by using the Exhaust Gas Temperature (EGT). The 182S has two recommended mixture settings: Recommended and Best Power.

Cessna 182S EGT Table

Mixture Description		Exhaust Gas Temperature
Recommended Lean (Pilot's Operating Handbook)		Peak EGT
Best Power	x	125 degrees F. Rich

This table suggests that for best economy we need to lean the mixture until the EGT reaches its peak temperature, and for Best Power we need to lean the mixture to peak and then back it down (richen it) until the EGT reads 125 degrees below peak. The EGT has a movable pointer (most movable pointers are called *bugs*) that you can move to establish where peak EGT is. This can help you remember what peak EGT is while you're busy scanning all the other instruments. To move the EGT bug, press U followed by + (plus sign) or - (minus sign). With the bug placed at peak EGT, it'll be easier to figure out where 125 degrees below peak really is.

The problem is that at 5,500 feet on this particular day we're flying (in summer), the EGT peaks well beyond the EGT's temperature scale. Nevertheless, we know from the cruise table that, at our power settings and altitude, we can fly with a 10.3 GPH fuel burn at 6,000 feet. So instead of using the EGT, we can use the fuel flow gauge to lean the engine. Slowly lean the mixture to reach the 11 GPH mark (we're a little below the 6,000 feet chart numbers, and it's better to err on the rich side than the lean side) while listening to the engine. If the engine starts to sound rough, you need to enrich the mixture for smooth operation.

4. Engine instruments/Ammeter (CHECK)

After leaning the engine, it's always best to look at all of the engine gauges. As before, we're interested in green indications, but be especially sure to watch for high cylinder-head temperatures. This will tip you off that you leaned the engine too much.

5. Fuel quantity
(CHECK)

In addition to overall quantity, if you have an imbalance in fuel between your tanks, now is the time to switch tanks to try to even them out. Although, theoretically, fuel should be taken evenly from both tanks, when ALL is selected, turns and banking can cause uneven usage. This issue isn't usually a big deal, so don't worry about it too much. And in any case, checking your fuel gauges should be a regular part of one of your sub-scans throughout your flight.

Standard rate turn at cruise in the 182S.

6. Altimeter (SET and CHECKED)

Because you're usually traveling a considerable distance while cruising, your altimeter setting may change. On a real flight, ATC or other ground services can update your altimeter settings en route. In Flight Simulator, you have to get ALT settings from ATIS reports from the airports along your route of travel.

Tip: *It's highly unlikely that you'd be able to make an entire flight and never have to perform a turn, so here's a tip regarding turns. To help you roll out of a turn on your desired heading, begin leveling your wings at one-half your bank angle. Let's use the standard rate turn at cruise speed for an example.*

A standard rate turn at cruise speed requires about a 17-degree bank (we'll call it 16). So if you were changing course from 360 to 180, you'd begin rolling out at heading 172 (360 - 8 = 180). Of course, you need to descend 1,000 feet as well to account for the new magnetic heading.

7. Nav/Com radios (TUNED and SET)

Descent

The next normal flight configuration is the descent. The descent (or cruise descent) is made at cruising speed. You go from cruising altitude to a lower cruising altitude, or until your transition to a landing approach descent. (There

Descent configuration instrument readings in the 182S.

is another kind of descent, too, called an *approach descent*. It is used in precision IFR operations.)

1. ATIS/Airport information (CHECK)

2. Approach briefing (COMPLETE)

This information comes from ATIS or ATC. If you're near your destination and on a VFR flight, you're interested in which runway is active. You also want to know if there are any advisories in effect that may have a bearing on your arrival.

3. Altimeter (SET and CHECKED)

This setting comes from ATIS or ATC.

4. Nav/Com radios (TUNED and SET)

If you have someone to talk to, set your radio to the appropriate ATC frequency and NAV settings. Since we're not using radio navigation, you can leave the NAV stuff alone. If you were near your destination airport, you'd switch to the tower frequency and request landing clearance.

5. Power (SET)

You know that, if you lowered the nose of the airplane, your airspeed would increase. Our definition of *cruise descent* is a descent made at cruising speed. So in order to descend at cruising speed, we need to reduce power. Aviation procedures specify that descents be made at the "optimum" rate and then at 500 FPM for the last 1,000 feet. Luckily (by design actually), the 182S's optimum descent rate is 500 FPM. (This is true for most single engine aircraft.)

Reduce power until the manifold pressure gauge shows about 15 inches. When you reduce power, the nose of the airplane will pitch downward by itself (remember that the throttle controls descent.) Split the horizon line on the AI with the AI's wings and keep it there until the airplane again reaches

equilibrium. You shouldn't have to mess with the elevator trim because we were using trim for cruise speed, and you should now be descending at cruise speed as well. Finally, because we've changed power and pitch, you'll need to add some left rudder and keep the ball in the TC centered.

6. Mixture (SET)

All things being equal, your mixture setting will automatically lean itself when you descend due to the denser air below. This can be dangerous if you didn't reduce the power setting. Generally, a leaner mixture at a higher power setting will become a slightly richer mixture at a lower power setting because the fuel flow (requirements) are reduced. Nevertheless, once you've established the cruise descent, re-check your mixtures. You'll notice that the EGT needle is back on the scale.

7. Fuel quantity/Selector (CHECK/BOTH)

This step will help remind you to return the fuel selector back to ALL in case you've forgotten.

8. Flaps—AS DESIRED:

0-10

10-20

20-FULL

We won't be needing any flaps right now because we're ahead of the airplane. We're descending before we need to. If we had to lose a lot of altitude quickly, we'd cut the power and apply flaps at the earliest possible time to increase our drag. Anyway, make sure you're watching the ASI, VSI and ALT. You don't want to descend beyond your target altitude. The 10 percent rule for leveling off applies to descents as well. So, to descend to the Meigs pattern altitude, you'll begin leveling off at 1,650 feet.

Approach

The final configuration we'll cover in this book is the approach. The approach can be thought of as the level approach (as opposed to the Approach Descent— normal flight configuration #5, listed at the beginning of the chapter) because

you'll be flying level. Approach speeds vary from plane to plane (and according to wind conditions), but they are always at a slower speed than the cruise.

Ideally, an approach speed should be at Vy. *Vy* is the best rate of climb. This way, if you have to abort your landing, you won't have to re-trim your airplane during the flurry. On the other hand, you also want your approach speed to make it easy to slow down for landing as well. We know that Vy is 80 and the recommended engine-out speed with flaps is 70, so we can logically use an approach speed of 70–80 KIAS.

Before Landing

Back to the example flight. You were leveling off at 1,600 feet. Now pitch the nose of the airplane up to halfway between the AI's horizon and the first pitch bar. Then go through the Before Landing checklist after the airplane slows down:

1. Seats, belts, harnesses (SECURE)

2. Fuel quantity/Selector (CHECK/BOTH)

Takeoffs and landings in the 182S are made with the fuel selector in the ALL position (Flight Simulator's term).

Tip: *GUMP-No relation to Forrest Gump, but you'd probably be called that around the airport if you landed your airplane with the gear retracted. GUMP is an acronym for the landing checklist.*
It stands for the following:

G-Gas
U-Undercarriage (landing gear)
M-Mixture
P-Prop(s)

These items are listed in the next four steps on the Before Landing checklist. However, when you're landing, there's a lot to do, so rather than read through a checklist, the most important list items can be covered by remembering GUMP.

3. Landing gear (DOWN)

Obviously, this doesn't apply to the 182S (which has fixed gear), but if you had retractable gear, you'd lower it now.

4. Mixture (RICH)

Part of the pre-landing checklist is designed to help you prepare for landing. The other part is to prepare you in case you need to abort your landing and go around (fly back up and make another approach). Setting your mixture is one of these steps. You want your mixture to be at Full Rich just in case you need to punch the throttle through

the firewall for a go-around. At this mixture, the engine won't sputter and die from being overly lean just when you need it the most.

5. Propeller (HIGH RPM)

This is another go-around precaution. High prop RPM is used for maximum power, and maximum power is what you'll need on a go-around.

6. Landing Lights (ON)

As we discussed earlier, during the day this is a personal preference.

7. Flaps—AS DESIRED:

    0-10

    10-20

    20-FULL

If you've held the nose halfway between the horizon and the first bar on the AI, we should be at a comfortable 75 KIAS with the current throttle and prop settings. When you have the airport in sight, enter the standard traffic pattern on a 45-degree angle.

After you're on the downwind leg of the traffic pattern, you're assured of being able to make the runway. Just when it comes time to turn to the base leg (when you can see the touchdown point at your 4 o'clock or 8 o'clock

The Flap About Flaps

There are two schools of thought about deploying flaps for landing. You might even classify them as teachings from the "school of optimism" and the "school of pessimism." Here's why: one school of thought believes that the earlier you can put your airplane into a landing configuration, the better off you'll be because you'll be ahead of the airplane. The more you can do before it becomes critical reduces the number of things you'll need to do later.

The second school of thought (the school of pessimism) says that you should only deploy your flaps when you are assured of actually being able to land. This theory states that if you are forced to go around, you won't have to spend time retracting the flaps.

According to the school of optimism, leaving the flaps up means the silly pessimists would have to cram all of that flap-setting into a relatively short period of time, increasing your workload rather than reducing it.

Who's right? Obviously if you could make every single landing and never had to go around, the optimists would be correct. But who really wants to take that kind of chance? There are plenty of pilots out there who feel like that. As for yours truly? Call me a pessimist.

Non-precision level approach configuration instrument readings in the 182S.

It's time to turn to the base leg when you can see the touchdown point at 4 o'clock.

position), systemically extend the flaps in 10-degree increments to 20 degrees. Don't let the nose drop. When you apply the first 10 degrees of flap, your airspeed will drop to 70; then it'll drop even more when you add the second flap.

At 65 KIAS pull back the throttle to about 10 inches and let the nose drop, but stay on top of everything. Use your pitch to maintain 65 KIAS. When you turn to final, drop the last flap. Watch your VSI: you don't want to descend faster than 500–800 FPM. If you are descending too fast, add two inches of throttle for a couple of seconds and then pull it back to 10 again.

You'll also need to add or reduce throttle based on how far away from the runway you are. If you don't think you'll make the runway, add throttle and go around. If you think you're going to land in the middle of the runway or further away, reduce throttle. You'll be tempted to lower or raise the nose, but use the throttle instead.

Landing

A wise man (all right a *wiseguy*) once said, "Any landing you can walk away from is a good landing." If that were true, *every* landing in Flight Simulator would qualify as a good landing. (Yea!) Actually, landing really amounts to a controlled crash. It's the level of control that you have when you *crash* that seems to make all of the difference. The idea behind the "perfect landing" is to try to slow the airplane down so it stalls just as the wheels touch the tarmac. Here's how you do it:

Just before you cross the start of the runway, reduce power to idle and gently raise the nose until it's one-half of a bar width above the horizon on the AI. You don't want to climb. However, there's a technique that really helps a lot of new pilots with their landings. Try playing a little game called " keep the airplane from landing."

It sounds pretty silly (especially when you're actively *trying* to learn to land) but here's how it works: instead of letting the airplane just drop in, if you try to keep it off the ground by increasing pitch, the airplane will stall just as it touches the ground. As long as you don't attempt this when you're too high in the air or allow the airplane to climb, it'll work perfectly. And when it does, the only clue you'll get as to when you actually touch down will be the screech of your tires. Don't get discouraged if you don't perfect it right away; keep practicing. Remember, as the General says "There ain't no such thing as a natural pilot." Here's a convenient breakdown of the four normal flight configurations for the 182S that we just covered. Note that each configuration

Normal Flight Configurations for the Cessna 182S

	Manifold Pressure	RPM	Pitch Attitude	Airsped	Vsi
Climb	23 in.	Full	1/2 between horizon/1st bar	90 KIAS	600 FPM
Cruise (5.5K')	23 in.	2,000	Level 1/2 bar below horizon	114 KIAS	0 FPM
Descent	15 in.	2,000	Level	114 KIAS	-500 FPM
Approach	15 in.	Full	1/2 between horizon/1st bar	75 KIAS	0 FPM

variable was chosen based on keeping as many of them exactly the same as the previous configuration as possible. This minimizes your workload and makes for more enjoyable flights.

Taxiing

Now that you're back down on terra firma, we can discuss a few things about taxiing. After taking off, taxiing will seem like a piece of cake. But here are some tips to help you get around better on the ground.

- Watch your speed. It's much better to be too slow than to move too fast. You can add a bit of power to get rolling, but once you're rolling, back the throttle down to reduce power. A power setting of 1,000 RPM works pretty well.
- Stay on the taxiway centerline. Wandering left or right of the center is not only bad form, but you could hit a wing tip.
- Trying to see ahead of you is really tough in the Extra 300S because it's a taildragger and its nose sticks up in the air when it's sitting on the ground. (Some people may see that as an "attitude" problem, but in aviation it's just a high-pitch attitude.) You can cheat by tilting the forward view: press Shift + Backspace. However, if you're into doing things the "real way," use your rudder to zig-zag around the taxiways while using the 2 o'clock and 10 o'clock views. Don't worry about people thinking you're drunk. This wandering is common practice for taildraggers.
- Use differential braking and individual throttle control to help turn the Learjet 45 and 737-400. Increasing the engine thrust on the outside engine and applying brake to the inside wheel can dramatically decrease your turn radius. If you really need the tightest possible turn, apply reverse thrusters on the inside engine as well.
- Don't forget to reduce power when you want to stop. You'll stop a lot faster that way than if you just apply the brakes. Besides, you wouldn't want to ding the wings of that shiny new Cessna!

Flying a Helicopter

Half-time helicopter hi-jinks.

The Bell 206B JetRanger is the first helicopter ever included in Flight Simulator. So even if you're a Flight Simulator fan from way back, flying this aircraft may be something totally new for you. But don't let that scare you; in forward flight a helicopter is very similar to flying an airplane. Therefore, you do have some valuable experience that you can call upon.

At this point, you have a pretty good idea of how the checklists are performed, so you should be able to run through the JetRanger's checklists on your own. Instead, let's cover some basic helicopter flying concepts, and also discuss some of the JetRanger's normal flight configurations.

Realism Settings

You might conclude that the highest realism setting would be harder to fly because it reproduces all of the quirks that real helicopter pilots and students have to deal with. But many pilots think the Flight Simulator helicopter is easier to fly at the highest realism setting. Try it both ways and decide for yourself.

The bottom line is this: don't let that *realism* label stop you. If a real pilot can deal with these quirks, there isn't any reason why you can't. All you have to do is be willing to devote some extra time and effort. The key is to take it a little at a time, just like any ordinary pilot would. Sooner or later, you'll get there.

Note: *For the sake of brevity, when talking about the helicopter, the terms collective and torque will be used interchangeably for percentage settings.*

Collective Perspective

Recall that there are parallels between a constant speed prop on an airplane and the main rotor system of a helicopter. Basically, where an airplane handles blade pitch with the prop pitch control, a helicopter uses the collective. The collective is a combination engine throttle and rotor blade pitch control. But because the RPM on a helicopter engine remains more or less constant while in flight, you only need to worry about controlling the collective. As you increase the collective, you increase downward thrust from the main rotor blades. But the thing to keep in mind here is that the collective controls altitude in exactly the same way that the application of throttle controls altitude in an airplane.

Note that it's possible to over-torque a helicopter's engine. In the simplest terms, torque is the amount of twisting pressure placed on the rotor drivetrain. The torque gauge in a helicopter indicate its limitations. As long as you remain below the red line and only go into the yellow arc *occasionally* you should be fine.

Cyclic Physics

A helicopter's *cyclic* controls the direction of the downward airflow generated by the main rotor system. When you're in forward flight, bank and pitch are controlled the same way as an airplane, where pitch controls airspeed. On the other hand, there are two differences you should be aware of: in a helicopter, forward level flight requires continuous forward pressure; and there is no equivalent to an airplane's elevator trim.

Anti-torque Talk

The tail rotor is best controlled by a set of rudder pedals, and self-centering pedals are distracting. A real helicopter has no *notch* in its center position, and the pedals are not self-centering. So the real thing has advantages and disadvantages over the typical desktop pilot setup.

The tail rotor controls yaw. As in an airplane, you press the pedal on the side toward where you want to turn. Many beginning pilots get confused when it comes to reverse flight. One way to stop the confusion is to always relate your position to the same location in the helicopter. Just as we did in the

airplane, use the nose as your reference. This way no matter which way you fly, you remember that the right pedal moves the nose right.

Another characteristic of helicopter flight is that tail rotor effectiveness is related to airspeed. As your airspeed increases, your tail rotor effectiveness decreases. This is due to a "weather vane" effect. During forward flight, the nose of the helicopter will always tend to point into the oncoming airflow in forward flight.

Finally, the effects of torque during takeoff (power on) and descending (power off) are the reverse of those in an airplane. When you add power in an airplane, the airplane will tend to yaw to the left, requiring right rudder input to correct. On helicopters made in the US (like the JetRanger), takeoff torque is backwards—left anti-torque pedal input is required instead. The reverse is also true: when you ease off the collective, you'll need to add right pedal.

Helicopter Flight Modes

A helicopter can fly in just about in any direction. For the sake of simplicity, let's just say there are basically two modes—hover and forward flight (flying backwards is the same as forward, only reversed). Of the two, hovering is by far the more difficult. We'll cover both, but let's start with the easier, forward flight.

The Takeoff Two-Step

The first stages of taking off in the helicopter are nearly identical to hovering, but the difficult balancing act of hovering only needs to be maintained for a couple of seconds during takeoff. To take off, smoothly add collective until 70–75 percent torque is achieved. Just as in an airplane, the more quickly you add power, the more

Transitioning to forward flight in a helicopter is like riding a wave.

torque effect you'll experience. Be prepared to add a slight amount of left pedal to counteract yaw. As the helicopter lifts its skids off the ground, push the stick slightly forward and make the AI's wings rest just on the horizon line. Depending on how skillfully you moved the stick forward, once you start moving you may need to add collective. Let's discuss why.

Transitioning to Forward Flight

Pushing forward on the cyclic moves the main rotors' thrust backwards. This pushes you forward. However, if you go forward too fast, you'll also lose altitude. In a way, this is similar to surfing. Of course you're riding on air, but in some ways air behaves like a fluid. Nevertheless, this analogy will require some imagination.

Picture yourself surfing in your JetRanger on the biggest wave ever. If you move the cyclic stick too far forward, you'll move forward at a quicker rate than the wave. Your forward velocity will increase, but you'll move down on the wave and lose altitude. However, if you pull the cyclic backwards, you'll move rearward, fall off the wave in that direction, and lose altitude. The big advantage that helicopters have over surfers is that you can compensate for a loss in altitude in a helicopter by adding more collective. Furthermore, you can retain the same altitude as long as you don't try to go too fast too soon.

Climb configuration for the Bell 206B JetRanger.

Climb

The JetRanger's best climb speed (its Vy) is 52 KIAS and its best engine-out glide range speed is 69 KIAS. So a good climb speed would be something above 52 KIAS, but not too much higher than 69 KIAS. The Aircraft Handbook in Flight Simulator suggests a climb speed of 60 KIAS, so we'll use that. The configuration that fits the

airspeed and has a reasonable climb rate is 70 percent torque with the pitch set level. This will net a 60 KIAS and a 500 FPM climb. However, torque decreases 3 percent per 1,000 feet of climb, so be prepared to increase torque regularly during the climb or your climb rate will deteriorate as you ascend.

Cruise

The JetRanger really isn't a "cross-country" type of vehicle, but a cruise configuration can help you get wherever you're going faster. The maximum cruise torque setting is 80 percent, and when you place the AI wings to rest just below the AI horizon, you'll net a speed of about 120 KIAS at 1,600 feet. (Meigs' pattern altitude— let's hope we don't scare any of those Cessnas!)

Cruise configuration for the Bell 206B JetRanger.

Descent

The cruise descent isn't something you'd really do much in real life due to the high speed and proximity to Vne (maximum never-exceed speed). However, if you're going to cruise fast, you might as well descend fast as well. All you need to do to change to cruise descent from cruise is

Cruise descent configuration for the Bell 206B JetRanger.

reduce torque to 75 percent. If you maintain cruise pitch, you'll remain at 120 KIAS, but you'll descend at a comfortable 500 FPM. Remember that when you descend, the effect of altitude on torque will reverse. Torque will increase 3 percent per 1,000 feet of descent, so watch it or you'll find yourself leveling out.

Approach

The Aircraft Handbook in Flight Simulator 98 recommends a 90 KIAS approach speed. Although single-engine airplanes fly slower approaches, you won't have to worry too much about them. The traffic pattern for helicopters is generally 500 feet AGL. To transition to a normal non-precision approach configuration, simply reduce torque to 55 percent. Keep pitch attitude where it was for cruise (or cruise descent) and you'll slow down.

Hovering

Hovering can be a little tricky because, in actuality, you're trying to balance on a column of air. Other than those you're about to read, there aren't really any other hints to help you with hovering. Do remember, though, not to fixate on any one control or indicator. You have to constantly react to what the helicopter is asking you for. What's required is an instrument scan and a scan of the outside world, all at the same time.

Non-precision approach configuration for the Bell 206B JetRanger.

The first thing to do is put the aircraft into the hover configuration. Scan the torque indicator and the ASI to make sure you're not flying forward. Next look at the VSI and make sure you're not climbing or descending. Add or reduce torque as necessary.

It is said that hovering a helicopter is like rubbing your belly and patting the top of

your head—while walking and chewing gum at the same time. Don't let anyone fool you; hovering *is* tough, but it's a little easier in real life than when you're sitting in front of a monitor because you have more feedback about the helicopter's status through your peripheral vision.

> **Tip:** *The best way to practice hovering is to do it just a foot off the ground. This way the ground can save you from some of the less dramatic bobbles by keeping you upright.*

There are only three other tips that can be passed along to help you learn to hover. The first has to do with peripheral vision. Rather than scanning outside the helicopter, you may find it easier to try using your peripheral vision to reinforce what you see on the AI. That puny little AI ball is hard to decipher, so any help you can get elsewhere should be welcome.

The way to do this is to make a mental picture of where the horizon is on the screen. Not so much exactly where it is, but just to get a general sense of where the colors of the sky meet the colors of the ground. What you're after is being able to pick up banking and pitch changes by comparing visual details of the physical layout to your mental picture. It's really tough to explain, but once you've experienced it, you'll understand.

The second tip is: don't overcorrect. Helicopter controls don't react quite like what you may be used to. The best way to explain this is that an opposite but equal control input will not always negate the original control input. For example, if the helicopter is banking to the left because you moved the stick 1" to the left, moving the stick 1" to the right won't put you back to level—it'll only make you bank to the right. To correct the first bank, you'd move the stick back to center, or only 1/4" to the right, instead. The amount you need to move the stick, to correct, depends on how early you react.

This leads us to the final tip: try to predict where the helicopter is about to move and correct it as soon as possible. It's much easier to correct little deviations than it is to correct big ones. That's easier said than done, but rest assured it *can* be done.

Landing the Helicopter

As you can imagine, landing is a very important skill to learn. Fortunately, landing a helicopter is actually pretty easy. What most pilots usually have trouble with is the transition from forward (or whatever direction you're

heading) flight to the state of hovering. In addition to excellent coordination, that transition requires a good instrument scan.

When you transition from forward flight to hover you'll usually experience a ballooning effect when the cyclic is pulled back to stop forward flight. To prevent this from happening, decrease collective before pulling back on the cyclic. The amount that the collective needs to be reduced depends on how fast you want to slow down.

If you're going pretty fast, don't be afraid to drop your collective all the way down. You won't fall out of the sky. The amount of back-cyclic you'll need should be gauged by the VSI. Pull back further if the VSI shows you're descending and push forward if you're climbing. Generally, the angle of attack that you'll end up with will be somewhere between one-half to three-fourths the distance between the AI's horizon line and the first pitch bar. Again, I can't cite specific numbers here because the starting airspeed and the desired rate of deceleration are unknown.

As you begin to slow down (you are scanning the ASI aren't you?), two things will happen. First, you'll need to lower the nose or you'll start moving backwards. This is a common problem that leads to pilot induced oscillations. More often than not with new pilots, this turns your helicopter into a big roto-tiller. One tip to pass along is that once your ASI reads zero, it won't register anything if you start flying backwards. So the best thing to do is look outside when the ASI reaches zero. Also, when you're looking outside for motion cues, it's better to look toward the sides rather than the front.

The second thing that'll happen when you slow down is you'll begin to descend regardless of your cyclic position. This results from the lack of airspeed. Naturally you'll need to apply collective. How much you apply depends on how high you are. Apply enough to reach hover or just to slow your descent. With some practice, you'll learn to time the cyclic push forward with level pitch attitude so they meet zero airspeed at the same time.

If you are just slowing to hover, add collective to the hover torque setting (60 percent) and let it settle down. Watch the VSI and make collective adjustments as necessary. On the other hand, if you want to descend to land, add collective to slightly below hover torque (50–55 percent). Compare your torque setting against your VSI while keeping an eye on the altimeter and the world outside. That's a lot of activities to keep track of simultaneously, but you have no choice in the matter. You don't want to descend so quickly that you won't be able to slow down before hitting the ground. Generally, a descent of

500 FPM is good until you get near the ground. When you reach about 25 feet AGL, increase collective back to hover torque. From this low hover, landing is a piece of cake.

The secret to achieving those "Airwolf" style landings is to add only enough collective to maintain a slow descent (this way you bypass hover altogether). The real trick is to gradually increase collective as you near the ground, then let off when you touch down. One of the most common mistakes new chopper pilots make is not reducing collective once they're on the ground. If you don't reduce collective, the helicopter remains light and is therefore very easy to tip over.

With any landing, the critical point you want to reach is a descent rate of less than 60 FPM (feet per minute), somewhere below 50 feet AGL. You can tell what 60 FPM is by looking at the VSI. It reads the same as the one in the 182S, but deciphering what your altitude is over an area you've never landed on before is a lot tougher. All you can do is decrease your VSI to something low and use your depth perception on the outside view. As you doubtless have already noticed, depth perception on a two-dimensional CRT screen is pretty tough to experience. You'll just have to do your best in these situations.

With any landing (airplane or helicopter), the approach is key. Make a bad approach, and your landing will be more difficult to perform (if not impossible). And landing in a helicopter doesn't exactly make your job easier. However, equipped with information listing the normal flight configurations for the JetRanger, you'll have a good foundation to hone your rotary-wing flying skills.

Normal Flight Configurations for the Bell 206B JetRanger

	Torque	Pitch Attitude	Airsped	Vsi
Climb	70 percent	Level	60 KIAS	1000 FPM
Cruise	80 percent	Just below horizon	120 KIAS	0 FPM
Descent	75 percent	Just below horizon	120 KIAS	-500 FPM
Approach	55 percent	Just below horizon	90 KIAS	0 FPM
Hover	60-65 percent	Level	0 KIAS	0 FPM

Chapter Six

EMERGENCY PROCEDURES

Microsoft Flight Simulator 98 allows you to fly a perfect airplane. If you wish, you need never experience any aircraft problems. So it's not absolutely necessary to read this chapter to be able to enjoy Flight Simulator 98. After all, why *would* anyone want to deal with a faulty airplane if he or she didn't have to? Actually, there are quite a few reasons why desktop pilots submit themselves to the rigors of handling in-flight emergencies. Some of the more experienced pilots enjoy the challenge of dealing with the unexpected. Others feel that this type of training builds their flying skills. Then there are those who are just interested in *what if* scenarios. Whatever your reasons, one thing's for sure—you'll either find this is one of the most thrilling aspects of aviation or you'll find yourself totally overwhelmed. Either reaction is totally natural.

It may come as a surprise to you that the Emergency Procedures section of an aircraft manual is usually the shortest section of the book. Whether that's because these manual writers feel that if you're really experiencing an emergency you won't have time to read through a lot of pages or because there isn't much you can do if things go really wrong, is a matter of debate. But one thing everyone agrees on is that it's far better to know what to do *before* something happens rather than to try to figure it out when your engine starts sputtering.

That's why we should talk a little about emergency procedures. But rather than go through the checklists like we did in the last chapter, let's just discuss some things that can come in handy that aren't written in the Emergency checklists.

Types of Emergencies

There are all kinds of emergencies you can experience in the air—anything from medical emergencies to terrorists. But we'll focus on aircraft-related flight emergencies.

There are basically four types of failures that can occur on aircraft:

- Structural
- Mechanical
- Electrical
- Pilot

Naturally, there are literally thousands of causes for any one of them, but the stringent mandatory practice of preventative maintenance and training makes air travel one of the safest forms of transportation around. Still, it doesn't hurt to be prepared. The simplest way to discuss this subject is to concentrate on the effects of failures on the aircraft and how you should deal with them.

When a failure is severe enough (total vs. partial) or occurs in a critical component, you can expect reduced performance, or a total loss, of an instrument or engine. The only exception to this rule is with structural failures.

Flight Simulator 98 does model structural failures, but they're pretty much limited to a single sequence of events that begins with overstressing the airplane and leads directly to *game over*. There are no control surface failures, cable breakage, or anything such as that to worry about (not that you can do much about these problems anyway).

So that basically leaves us with two other categories of losses modeled in Flight Simulator 98—engine and instrument losses. (Fires are not modeled.) When dealing with any in-flight emergency you have two priorities:

1. Keep the airplane flying,

and

2. Land as soon as possible.

Anything you'll ever read about aircraft emergency operational procedures is generally designed with those two goals in mind. No matter what kind of emergency you have, if you remember these two *mission goals*, you're more likely to make the right decisions.

Loss of Instruments

After learning to rely on your instruments for flight, the loss of any of them can really make you feel insecure. The way that pilots are taught to deal with such a loss is through what is known as *partial panel training*. Panel naturally refers to

the instrument panel, so partial panel training means learning to fly while one or more of the standard instrument group instruments is dead.

The first thing that crosses the mind of student pilots—when told they will undergo partial panel training—is usually something like this: "Why do I need to learn that? I'm getting my VFR license."

One of the partial panel training scenarios that student pilots are given is known as *unusual attitude/no AI recovery*. In this exercise, the instructor puts the aircraft in an unusual attitude and then asks the student to return the aircraft to level flight using nothing but the instruments and without the benefit of the AI.

Even though you may only fly VFR, what would happen to you if you happened to wander into a cloud by mistake? Granted, such an occurrence doesn't mean instant death, but if you became disoriented, you could lose the use of the AI. If you spin an airplane with an uncaged attitude indicator, the AI may end up spinning uselessly like a pinwheel. That's because most AI's will tumble if you exceed their pitch or bank limits, making them useless for controlling the airplane.

The AIs in Flight Simulator have no such problems, but in real-world flight training your flight instructor would say something like "Oh, oh, there goes your attitude indicator," and then would cover up your AI with a card. This would simulate a failed instrument and prevent you from "cheating" by sneaking a peek.

There are three ways that Flight Simulator allows you to simulate instrument failures. One is a simulation of simulated failure, the second is an individual instrument failure, and the third is a system-wide failure. The first two

The Hidden option covers the AI.

Tip: *When practicing partial panel flight, you're better off using Flight Simulator's Hidden option rather than the Inoperative option unless you're testing someone on inoperative instrument symptom recognition. That's because you may tend to scan the inoperative instrument just out of habit. In the real world it's standard to place a slip of paper or a card over the dead instrument.*

The AI in this picture is Inoperative.

options are described as Hidden and Inoperative, respectively.

The Hidden option re-creates what a flight instructor would do to simulate a failed instrument. It literally covers the selected instrument.

The Inoperative option simulates an inoperative instrument. We've pictured an inoperative AI. Because the AI is a gyro instrument, when the gyro powers down or fails, the AI will lie on its side. If you're not familiar with the symptoms of an inoperative instrument, the accompanying table lists instrument failure symptoms to help you recognize them.

Instrument Failure Symptoms

Instrument	Symptoms
Attitude Indicator	Lies on its side, tumbles, or rotates like pinwheel
Altimeter	Is stuck, or behaves like VSI
Airspeed Indicator	Is stuck, jumpy indications, behaves like ALT, or no airspeed
Vertical Speed Indicator	Is stuck or behaves like ALT
Directional Gyro	Is stuck, inaccurate, or spins wildly
Turn Indicator/Coordinator	Needle doesn't center/does not indicate turns

System-wide failures and individual instrument failure options are set in the Instrument Display tab of Aircraft Settings in the Aircraft menu. System failures are categorized as Fuel, Electrical, Vacuum, and Pitot-Static.

The second table lists the instruments in Flight Simulator that would become useless with each type of system failure. Note that the Learjet 45 and Boeing 737 have electric AIs and DGs. All other AIs and DGs in Flight Simulator are vacuum-driven. Although the 45's and 737's systems are pitot-static and electric, all the displays in the 45 are electric, so if you lose your electrical system, you lose everything. But redundant electrical components make a total loss of all electrical power in the 45 very unlikely.

Flight Simulator's Instrument and System Failure Relationships

Instrument	Vacuum	System Electrical	Pitot - Static
Attitude Indicator	X	X (45 & 737)	
Altimeter			X
Airspeed Indicator			X
Vertical Speed Indicator			X
Directional Gyro	X	X (45 & 737)	
Turn Indicator/Coordinator	X		

OK, now that we know what to look for and what may go bad when, let's talk about how to deal with instrument losses and also how to prevent some of them.

Losing the AI

Losing your AI is probably the most traumatic of all instrument losses because most instrument scans are based primarily around the AI. Nevertheless, if your other instruments are working, you can still get secondary bank and pitch

System-wide failures and individual instrument failure options are set in the Instrument Display tab.

information. Bank information can be provided by the TC, and pitch information can come from the ASI, VSI, and ALT. All modern TCs are electric. Older versions were vacuum-driven, so in addition to losing the AI, and DG, you'd lose the TC as well. That's not a good situation to be in because you'd have no bank information whatsoever. (The slip indicator doesn't give bank angle information.)

The biggest problem you'll have if you lose the AI is with setting normal flight configurations. That's because pitch attitude is one of the configuration

components. Nevertheless, if you know the airspeeds and climb/descent rates for each configuration, you can still be pretty accurate (because you know the power settings).

Losing the ALT

Having to fly with a total loss of the ALT is pretty rare. Because it's a static air source instrument, introducing any alternate static air source will partially cure all ALT problems except for mechanical damage to the ALT itself. In a real aircraft, opening the alternate static source is as simple as flipping a valve open. And even if that doesn't work, breaking the glass on the ALT will accomplish the same thing.

Of course you can't do anything like that in Flight Simulator, so partial panel training without an ALT would be pretty pessimistic. Nevertheless, there is no real alternative to the ALT. The best you can do is use the VSI and descend slowly until you can reach VFR conditions.

Losing the VSI

Losing your VSI isn't a big deal. The VSI is arguably one of the most expendable instruments in a standard instrument cluster. Because the VSI is also a static air source instrument, if the alternate static source valve doesn't remedy the situation, breaking the VSI glass is another alternative. Furthermore, note that, in the case of a static system failure (where both the VSI and ALT would be effective), breaking either VSI or ALT glass will provide an alternate static source to the system. But if you have the option, breaking the VSI glass should be your first choice. In addition to being the most expendable instrument, it's also the cheapest to replace.

The only instruments that can provide ASI-style trend information are the ALT and the AI. The combination of pitch, airspeed, and altitude changes can provide ballpark VSI information. If you couple all of these with a clock, you can be pretty accurate with your vertical speeds. However, if you know your configurations, the VSI should fall into place if you have the correct power and pitch, especially when the proper airspeed is indicated.

Losing the ASI

Like the loss of the ALT, there isn't any direct feedback provided by other instruments to make up for the loss of the ASI. The only things you can do are to use your configurations (power and pitch) and watch your engine gauges. Listening for engine speed changes can also offer valuable clues to your airspeed as well. When it comes time to land, it's better to land hot (fast) than it is to stall before reaching the runway. When in doubt, go with extra airspeed.

Losing the DG

The DG can be thought of as an instrument of convenience. You can very easily use a magnetic compass in place of the DG as long as you're aware of its quirks (compass errors). But an easier method is to first fly in level, unaccelerated flight to get your bearings straight and then make all course changes at standard rate using the clock as your guide. After leveling out, you can check to see how you did.

Losing a TC

The loss of a turn instrument probably doesn't rank as high on the panic meter as some of the other instruments, but it still deserves a mention. The main thing you have to worry about is getting yourself into a spin from severely uncoordinated flight. But because the slip indicator isn't powered, you'll always have it to look at. The only thing about the TC that you'll miss is the two-minute turn reference. If you're familiar with how much bank is required on the AI to produce a standard rate turn in the normal flight configurations, you're less likely to miss the bank indicator portion of the TC.

Preventing System Failures

The only system in Flight Simulator in which you can prevent failures is the pitot-static system. What you can do is really more a preventative measure than a cure. Failures of the pitot-static system are a result of a pitot tube obstruction or a static vent obstruction. There isn't anything you can do about preventing a static vent obstruction in Flight Simulator, but you do have some control over the pitot tube.

The pitot heat switch on the 737 is located on this overhead center console.

Although bugs and debris have been known to clog pitot tubes, they can only be diagnosed while you're outside the aircraft. On the other hand, water and ice are also known to cause pitot tube blockage. Applying pitot heat whenever there's visible moisture and the temperature is 0 degrees C or colder will help prevent pitot blockage from ice formations.

The aircraft that are equipped with pitot tube heaters are the Learjet 45 (it's located on the far left side of the instrument panel), the 737 (on the overhead center), the 182S, and 182RG (the last switch to the right of the lighting switches). To apply pilot heat via the keyboard, press Shift+H. Remember that although pitot heat may remove ice, it is designed to work *before* ice builds up. Speaking of flying in ice, let's talk about that next.

Surviving Icing Conditions

None of the aircraft in Flight Simulator are certified to fly in icing conditions. But if you happen to find yourself picking up ice, here are some tips:

- Turn pitot heat on as soon as you realize there may be ice out there. It doesn't hurt to keep it on, and it's always better to be safe than sorry.
- Make a 180-degree turn back (using a standard rate turn for one minute if you've lost your DG) or move to an altitude where ice formation will be unlikely. Specifically you want to get into air that's above 0 degrees C (32 degrees F) or below (colder) than -10 degrees C (15 degrees F). Be aware that, if you have ice on your wings, climbing may be impossible.
- Increase engine speed to minimize ice formation on your propeller.
- Fly everything at a higher airspeed than normal. Just a little bit of ice can dramatically raise your minimum stall speed.
- Don't extend your flaps for landing. Ice-laden flaps have been known to reduce elevator control by disturbing airflow over the aircraft's tail.

Loss of Engine

Losing your engine in single-engine aircraft certainly rates up there as one of the oddest sensations. For a split second, all you notice is how quiet things have become all of a sudden, and all you hear is the rush of air blowing around the airplane. A fraction of a second later the brain kicks in, and you realize what's happened. That's when you begin to act on your training.

Mixture-Prop-Throttle!

Drill these three words into your head—*mixture, prop*, and *throttle*. Unless you were just cruising at some high flight level (18,000 feet and above), you probably won't have time to read through the emergency procedure checklists. *Mixture-prop-throttle* becomes your mental checklist. But before we get to that, you have to remember that your number one goal is to keep the airplane flying.

The first thing to do is to adjust your airspeed to obtain the best glide speed for your aircraft. This may require you to lower the nose, even if you're already near the ground. This may sound suicidal, but would you rather go in under control or with no control resulting from a stall?

Although there are many, many reasons that an engine can stop working, the only ones you have any control over are fuel management, carburetor ice, and magnetos. *Mixture*, of course, refers to fuel mixture. A common cause of engine problems is fuel starvation. If your engine has stalled from running too lean, you need to enrich the mixture. So when you think mixture, automatically apply Full Rich mixture.

The second word in our quick checklist is *prop*. If you have an engine problem and the engine is still producing power (spinning even though it may be sputtering), you want to get maximum power/thrust out of it, so push the props to full RPM. On the other hand, if the engine has quit, feathering the prop (maximum pitch) can increase your

Note: *On many real airplanes, the prop must be spinning in order to fully feather it. Another problem is that some of these engines become very difficult to restart once they're in the feathered position. On the other hand, if your restart attempt fails, you're stuck with an unfeathered prop that won't feather because it needs to be spinning to feather again in the first place. Fortunately, you won't have to choose between such trade-offs in Flight Simulator.*

Note: *Some manufacturers recommend that during an emergency you switch the fuel valve into the off position and put mixtures and throttle into minimum positions, to reduce the likelihood of fire.*

gliding ability by 15 percent or more. If you don't feather the prop, it will windmill and cause drag.

The last word on the mental checklist is *throttle*. There's no mistaking what that means—push the throttle to the firewall. Again, if your engine is sputtering along, you may be able to get a few extra seconds of power out of it. Pushing the throttle to maximum may achieve something. You're running out of options anyway, so it's worth a shot.

During all of this activity you should be looking for a place to land. Generally you can land anywhere in Flight Simulator except on water or smack into a building, If you have time, in a real airplane you'd switch on the fuel pumps and apply carburetor heat. (Flight Simulator's 182RG has carburetor heat. Press H to activate it.) Other than that, get ready for a landing.

Other things you should know are whether flaps are recommended for engine-out landings. As for landing gear positions, there are many arguments in favor of and against landing gear extension for off-runway, soft field landings. Some people feel you have a better chance of not flipping over if you land with the gear retracted. Others feel that having the landing gear extended gives you more structure to absorb crash impact force. Whatever your choice, if your landing gear is inoperable, you may be able to manually pump the landing gear up or down by repeatedly pressing Ctrl + G.

Surviving an Inoperative Engine on Multiengine Aircraft

When a single engine fails in a multiengine aircraft, you follow the same basic procedures as engine failures in a single engine aircraft, but there are some differences. The first thing that may comfort you is many multiengine aircraft will fly with only one running engine. This greatly improves your options and, consequently, your odds of survival. Both the Learjet 45 and the Boeing 737 will fly, and even climb (albeit at a very reduced rate), with only one operational engine. In addition to offering performance gains, added safety is another major appeal of the multiengine aircraft.

Whenever you suspect an engine problem, the first order of business is to go over your quick emergency checklist—mixture, props, and throttle—for

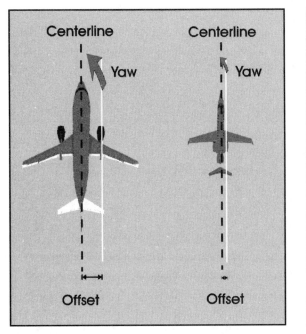

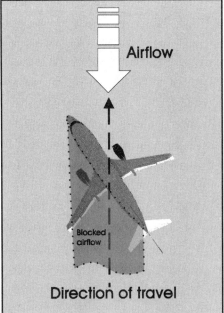

The further an engine is from the centerline of the aircraft, the more yaw it will produce when operating alone.

Excessive yaw can cause the fuselage to block or reduce the airflow over the affected engine's wing.

both engines. Even though all of the multiengine aircraft in Flight Simulator are turbine powered (so there are no mixtures or props to deal with), the overall emergency strategy remains the same. You want to try to maximize whatever engine power (if any) the affected engine can provide.

Simultaneously, you need to also maneuver the aircraft into its best single engine rate-of-climb speed by lowering or raising its nose (160 KIAS for the 737, and 134 KIAS on the model 45). Once you have the aircraft stabilized (out of immediate danger of crashing), you then need to detect and secure the inoperative engine. Obviously it's extremely important to secure the correct engine. If you secure the wrong engine, you'll be flying a glider. Let's see what you're up against.

We'll want to consider the effects of asymmetrical thrust on a multiengine aircraft. Basically, the further the operating engine is from the centerline of the aircraft, the more yaw it will produce. For example, the single engine yaw

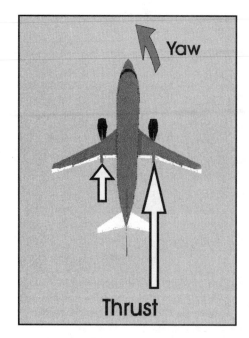

An airplane will yaw toward the engine producing the least amount of thrust. And the greater the differential of thrust, the greater the degree of yaw.

Tip: *Try to turn only in the direction of the good engine. Turns in the opposite direction are possible, but they require additional rudder input to avoid skidding in the turn. This is rudder that you may not be able to provide.*

produced on the 737 will be greater than that on the model 45 because the engines on the 737 are out on the wings while the engines on the 45 are on the fuselage.

As you know, the danger of too much yaw is the increased likelihood of entering a spin. Excessive yaw can cause the fuselage to block or reduce the airflow over the affected engine's wing.

A second consideration is that the larger the differential of thrust between the two engines, the more yaw will be produced. This is over and above the engine offset factor. As you'd expect, the main flight control for correcting yaw is the rudder. The correct rudder to apply is the opposite side of the inoperative engine. A good way to remember this is to use the memory aid, "step on the good engine." In other words, apply rudder to the same side as the running engine.

But there are things you can do to help minimize the amount of corrective rudder required.

- Reduce throttle on the good engine. By reducing the differential of thrust, you'll reduce yaw.
- Bank toward the good engine. All that you need is about 5 degrees, but the actual amount of bank required depends on where your engines are mounted (engine offset) and how much thrust is being produced by the good engine.

Autorotation Tips

If you lose the engine in a helicopter, you don't automatically become a rock and fall to the ground. A helicopter can *autorotate*. Although some people equate autorotation to falling like a rock, when it's performed properly, to an

outside observer there is no visible difference in the landing. In fact the JetRanger's excellent ability to autorotate has made it the safest aircraft in the world (calculated by injuries and fatalities per hour flown).

It's preferable to lose an engine in a helicopter because of its ability to land more or less vertically. This ability dramatically reduces the amount of clear terrain required to land. While an airplane may require 1,000 feet or more to come to a stop, a helicopter can land in an area as short as 100 feet.

The Pilot Help does a very good job of outlining autorotation procedures. The quick checklist (mixture-prop-throttle) we used for airplanes still applies. What you have to remember though is that throttle is throttle and prop is collective. Mixture doesn't apply because the JetRanger is a turbine.

The critical numbers you need to know are that 69 KIAS is the maximum distance glide speed and that transition to 52 KIAS (minimum sink rate speed) is when you're over your desired landing area. Under no circumstances should you exceed 100 KIAS, but forward speed must be maintained in order to maintain rotor speed and momentum. Conversely, never go below 52 KIAS until you're ready to put it down.

Two final autorotation tips are:

- When the engine fails, always reduce collective smoothly and as soon as possible to help maintain rotor RPM.
- Just as when flying an airplane, a slip or skid produces drag and causes a drop in airspeed. That, in turn, increases your sink rate and ultimately shortens your glide.

Tail Rotor Failure

Next to losing your main rotor blades (and that only occurs if you hit something with them or have a defect—extremely rare), tail rotor failure is probably the scariest thing that can happen to a helicopter pilot. That's because you lose yaw control.

The only thing you can do to help this problem is maintain a minimum airspeed above 52 KIAS. Your forward momentum will keep your helicopter from coming around on you because of what can be described as *weathervane effect*. As long as there is enough forward airflow, the tail will remain behind your flight path where it belongs.

Finally, (and this technique is even more important here than during autorotation), bring the helicopter in close to the ground before slowing down. As soon as you lose airspeed, you'll start spinning. When that loss of control

occurs, you want to be as close to the ground as possible. The ground is the only thing that will stop your spinning. Just be glad that tail rotor failures generally give you some warning before they happen. Watch for excessive vibrations, loss or decrease of antitorque pedal control or excessive transmission oil temperature.

Perhaps the most worrisome part about tail rotor failures is you can't practice tail rotor failure landings. The best you can do is know your autorotation procedures well and put the aircraft down as soon as you even suspect a problem. It's better to be wrong about a problem on the ground than in the air.

Chapter Seven

FLIGHT PLANNING

There are some parts of flight planning that are universal, regardless of your method of navigation. Some of these aspects, such as having enough fuel on board to reach your destination, may seem like common sense. However, you'd be surprised how many new pilots don't even consider them or their consequences.

Aircraft flight performance is closely woven with flight planning. So, even if you're just interested in flying around for fun, the performance aspects that we'll review in this chapter may still be of value to you.

Airport Information

All flight plans must have a point of origin and a point of destination. Choosing a destination airport may seem like a no-brainer—fly to the airport closest to the place you want to visit. But many new pilots seem to overlook whether the chosen destination airport can handle their aircraft. You've got to check runway lengths and airport elevation.

Runway length and surface are important because you need to know if the runway is long enough and hard enough for your type of aircraft to land on.

Useful information for over 3,000 airports around the world can be accessed through the Airport/ Facility Directory.

Airport/Facility Directory

Illinois   ○ Airports   ○ Navaids

Chicago, Illinois - Merrill C Meigs

ID	Elevation	Latitude	Longitude	ATIS Freq.
KCGX	+593	N41* 51.53'	W87* 36.45'	127.350

Runway	Length	Surface	ILS Freq.	ILS ID
18	0003899	Concrete	***	***
36	0003899	Concrete	***	***

Chicago, Illinois - Chicago O'Hare Intl

ID	Elevation	Latitude	Longitude	ATIS Freq.
KORD	+668	N41* 58.78'	W87* 54.27'	135.400

Runway	Length	Surface	ILS Freq.	ILS ID
14R	0013000	Asphalt	109.75	IORD

Map   < Back   Close

Directory airport listings provide runway directions, runway lengths, runway composition, field elevations, global positioning location, and ATIS frequencies.

ght Simulator 98
World Options Views Help
  Time & Season...
  Go to   ▶
  Airport/Facility Directory...
  Weather...
  Weather Areas...
  Scenery Complexity...
  Dynamic Scenery...
  Scenery Library...

Access to the Airport/Facility Directory is found in the World menu.

And just as important, you'll have to take off from this same runway on your way back home or to your next destination.

Airport elevation is also important. As we've seen already, power output is affected by altitude as is lift. (Thin air = fewer air molecules to produce lift.) So if your destination airport is at a high elevation, a fully loaded airplane may literally not be able to get off the ground.

Microsoft Flight Simulator 98 provides airport information through its Airport/Facility Directory. These listings will provide you with runway directions, runway length, runway composition, field elevations, and other types of information worth knowing (such as global positioning location and ATIS frequencies). To access the Airport/Facility Directory, click Airport/Facility Directory from the World menu.

Short Field Takeoff and Landing

Now that you have the pertinent airport runway info, we should talk about how to calculate your chances of success when taking off and landing. Short field takeoffs and landings are often referred to as *maximum effort* (performance) maneuvers. The term generally applies to the aircraft, but the pilot's actions matter as well.

Short field maneuvers specify the minimum required runway lengths for taking off and landing under the stated conditions. However, you should be aware that the test pilots who compiled these numbers are professionals. It's best to take these numbers with a grain of salt and lengthen them a bit to compensate for your less-advanced skills. (Besides, it's better to estimate too long than too short when it comes to runways.)

On the other hand, the numbers provided in these charts are based on the airplane's maximum takeoff weight and maximum landing weight. If, for example, you're carrying less fuel, you may achieve better performance than what's listed. These numbers were also compiled under zero wind conditions. As you can imagine, a landing with a tailwind will increase your landing distance. So, as always, your mileage may vary.

When you look over the performance charts in the following pages, note how performance degrades with both temperature and altitude. Warm air is less dense than cold air, and thin air has fewer air molecules for your prop to "bite" into and to support your wings.

Short Field Takeoffs

There are two airspeeds that are of particular interest to pilots during takeoff. They are known as Vx (best angle of climb) and Vy (best rate of climb). You should be familiar with Vy from the discussions about takeoff in the last chapter. Vy is the airspeed with the greatest amount of excess HP (horsepower) that's available to your plane for climbing.

Vx, on the other hand, trades airspeed and distance traveled for altitude. This is exactly the tradeoff you need to clear an obstacle. But to get off the ground in the shortest possible distance, you'll need to follow the procedure outlined below.

Short field performance tables are based on having a 50-foot-high obstacle that you need to clear at the end of the runway. The idea is that, by providing an obstacle with a known height, you will have some indication of the angle of climb you can expect to achieve, whether or not you really have an obstacle to clear.

Tip: *A good way to remember the difference between Vx and Vy speeds is the letter X has more angles than the letter Y, so you can remember Vx as the best angle of climb.*

The thermometer located on the upper right corner of the 182S's instrument panel displays outside air temperature.

The table labeled Cessna 182S Short Field Takeoff Distance provides performance data at these basic settings:

- Flaps set at 20 degrees
- Prop set to 2400 RPM
- Full throttle
- Mixture leaned to maximum power (peak EGT) before takeoff at full throttle
- Lift-off speed of 49 KIAS
- Level off and accelerate to 58 KIAS
- Climb at 58 KIAS until obstacle is cleared

Cessna 182S Short Field Takeoff Distance at 3,100 lbs. - 0 Wind

Pressure Alt. Ft.	0°C (32°F)		10°C (50°F)		20°C (68°F)		30°C (86°F)		40°C (104°F)	
	Grond Roll Ft.	Total Ft. to Clear 50 ft. Obst.	Grond Roll Ft.	Total Ft. to Clear 50-Ft. Obst.	Grond Roll Ft.	Total Ft. to Clear 50-Ft. Obst.	Grond Roll Ft.	Total Ft. to Clear 50-Ft. Obst.	Grond Roll Ft.	Total Ft. to Clear 50-Ft. Obst.
S.L.	715	1365	765	1460	825	1570	885	1680	945	1800
1,000	775	1490	835	1600	900	1720	965	1845	1030	1980
2,000	850	1635	915	1760	980	1890	1055	2035	1130	2190
3,000	925	1800	995	1940	1070	2090	1150	2255	1235	2435
4,000	1015	1990	1090	2150	1175	2325	1260	2515	1355	2720
5,000	1110	2210	1195	2395	1290	2595	1385	2820	1485	3070
6,000	1220	2470	1315	2690	1415	2930	1520	3200	1635	3510
7,000	1340	2785	1445	3045	1560	3345	1675	3685	—	—
8,000	1480	3175	1595	3500	1720	3880	—	—	—	—

Short Field Landings

Like the short field takeoff, short field landing performance tables are also based on a 50-foot obstacle that you need to clear at the end of the runway. But in the case of a landing, you are crossing the obstacle on your way down to the runway. Again, by providing an obstacle that has a known height, you get an indication of the angle of descent you can expect whether or not you really have an obstacle to clear. In the table labeled Cessna 182S Short Field Landing, field landings are performed with:

- Flaps set to FULL
- Power Off
- Descent speed 60 KIAS at obstacle
- Maximum braking once all wheels touch down (retract flaps for maximum braking)

Cessna 182S Short Field Landing Distance at 2,950 lbs. - 0 Wind

Pressure Alt. Ft.	0°C (32°F)		10°C (50°F)		20°C (68°F)		30°C (86°F)		40°C (104°F)	
	Ground Roll Ft.	Total Ft. to Clear 50-Ft. Obst.	Ground Roll Ft.	Total Ft. to Clear 50-Ft. Obst.	Ground Roll Ft.	Total Ft. to Clear 50-Ft. Obst.	Ground Roll Ft.	Total Ft. to Clear 50-Ft. Obst.	Ground Roll Ft.	Total Ft. to Clear 50-Ft. Obst.
S.L.	560	1300	580	1335	600	1365	620	1400	640	1435
1,000	580	1265	600	1365	620	1400	645	1440	665	1475
2,000	600	1370	625	1450	645	1440	670	1480	690	1515
3,000	625	1410	645	1445	670	1485	695	1525	715	1560
4,000	650	1450	670	1485	695	1525	720	1565	740	1600
5,000	670	1485	695	1525	720	1565	745	1610	770	1650
6,000	700	1530	725	1575	750	1615	775	1660	800	1700
7,000	725	1575	750	1615	780	1665	805	1710	830	1750
8,000	755	1625	780	1655	810	1715	835	1760	865	1805

Maximum Performance

Faster, higher, stronger, and more powerful are adjectives that describe one of those basic cravings generally shared by aviation enthusiasts—maximum performance. Although a single engine Cessna is not what most people consider the pinnacle of aviation performance, it isn't the most under-powered aircraft in existence, either.

The following performance charts will help you understand the factors that affect aircraft performance. Recall that aircraft performance is highly dependent on atmospheric conditions, flight configuration, and flight attitude.

First let's take a look at how atmospheric conditions affect performance. The table labeled "Cessna 182S Maximum Rate of Climb at 3,100 lbs." charts the Cessna 182S's maximum rate of climb at maximum weight, from sea level to 14,000 feet. Note how the rate of climb diminishes as altitude and temperature rise. Although the engine power output on a normally aspirated engine shows degradation sooner (at lower altitudes) than non-normally aspirated engines, the downward trend as altitude and temperatures rise remains constant.

Cessna 182S Maximum Rate of Climb at 3,100 lbs.

Pressure Alt. Feet	Climb Speed KIAS	Rate of Climb			
		-20°C (-4°F)	0°C (32°F)	20°C (68°F)	40°C (104°F)
S.L.	80	1055	980	905	835
2,000	79	945	875	805	735
4,000	78	840	770	705	635
6,000	77	735	670	605	535
8,000	75	625	560	495	430
10,000	74	520	455	390	330
12,000	73	410	350	285	225
14,000	72	310	250	190	130

The other performance factors include flight configuration and flight attitudes. Although you don't need to worry about weight and balance issues in Flight Simulator (total weight and center of gravity/C.G. aircraft loading), you do need to know how other aspects of flight configuration can affect your aircraft's performance.

These factors are illustrated in minimum stall speed charts. The table labeled "Cessna 182S Stall Speeds at 3,100 lbs. (most forward C.G.)" lists the minimum stall speeds for the Cessna 182S in KIAS and KCAS (Knots Calibrated Airspeed) for three flap positions and four angles of bank.

The factors that are of the most interest are how stall speeds are lowered with the application of flaps and how stall speeds increase with the angle of bank. These results shouldn't come as a surprise since you know that flaps increase lift and that the angle of bank reduces the upward component of lift—requiring more lift to remain flying.

Cessna 182S Stall Speeds at 3,100 lbs. (Most Forward C.G.)

			Angle Of Bank					
	0°		30°		45°		60°	
Flaps	KIAS	KCAS	KIAS	KCAS	KIAS	KCAS	KIAS	KCAS
UP	43	56	46	60	51	67	61	79
20°	35	52	38	56	42	62	49	74
FULL	36	50	39	54	43	59	51	71

Fuel Management

The other aspect of flight planning that most desktop pilots tend to overlook has to do with fuel. Although the consequences of running out of fuel in Flight Simulator aren't as critical as when flying in real life, fuel management can add a strategy element to your virtual flights of fancy.

Fuel requirements as mandated by the FAA are:

- For VFR day flight, enough fuel is required on board to make it to your first point of intended landing, plus an additional 30 minutes flight time under normal cruise consumption.
- For VFR night flight, fuel requirements are the same as day VFR, but the additional obligatory fuel increases to 45 minutes.
- Helicopter flights (day or night) require an additional 20 minutes of fuel.

Note: *Unless you enable the Engine Stops When Out Of Fuel option on the Realism tab in Aircraft Settings (on the Aircraft menu), your engine will continue running even if you do run out of fuel.*

Note: *KCAS—Knots Calibrated Airspeed is Knots Indicated Airspeed corrected for position and instrument error. Position error is introduced by the AOA changes causing the pitot tube to read airspeed at other than optimum AOA. Instrument error has to do with the calibration of the instrument itself (in this case, the ASI). Every instrument usually has some type of error, but errors are generally small enough not to cause any problems during normal flight. But when it comes to stall speeds, pilots usually take those numbers as written in stone. So aircraft manufacturers are very careful about how they present that data.*

To give you an idea of the kinds of instrument errors typical of an ASI, ASIs usually indicate accurate airspeeds throughout the normal range of airspeed operation; however, with very fast or very slow airspeeds, they tend not to be as accurate. ASIs are not totally unreliable, but they are not absolute.

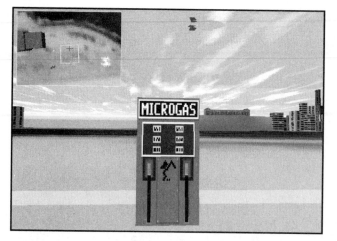

Coming to a complete stop within a yellow fuel and servicing facility square will get you some Microgas.

- IFR flights (regardless of time of flight) require that enough fuel be carried on board to complete the flight to the first airport and to make it to a second (alternate) airport, plus an additional 45 minutes of fuel at cruise speed consumption rates.

Re-fueling

There are two ways to add fuel to an aircraft in Flight Simulator. One is with the fuel dialogue tab under Aircraft Settings on the Aircraft menu. The other is by coming to a complete stop within the yellow fuel-and-servicing facility square found at airports. Some facilities will be recognizable by a Microgas fuel pump located within the yellow square. Others will have only a giant letter *F* painted in the center of the yellow square on the tarmac.

Cruise Performance

The majority of a cross-country flight is spent flying in cruise configuration. Unlike climbs, cruise does not always require maximum engine power and rich mixture settings for safety. That's why if there are any fuel savings to be made, they're usually made during the cruise part of a flight.

Remember that engine power, wing lift, prop thrust, and mixture settings vary with altitude. And as we've seen, atmospheric conditions such as temperature affect performance as well. The problem is that the atmospheric pressure at a particular altitude varies with the current barometric pressure in the area. That's why you calibrate your altimeter. If a particular altitude always had the same air pressure, there wouldn't be any need to adjust your altimeter settings.

Here's an example. An altimeter is designed to reflect the fact that the atmospheric pressure drops approximately one inch of mercury per 1,000 feet

of altitude. On what's called a standard day (a fictional day created for atmospheric comparisons) the barometric pressure at sea level is 29.92 inches of mercury.

So, knowing the rate that pressure decreases per 1,000 feet, we know that at 5,000 feet the air pressure will be approximately 24.92. But on a day where the barometric pressure at sea level is higher (or lower) than the fictional standard, the actual pressure felt by your airplane at 5,000 feet will differ from what's expected. This, in turn, will affect performance.

Some Standard Standards

Flying is affected by a non-ending supply of constantly changing variables. Luckily, a few things remain consistent...

A Standard Day:
Temperature at sea level = 15 degrees C (59 degrees F)
Barometric pressure at sea level = 29.92" Hg. (mercury) 14.7 lb/sq.in.

Standard Rules of Thumb:
- *Lapse Rate—temperature decrease at the rate of 2 degrees C. (3.5 degrees F) per 1,000 feet of altitude.*
- *Barometric pressure decreases at the rate of 1 inch of mercury per 1,000 feet of altitude.*
- *The amount of runway behind you is useless to you.*

Therefore, rather than deal with huge charts and graphs for every possible combination of barometric pressure and temperature, a special technique called *pressure altitude* is used instead.

Pressure altitude is based just on air pressure rather than actual altitude. In other words, if the air pressure at a particular altitude is 24.92, it doesn't matter whether you're really at 3,000 feet. To your airplane, the air pressure seems like flying at 5,000 feet.

You find out your current pressure altitude in Flight Simulator the same way it's done in real life. You simply set your altimeter to 29.92 (the barometric pressure at sea level for a standard day) and read your altitude. What you get is your pressure altitude.

Changing your altimeter setting to something other than the current altimeter setting given by ATIS is pretty difficult to do with the little altimeter on your computer screen. It's much easier to go to the Aircraft menu, choose Aircraft Settings, Realism tab and just type 29.92 into the altimeter setting. But don't forget to set your altimeter back to the proper setting when you're done, or you may be making a landing (with way too much vertical velocity) sooner

than you expect! The quickest way to reset the altimeter is to press the B key when you've closed the Aircraft menu.

The way to use the following Cruise Performance tables is to first find your pressure altitude. Use the chart that corresponds closest to your pressure altitude. Next check the OAT (outside air temperature) on your instrument panel thermometer. Use the column that's closest to your current temperature reading. Finally, select a prop RPM. Slower RPMs will produce less noise and the best fuel economy. High RPMs will net you more speed, but with lower fuel efficiency. All that's left is to choose a power setting. Base your decision on your desired airspeed or fuel consumption.

Cruise performance data is based upon:

- 3,100 lb. maximum weight
- Recommended Lean mixture (peak EGT)
- Maximum cruise power is 80 percent. Power numbers above 80 percent are for interpolation only.

RPM—Revolutions Per Minute
MP—Manifold Pressure
%BHP—Percentage Brake Horsepower
KTAS—Knots True Airspeed
GPH—Gallons Per Hour

Cruise Performance Cessna 182S—Pressure Altitude Sea Level

RPM	MP	20°C Below Standard Temp. -5°C			Standard Temp. 15°C			20°C Above Standard Temp. 35°C		
		%BHP	KTAS	GPH	%BHP	KTAS	GPH	%BHP	KTAS	GPH
2400	27	—	—	—	82	133	13.7	76	132	12.7
	26	—	—	—	78	131	13.0	72	129	12.1
	25	80	129	13.3	73	128	12.3	68	126	11.5
	24	75	126	12.6	69	125	11.7	64	123	10.9
	23	70	123	11.9	65	122	11.0	60	119	10.3
	22	66	120	11.2	61	117	10.4	56	116	9.8
	21	61	116	10.5	57	114	9.9	52	112	9.3
	20	57	112	9.9	53	110	9.3	49	107	8.7
2300	27	—	—	—	79	132	13.2	73	130	12.2
	26	81	130	13.6	75	129	12.5	69	127	11.6
	25	77	127	12.8	71	126	11.9	65	124	11.1

Cruise Performance Cessna 182S—Pressure Altitude Sea Level, continued

RPM	MP	20°C Below Standard Temp. -5°C			Standard Temp. 15°C			20°C Above Standard Temp. 35°C		
		%BHP	KTAS	GPH	%BHP	KTAS	GPH	%BHP	KTAS	GPH
	24	72	124	12.2	67	123	11.3	62	120	10.6
	23	68	121	11.5	63	119	10.7	58	17	10.0
	22	64	118	10.9	59	116	10.2	54	114	9.5
	21	59	114	10.2	55	112	9.6	51	110	9.0
	20	55	110	9.6	51	108	9.0	47	105	8.5
2200	27	82	131	13.7	76	129	12.7	70	128	11.8
	26	78	128	13.0	72	127	12.1	66	125	11.2
	25	74	125	12.4	68	124	11.5	63	121	10.7
	24	70	122	11.7	64	121	10.9	59	119	10.2
	23	66	119	11.1	60	117	10.4	56	115	9.7
	22	61	116	10.5	57	114	9.9	52	112	9.3
	21	57	112	10.0	53	110	9.3	49	108	8.8
	20	53	109	9.4	49	106	8.8	45	103	8.3
2100	27	78	128	13.0	72	127	12.1	66	125	11.3
	26	74	126	12.4	68	124	11.5	63	122	10.8
	25	70	123	11.8	65	121	11.0	60	119	10.3
	24	66	120	11.2	61	118	10.5	56	116	9.8
	23	62	117	10.7	58	115	10.0	53	112	9.4
	22	58	113	10.1	54	111	9.5	50	109	8.9
	21	55	110	9.6	50	108	9.0	47	105	8.4
2000	27	74	126	12.4	68	124	11.5	63	122	10.8
	26	70	123	11.8	65	122	11.0	60	119	10.3
	25	67	120	11.3	61	118	10.5	57	116	9.9
	24	63	118	10.7	58	115	10.0	54	113	9.4
	23	59	114	10.2	55	112	9.6	50	110	9.0
	22	56	111	9.7	51	109	9.1	47	106	8.5
	21	52	107	9.2	48	105	8.6	44	101	8.1

Cruise Performance Cessna 182S—Pressure Altitude 2,000 feet

RPM	MP	20°C Below Standard Temp. -9°C			Standard Temp. 11°C			20°C Above Standard Temp. 31°C		
		%BHP	KTAS	GPH	%BHP	KTAS	GPH	%BHP	KTAS	GPH
2400	26	—	—	—	80	135	13.4	74	133	12.4
	25	82	133	13.8	76	132	12.7	70	130	11.8
	24	78	130	13.0	71	129	12.0	66	126	11.2
	23	73	127	12.3	67	126	11.4	62	123	10.6
	22	68	124	11.6	63	121	10.8	58	119	10.1
	21	64	120	10.9	59	118	10.2	54	115	9.5
	20	59	116	10.2	55	114	9.6	50	111	9.0
2300	26	—	—	—	77	132	12.9	71	131	12.0
	25	79	131	13.2	73	130	12.2	67	128	11.4
	24	75	128	12.5	69	127	11.6	64	124	10.8
	23	70	125	11.8	65	123	11.0	60	121	10.3
	22	66	122	11.2	61	119	10.4	56	117	9.8
	21	62	118	10.6	57	116	9.9	52	113	9.3
	20	57	114	9.9	53	112	9.3	49	109	8.7
2200	26	80	132	13.4	74	130	12.4	68	129	11.5
	25	76	129	12.7	70	128	11.8	65	125	11.0
	24	72	126	12.1	66	125	11.2	61	122	10.5
	23	68	123	11.4	62	121	10.7	58	119	10.0
	22	64	120	10.8	59	118	10.1	54	115	9.5
	21	59	116	10.2	55	114	9.6	51	111	9.0
	20	55	112	9.7	51	110	9.0	47	106	8.5
2100	26	76	129	12.8	70	128	11.8	65	125	11.0
	25	72	126	12.1	67	125	11.3	62	123	10.5
	24	68	124	11.5	63	121	10.8	58	119	10.1
	23	64	121	11.0	59	118	10.2	55	116	9.6
	22	60	117	10.4	56	115	9.7	51	112	9.1
	21	56	114	9.8	52	111	9.2	48	108	8.7
	20	53	110	9.3	48	107	8.7	45	103	8.2
2000	26	72	126	12.2	67	125	11.3	62	123	10.6
	25	69	124	11.6	63	122	10.8	58	120	10.1
	24	65	121	11.0	60	119	10.3	55	116	9.7
	23	61	117	10.5	56	115	9.8	52	113	9.2
	22	57	114	10.0	53	112	9.3	49	109	8.8
	21	54	111	9.4	49	108	8.8	46	104	8.3

Cruise Performance Cessna 182S—Pressure Altitude 4,000 feet

RPM	MP	20°C Below Standard Temp. -13°C			Standard Temp. 7°C			20°C Above Standard Temp. 27°C		
		%BHP	KTAS	GPH	%BHP	KTAS	GPH	%BHP	KTAS	GPH
2400	25	—	—	—	78	136	13.1	72	134	12.1
	24	80	134	12.4	74	133	12.4	68	130	11.5
	23	75	131	12.7	69	130	11.7	64	127	10.9
	22	71	128	11.9	65	125	11.1	60	123	10.4
	21	66	124	11.2	61	122	10.5	56	119	9.8
	20	61	120	10.5	57	118	9.9	52	115	9.2
2300	25	81	135	13.6	75	133	12.6	69	132	11.7
	24	77	132	12.9	71	131	12.0	66	128	11.1
	23	73	129	12.2	67	127	11.3	62	125	10.6
	22	68	126	11.5	63	123	10.7	58	131	10.1
	21	64	122	10.9	59	120	10.2	54	117	9.5
	20	59	118	10.2	55	115	9.6	50	113	9.0
2200	25	78	133	13.1	72	131	12.1	67	129	11.3
	24	74	130	12.4	68	128	11.5	63	126	10.8
	23	70	127	11.8	64	124	10.9	59	122	10.2
	22	66	124	11.1	60	121	10.4	56	119	9.7
	21	61	119	10.5	57	117	9.8	52	115	9.2
	20	57	116	9.9	53	113	9.3	49	110	8.7
2100	25	74	130	12.5	68	129	11.6	63	126	10.8
	24	70	127	11.9	65	125	11.0	60	123	10.3
	23	66	124	11.2	61	122	10.5	56	119	9.8
	22	62	120	10.7	57	118	10.0	53	116	9.4
	21	58	117	10.1	54	115	9.5	50	111	8.9
	20	54	113	9.5	50	111	8.9	46	106	8.4
2000	25	71	127	11.9	65	125	11.0	60	123	10.3
	24	67	125	11.3	61	122	10.5	57	120	9.9
	23	63	121	10.8	58	119	10.1	54	116	9.4
	22	59	118	10.2	55	115	9.6	50	112	9.0
	21	55	114	9.7	51	112	9.1	47	108	8.5

Cruise Performance Cessna 182S—Pressure Altitude 6,000 feet

RPM	MP	20°C Below Standard Temp. -17°C			Standard Temp. 3°C			20°C Above Standard Temp. 23°C		
		%BHP	KTAS	GPH	%BHP	KTAS	GPH	%BHP	KTAS	GPH
2400	23	78	135	13.0	72	134	12.1	66	131	11.2
	22	73	132	12.3	67	129	11.4	62	127	10.6
	21	68	128	11.6	63	126	10.8	58	123	10.1
	20	64	123	10.9	59	121	10.1	54	119	9.5
	19	59	120	10.2	54	117	9.5	50	113	8.9
2300	23	75	133	12.6	69	131	11.6	64	129	10.9
	22	70	130	11.9	65	127	11.0	60	125	10.3
	21	66	126	11.2	61	124	10.4	56	121	9.8
	20	61	122	10.5	57	119	9.8	52	116	9.2
	19	57	117	9.9	52	115	9.3	48	111	8.7
2200	23	72	131	12.1	66	128	11.2	61	126	10.5
	22	68	127	11.4	62	125	10.7	58	122	10.0
	21	63	123	10.8	58	121	10.1	54	119	9.5
	20	59	120	10.2	54	117	9.5	50	114	9.0
	19	55	115	9.6	51	112	9.0	47	108	8.4
2100	23	68	128	11.6	63	126	10.8	58	123	10.1
	22	64	124	10.9	59	122	10.2	55	119	9.6
	21	60	121	10.4	56	118	9.7	51	115	9.1
	20	56	117	9.8	52	114	9.2	48	110	8.6
	19	52	112	9.2	48	109	8.6	44	104	8.1
2000	23	65	125	11.0	60	123	10.3	55	120	9.6
	22	61	121	10.5	56	119	9.8	52	116	9.2
	21	57	118	9.9	53	115	9.3	49	111	8.7
	20	53	114	9.4	49	110	8.8	45	106	8.3
	19	50	109	8.9	46	105	8.3	42	99	7.8

Cruise Performance Cessna 182S—Pressure Altitude 8,000 feet

RPM	MP	20°C Below Standard Temp. -21°C			Standard Temp. -1°C			20°C Above Standard Temp. 19°C		
		%BHP	KTAS	GPH	%BHP	KTAS	GPH	%BHP	KTAS	GPH
2400	21	71	132	11.9	65	130	11.1	60	127	10.4
	20	66	127	11.2	61	125	10.4	56	123	9.8
	19	61	124	10.5	56	121	9.8	52	117	9.2
	18	56	119	9.8	52	116	9.2	48	111	8.6
2300	21	68	130	11.5	63	127	10.7	58	125	10.0
	20	64	126	10.8	58	123	10.1	54	120	9.5
	19	59	121	10.2	54	119	9.5	50	115	8.9
	18	54	117	9.5	50	113	8.9	46	108	8.4
2200	21	65	127	11.1	60	125	10.4	56	122	9.7
	20	61	123	10.5	56	121	9.8	52	117	9.2
	19	57	119	9.9	52	116	9.2	48	111	8.7
	18	52	114	9.3	48	110	8.7	45	104	8.1
2100	21	62	124	10.6	57	122	9.9	53	118	9.3
	20	58	120	10.1	53	118	9.4	49	113	8.8
	19	54	116	9.5	50	113	8.9	46	108	8.3
	18	50	111	8.9	107	107	8.3	42	99	7.8
2000	21	59	121	10.2	54	119	9.5	50	115	8.9
	20	55	117	9.6	51	114	9.0	47	109	8.5
	19	51	113	9.1	47	109	8.5	43	102	8.0

Cruise Performance Cessna 182S—Pressure Altitude 10,000 feet

RPM	MP	20°C Below Standard Temp. -25°C			Standard Temp. -5°C			20°C Above Standard Temp. 15°C		
		%BHP	KTAS	GPH	%BHP	KTAS	GPH	%BHP	KTAS	GPH
2400	20	68	132	11.5	63	130	10.7	58	127	10.0
	19	63	128	10.8	58	125	10.1	54	121	9.5
	18	59	123	10.1	54	120	9.5	50	115	8.9
2300	20	66	130	11.1	60	127	10.4	56	124	9.7
	19	61	125	10.5	56	123	9.8	52	118	9.2
	18	56	120	9.8	52	117	9.2	48	112	8.6

Cruise Performance Cessna 182S—Pressure Altitude 10,000 feet, continued

RPM	MP	20°C Below Standard Temp. -25°C			Standard Temp. -5°C			20°C Above Standard Temp. 15°C		
		%BHP	KTAS	GPH	%BHP	KTAS	GPH	%BHP	KTAS	GPH
2200	20	63	127	10.8	58	125	10.0	53	121	9.4
	19	59	123	10.1	54	120	9.5	50	115	8.9
	18	54	118	9.5	50	114	8.9	46	108	8.4
2100	20	60	124	10.3	55	121	9.6	51	117	9.0
	19	56	120	9.7	51	116	9.1	47	111	8.5
	18	52	115	9.1	47	110	8.6	44	102	8.0
2000	20	57	121	9.9	52	117	9.2	48	113	8.7
	19	53	117	9.3	49	112	8.7	45	105	8.2
	18	49	111	8.8	45	106	8.2	42	97	7.7

Cruise Performance Cessna 182S—Pressure Altitude 12,000 feet

RPM	MP	20°C Below Standard Temp. -29°C			Standard Temp. -9°C			20°C Above Standard Temp. 11°C		
		%BHP	KTAS	GPH	%BHP	KTAS	GPH	%BHP	KTAS	GPH
2400	18	61	127	10.4	56	124	9.7	51	119	9.1
	17	56	122	9.7	51	117	9.1	47	111	8.5
	16	51	115	9.0	47	110	8.5	43	101	7.9
2300	18	58	124	10.1	54	121	9.4	49	116	8.8
	17	54	119	9.4	49	114	8.8	45	106	8.3
	16	49	112	8.8	45	105	8.2	41	99	7.7
2200	18	56	122	9.8	52	118	9.1	48	111	8.6
	17	52	116	9.1	47	111	8.6	44	102	8.0
2100	18	53	119	9.4	49	114	8.8	45	106	8.2
	17	49	112	8.8	45	106	8.2	42	99	7.7
2000	18	51	115	9.0	46	109	8.4	43	100	7.9

Cruise Performance Cessna 182S—Pressure Altitude 14,000 feet

RPM	MP	20°C Below Standard Temp. -25°C			Standard Temp. -5°C			20°C Above Standard Temp. 15°C		
		%BHP	KTAS	GPH	%BHP	KTAS	GPH	%BHP	KTAS	GPH
2400	16	53	119	9.3	48	114	8.7	45	104	8.2
	15	48	111	8.6	44	102	8.0	40	99	7.5
2300	16	51	116	9.0	47	109	8.5	43	102	7.9
2200	16	49	113	8.8	45	105	8.2	41	100	7.7
2100	16	46	109	8.4	43	100	7.9	39	98	7.4

Calculating Fuel Requirements

To roughly calculate the amount of fuel needed for a trip, measure the distance in knots and divide that by your cruise speed. This will tell you how long your flight will take. Multiply the result by the fuel usage figure, and you'll have a fast ballpark answer.

Naturally, other factors such as winds aloft and how high you plan to cruise will affect your total fuel requirements. There's not much you can do about wind in your calculations unless you can figure out how it will affect your ground speed. This is not an easy task if you're on the ground and have no flight computer, unless the winds are direct headwinds (which decrease your ground speed equal to wind speed) or direct tailwinds (which increase your ground speed equal to wind speed).

But you *can* calculate your fuel requirements for the rest of your trip. The problem with the "quick-and-dirty" method of figuring out fuel requirements is that you don't start a flight at cruising altitude. Therefore, you neglect to factor in the fuel burned when starting the engine, taxiing to the runway, performing the engine run-up check, and taking off. What's more, extra fuel is also required during your climb to cruise.

However, calculating fuel isn't as difficult as it may sound. First, you can figure that it takes 1.7 gallons of fuel on average for startup, taxi, and takeoff. (Naturally you'd factor in a little more usage if you had a long delay for takeoff clearance—not usually a problem in Flight Simulator.)

Fuel consumption for the climb to altitude can be calculated by what are called Time, Fuel, and Distance charts. Use the table labeled "Time, Fuel, and Distance to Climb at 3,100 lbs. Cessna 182S—Maximum Rate of Climb" when climbing at maximum rate, and the table labeled "Time, Fuel, and Distance to

Climb at 3,100 lbs. Cessna 182S—Normal Climb (90 KIAS)" when climbing at a more practical 90 KIAS.

With this information, you can subtract the distance to climb from your total trip distance and then calculate the cruise fuel usage with the quick-and-dirty method. Add the two results together plus the 1.7 gallons startup/run-up gas, and you'll have a pretty good fuel requirement estimate—provided there's no wind!

Time, fuel, and distance to climb calculations are based on:

- Zero wind
- Mixture leaned for smooth engine operation and increased power
- Increasing time, fuel, and distance by 10 percent for each 10°C above standard temp.

Time, Fuel, and Distance to Climb at 3,100 lbs. Cessna 182S—Maximum Rate of Climb

Pressure Alt. Feet	Climb Speed KIAS	Rate Of Climb FPM	From Sea Level Time In Min.	From Sea Level Fuel Use Gallons	From Sea Level Distance N.M.
S.L.	80	925	0	0.0	0
2,000	79	835	2	0.8	3
4,000	78	750	5	1.5	7
6,000	77	660	8	2.3	11
8,000	75	565	11	3.2	16
10,000	74	470	15	4.2	21
12,000	73	375	20	5.2	29
14,000	72	285	26	6.5	38

Time, Fuel, and Distance to Climb at 3,100 lbs. Cessna 182S—Normal Climb (90 KIAS)

Pressure Alt. Feet	Climb Speed KIAS	Rate Of Climb FPM	From Sea Level Time In Min.	From Sea Level Fuel Use Gallons	From Sea Level Distance N.M.
S.L.	90	665	0	0.0	0
2,000	90	625	3	0.8	5
4,000	90	580	6	1.6	10
6,000	90	540	10	2.5	16
8,000	90	455	14	3.5	23
10,000	90	370	19	4.6	31

Specifications and Airspeed Limitations

The following pages contain the specifications and airspeed limitations for the three new aircraft in Flight Simulator. Although some specifications (such as interior dimensions) are given strictly for academic purposes, the other information (such as airspeed limitations) is extremely useful for flight planning and flight configuration.

Cessna 182S Skylane.

Cessna 182S Skylane

Engine: Textron Lycoming

Model Number:	IO-540-AB1A5
Maximum Power:	230 BHP rating
Propeller:	McCauley, 2-Bladed Constant Speed
Landing gear:	Fixed tricycle, steerable nosewheel

Cessna 182S Engine Instrument Markings

Instrument	Red Line (Minimum)	Green Arc (Normal Operating)	Red Line (Maximum)
Tachometer	—	2,000 - 2400 RPM	2,400
Manifold Pressure	—	15-23" Hg.	—
Cylinder Head Temp.	—	200-500°F	500°F
Oil Temp.	—	100-245°F	245°F
Oil Pressure	20 PSI	50-90 PSI	115 PSI
Fuel Quantity	E (2.0 gal. Unusable each tank)	—	—
Fuel Flow	—	0-15 GPH	—
Suction Gauge	—	4.5-5.5" Hg.	—

Crew:	1
Seats:	4
Length:	29 ft.
Height:	9 ft. 3 in.
Wingspan:	36 ft.
Wing area:	175.5 sq. ft.
Max ramp weight:	3,110 lb.
Max takeoff weight:	3,100 lb.
Max landing weight:	2,950 lb.
Std. empty weight:	1,882 lb.
Useful load:	1,228 lb.
Wing loading:	17.8 lb./sq. ft.
Power loading:	13.5 lb./hp.
Max fuel capacity:	92 gal.
Max usable fuel:	88 gal.
Max rate of climb (SL):	924 ft. /min.
Service ceiling:	18,100 ft.
Max operating speed (SL):	145 knots
Range (75% power at 6,000 ft.)	140 knots
Best cruise altitude:	8,000–10,000 ft.

Interior:

Cabin length:	11 ft. 1 in.
Cabin maximum width (centerline):	3 ft. 6 in.
Cabin width (floor level):	3 ft.
Cabin height:	4 ft. 0.5 in.

Cessna 182S Skylane Airspeed Limitations

Vne	175 KIAS	Never Exceed Speed
Vno	140 KIAS	Maximum Structural Cruising Speed (never exceed, unless in smooth air)
Va at 3100 lbs.	110 KIAS	Maneuvering Speed
at 2,600 lbs.	101 KIAS	
at 2,000 lbs.	88 KIAS	
Vfe(1)	10 deg <140 KIAS	Maximum Flap Extension speeds
Vfe(2)	20 deg <120 KIAS	
Vfe(3)	Full <100 KIAS	

Cessna 182S Skylane Airspeed Limitations, continued

Vr	50-60 KIAS	Rotation speed
Vx at SL	63 KIAS	Best angle of climb
at 10,000 ft.	66 KIAS	
Vy at SL	80 KIAS	Best rate of climb
at 10,000 ft.	72 KIAS	
Max glide (flaps up)		Best glide engine out, flaps up
at 3100 lbs.	75 KIAS	
at 2600 lbs.	60 KIAS	
at 2000 lbs.	62 KIAS	
(flaps down) at 3100 ft.	70 KIAS	
Approach no engine (flaps up)	70 KIAS	
(10 deg flaps)	65 KIAS	
Vs	54 KCAS	Stall clean
Vso	49 KCAS	Stall landing configuration
Vref	Approx. 60 KIAS until flair	Landing speed
Max demonstrated crosswind velocity (takeoff and landing)	15 Knots	

Bell 206B JetRanger

Engine: Allison
Model Number: 250-C20B or
                                   250-C20J turbine
Maximum Power: 420 SHP flat-rated
                      to 317 SHP (236 kW)
Maximum Continuous Power:
                      85% Torque (270 hp.)
Maximum Power (5 minutes):
                      100% Torque
Maximum Takeoff Power:
                      100% Torque (317 hp.)
Normal Cruise Power:
                                   80% Torque

Bell 206B JetRanger.

Maximum Rotor RPM (power on):	100%
Minimum Rotor RPM (power on):	97%
Maximum Rotor RPM (power off):	107%
Minimum Rotor RPM (power off):	90%
Crew:	1
Seats:	5
Length:	31.29 ft.
Height:	11.63 ft.
Rotor Span:	33.33 ft.
Skid Width:	6.28 ft.
Maximum Gross Weight:	3,200 lbs.
Empty Weight:	1750 lbs.
Useful Load:	1,450 lbs.
Fuel Capacity:	91 gal.
Average Fuel Consumption	260-285 lbs./hr. (38-42 gal./hr.)
Maximum Rate of Climb:	about 1,300 fpm.
Maximum Operating Altitude:	20,000 ft.
Maximum Speed:	130 knots
Normal Operating Speed:	0-130 knots

Bell 206B JetRanger Airspeed Limitations

Vne	130 KIAS	Never exceed speed
Vy (also least sink)	52 KIAS	Best Rate of climb
Max glide (distance)	69 KIAS	

Learjet 45

Engines:	2 AlliedSignal/Garrett
Model Number:	TFE 731-20 turbofans
Maximum Power:	3.500 lb. st. (15.6 kN) each
Takeoff thrust flat-rated to 88 degrees F	
(31 degrees C):	3,650 pounds (APR rating) each
Crew:	2
Passengers:	Up to 9
Length:	58 ft.
Height:	14.1 ft.
Wingspan:	47.75 ft.

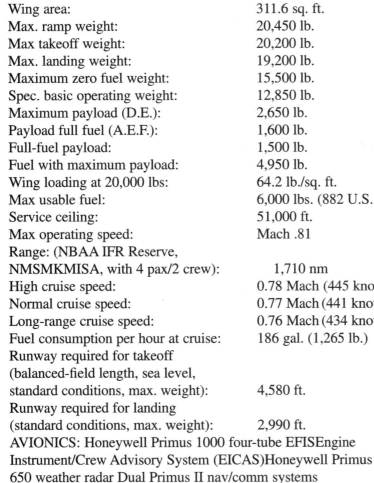

Wing area:	311.6 sq. ft.
Max. ramp weight:	20,450 lb.
Max takeoff weight:	20,200 lb.
Max. landing weight:	19,200 lb.
Maximum zero fuel weight:	15,500 lb.
Spec. basic operating weight:	12,850 lb.
Maximum payload (D.E.):	2,650 lb.
Payload full fuel (A.E.F.):	1,600 lb.
Full-fuel payload:	1,500 lb.
Fuel with maximum payload:	4,950 lb.
Wing loading at 20,000 lbs:	64.2 lb./sq. ft.
Max usable fuel:	6,000 lbs. (882 U.S. gal.)
Service ceiling:	51,000 ft.
Max operating speed:	Mach .81
Range: (NBAA IFR Reserve, NMSMKMISA, with 4 pax/2 crew):	1,710 nm
High cruise speed:	0.78 Mach (445 knots)
Normal cruise speed:	0.77 Mach (441 knots)
Long-range cruise speed:	0.76 Mach (434 knots)
Fuel consumption per hour at cruise:	186 gal. (1,265 lb.)
Runway required for takeoff (balanced-field length, sea level, standard conditions, max. weight):	4,580 ft.
Runway required for landing (standard conditions, max. weight):	2,990 ft.

AVIONICS: Honeywell Primus 1000 four-tube EFISEngine Instrument/Crew Advisory System (EICAS)Honeywell Primus 650 weather radar Dual Primus II nav/comm systems

Interior:

Cabin length (cockpit divider to end of pressurized compartment):	19 ft. 9in.
Cabin maximum width (centerline):	5 ft. 1 in.
Cabin width (floor level):	3 ft. 4 in.
Cabin height:	4 ft. 11 in.
Floor area (excluding cockpit):	65.8 26.1
Total volume (cockpit divider to end of pressurized compartment):	410 ft.

Learjet 45 Airspeed Limitations

Vne	Mach .81	Never-exceed speed
Vno		Maximum structural speed
Va		Maneuvering speed
Vfe(1)	8 deg. <200	Maximum Flap Extension speeds
Vfe(2)	20 deg. <185 KIAS	
Vfe(3)	40 deg. <150 KIAS	
Vr	143 KIAS	Rotation speed
Vx		Best Angle of climb
Vy		Best Rate of climb
Max glide		
Vmc		Minimum controllable airspeed 1 engine
Vs		Stall clean
Vso		Stall landing configuration
Vref (landing speed)	Approx. 125 KIAS at 14000 lbs.	Landing speed
Vle	260 KIAS	
Vlo	200 KIAS	
V1	136 KIAS	Takeoff decision speed
V2	134 KIAS at 16,900 lbs.	
V2+30	164 KIAS at 16,900 lbs.	
Vsse	146 KIAS inoperative speed	Intentional one-engine

Learjet 45.

Information Sources:

1997 Cessna 182S Skylane Information Manual

Learjet, Inc. at http://www.learjet.com/45_stat.html

Pilot Help: Flight Simulator 98

Chapter Eight

FLYING "THE SYSTEM"

When someone refers to "The System," it's natural to assume that they're referring to the Air Traffic Control System (or ATC). But in reality, The System is really a combination of both the ATC and the entire aviation navigation system infrastructure. Although the whole ATC system was designed for traffic control, you can break it down into two distinct systems—traffic control and the navigation system. You could argue that they're one and the same, but we're going to preserve the distinction between them because it's possible to fly using the aviation navigation infrastructure and never have contact with ATC.

Until you've actually flown within The System as a pilot, there's no way to really appreciate what a marvelous and complex system exists in the skies above us. Day and night, rain or shine, there are *thousands* of aircraft flying around up there at any given moment, so it's really a tribute to the efficiency of the ATC system that there aren't more mid-air collisions or near misses.

If there's one shortcoming in Microsoft Flight Simulator 98, it has to be in its modeling of ATC. Understandably, modeling such a dynamic and complex system would be an enormous undertaking (which, incidentally, no other simulator has been able to re-create well, either). What's more, most casual pilots probably wouldn't even care if it were modeled 100 percent accurately. Although a major portion of real world aviation revolves around ATC, you should consider yourself lucky that in Flight Simulator you have the freedom to do what you please. So there's the tradeoff. And as cool as the ATC system is, you probably end up the winner on this trade.

Flight Simulator is totally oblivious to ATC. What is modeled can give you an idea of what's involved in real world cockpit management, but you have the choice to follow procedure or totally ignore it. Let's go over what parts of The System are modeled.

> **Note:** *Even though you don't need to talk to ATC during Adventure Flights, that radio chatter you hear is extremely realistic. So if you want a taste of what it's really like, go on an Adventure.*

The Learjet 45's radios are located on the instrument panel.

Now on the Air...

Now that you've been up in the air, let's talk about getting you *on the air*—on the radio, that is. In real aviation, there are lots of people to talk to out there: Clearance Delivery, Ground Control, departure airport Control Tower, Departure Control, Approach control, the destination airport's Control Tower, and finally, your destination airport's Ground Control. In Flight Simulator, you don't have to talk to anyone if you don't want to, but if you do, the control towers are the only locations you can contact. But we're getting ahead of ourselves. Let's talk about radio equipment first.

All the aircraft in Flight Simulator (except for the sailplane, the Camel—which has no radio at all, the Learjet 45, and the 737-400) are equipped with a Bendix/King radio stack. The other units, although they look different, all function the same way. So we'll just stick with the most common unit for our discussions.

To display the radio stack, click the Avionics Master switch on the instrument panel (if the plane you're flying has such a switch), or from the Views menu, click Instrument Panel, then select radio stack. The Learjet 45's radios are located on the instrument panel.

The Bendix/King radio stack includes (from top to bottom):

Most of the aircraft in Flight Simulator 98 are equipped with a Bendix/King radio stack.

- Two Bendix/King KX 155A VHF COM/NAV radios
- One Bendix/King KR 87 ADF (Automatic Direction Finder)
- One DME (Distance Measuring Equipment) indicator
- One Bendix/King KT 76C Mode C transponder
- One Bendix/King KAP 2-axis autopilot

At first glance, the radio stack probably seems like a whole mess of knobs, buttons, and numbers. We'll take a look at each unit one at a time. Aside from their designations—COM1 and COM2, and NAV1 and NAV2—the top two units are identical. Each of these radios is divided into two sections. The left halves are the COM radios, and the right halves are the NAV radios. The NAV radios receive radio navigation signals; the COM radios transmit and receive voice communications.

COM1, COM All!

Although theoretically you have two COM radios, only COM1 is functional in Flight Simulator. Luckily, that isn't a problem because the only things you'll be tuning in for on the COM radio are ATIS reports.

> **Tip:** *On a long flight, listen to ATIS information along your route to be kept apprised of weather conditions and altimeter settings.*

ATIS

ATIS means *Automated Terminal Information System*. ATIS provides you with the current weather, ceiling (clouds), visibility, temperature, dew point (a temperature/humidity index), magnetic wind direction and velocity, altimeter settings, runway use, and cautionary advisories about the airport you tune in. There is a complete listing of airport ATIS frequencies in Flight Simulator, listed in the Airport/Facility Directory. The normal procedure is to listen to ATIS reports prior to taxi on departure and prior to arrival at a destination airport. In other words, listen to ATIS *before* contacting the tower to request takeoff or landing clearance.

There are three ways to tune COM frequencies—by mouse, keyboard, or menu.

- To tune COM frequencies by mouse, click the digit position of the number you want to change. When it is selected, it will change color from red to yellow. To increase the number, click to the right of the digit, and to decrease the number, click to the left of the digit.
- To tune COM frequencies by keyboard, press C on the keyboard to select the digit you want to change. Each keypress will cycle the selection one digit position to the right. When you've selected the digit you want to change, press the + (plus sign) key or - (minus sign) key to advance or decrease the number.
- To tune COM frequencies from a menu, select Communications from the Aircraft menu. Click the COM1 Frequency box and type in the frequency.

Requesting Takeoff or Landing Clearance

Not all tower communications require that you actually adjust the COM radio. COM1 can only be used for listening to ATIS, so it doesn't matter whether you tune in an actual tower frequency or not to request clearance.

To request takeoff or landing clearance:

1. Click the Aircraft menu.

2. Select Communications.

3. Click the radio button of the clearance you want to request.

4. Click OK.

After requesting takeoff clearance, the tower will acknowledge your call and give you instructions. "Taxi to runway of your choice" should be obvious, a rough translation being, "Take off anywhere you want." But being the procedure-hounds that we are, you'll want to taxi to the runway in use mentioned in ATIS.

"Hold short" means, "Stay off the runway until you're told you can get on it." "Squawk 0277" has to do with the transponder, so let's talk about that next.

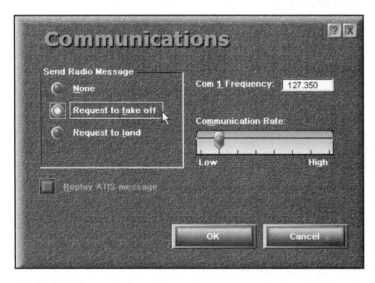

Flight Simulator 98 doesn't require you to perform a lot of "radio work," but you do need to request clearance for takeoffs or landings.

`Microsoft Flight Simulator, taxi to runway of your choice and hold short.  Squawk 0277 ...`

After requesting takeoff clearance, the tower will give you instructions similar to these.

Transponder

In most areas where there is radar coverage, ATC uses radarscopes to keep track of all aircraft in the area. You've seen these hundreds of times in the movies. You know—those green circular screens that have the little *blips* on them when the overpaid actor playing the controller exclaims something like, "It's going off the screen! Call the President!"

Radarscopes are pretty fancy these days. Many even have colors beyond the traditional sea green! They can display

your position and your altitude, but they aren't totally self-sufficient. This is where the transponder fits into the puzzle. A transponder (XPDR) is the airborne component of the ATC Radar Beacon System (ATCRBS). Although the ATCRBS can "see" an aircraft within its range, a transponder makes your airplane easier to identify.

When a transponder receives what's called an *interrogator pulse* from ATC radar, it replies with a four-digit code. This code is the number that appears on the face of the transponder. Therefore, when ATC tells you to "Squawk 0277," they're instructing you to set your transponder to 0277. This way they can identify you (by your transponder code) in relation to the other blips on their radarscope.

Normally, for radar to scan your altitude would require a pretty sophisticated system that would have to triangulate your position in space. A much simpler method uses what's known as a Mode C or *altitude reporting/encoding* transponder. This type of transponder takes your altimeter reading and reports that information, along with the four-digit code reply. So to ATC, your altitude on their scope is only as accurate as your altimeter.

Like the COM radio, transponder codes can be set three ways—by mouse, keyboard, or menu.

- To set transponder codes by mouse, click the digit position of

Radio Nostalgia

One of the most difficult skills a real pilot has to learn is how to use the radio. It's not the operation of the hardware or the fact that you have to talk on the radio and fly at the same time that's difficult. It's that when you first hear ATC jabber, it sounds like people reciting numbers to each other at 100 miles per hour. (Of course, the static, feedback, and mumbling that goes on while the drone of your poor little engine chugs along in the background doesn't help matters either.)

For me, though, the most difficult thing about learning to use the radio was that I couldn't help feeling self-conscious about broadcasting my voice over the airwaves. This didn't have anything to do with being afraid that my voice would crack or I'd stutter from being nervous or anything like that. Instead, I was afraid I'd say something wrong or unintelligible that would make ATC stop their flow of jabber to ask me to repeat my message! ATC can understand all of that other babbling, but what if they can't understand what I said? I'd have to be doing something seriously wrong. How embarrassing!

Admittedly, it was a silly thought, and it didn't last beyond my second flying lesson. But I bring it up to illustrate that using the radio adds a whole other aspect to flying that most people never consider. There's more to flying than just pushin' throttles and kickin' pedals.

Note: *Real transponders have what's called an Ident button. It's the button on the far left of the transponder code display (non-functional in Flight Simulator 98). Pressing this button will "highlight" your transponder blip to ATC. This Ident is different than Identify on NAV radios. You're only to press the transponder Ident button when requested by ATC.*

Note: *All of the transponders in Flight Simulator 98 use Mode C encoding, but altitude reporting isn't used for anything.*

the number you want to change. When the desired number is selected, it will change color from red to yellow. The numbers will only cycle upwards, and you can only select the numbers 0 through 7.

- To set transponder codes by keyboard, press T on the keyboard to select the digit you want to change. Each keypress will cycle the selection one digit position to the right. When you've selected the digit you want to change, press the + (plus sign) key or the - (minus sign) key to increase or decrease the number.
- To set transponder codes from the menu, select Navigation from the Aircraft menu. Select the Transponder/ADF tab, click the Transponder Code box, and type in the squawk code.

Your transponder lets ATC know exactly who—and where—you are.

Unless you squawk the correct transponder code after requesting takeoff clearance, you will not be cleared for takeoff. If you do not squawk the correct code, Flight Simulator ATC will send you a message reminding you what the squawk code should be.

Listed below are standard transponder codes along with their meanings:

- 1200—VFR flight. Use this code when

flying VFR and if you have not been instructed to squawk another code by ATC.

`Microsoft Flight Simulator set transponder code to 0277`

If you do not squawk the correct code, the ATC in Flight Simulator will send you a reminder.

- 7500—Hijacking. This is the code to report that your aircraft is being hijacked.
- 7600—Radio out. Squawking this code lets ATC know your radio is disabled.
- 7700—General Emergency. 7700 will normally trigger an alarm or special indicator at the ground radar facility.

Tip: *Flight Simulator requires you to squawk the proper transponder code before you receive takeoff clearance, but in real life you keep your transponder on standby mode or off until you're cleared for takeoff. Otherwise, you'd show up on ATC radar even though you were still on the ground. This practice helps avoid radar clutter and hopefully makes ATC's job easier.*

Navigating Systems

There are three ways to navigate in the Flight Simulator 98 world: pilotage, dead reckoning, and radio navigation. Although you can get around using any one of them, most pilots rely on combinations of the three methods.

Pilotage

Pilotage is the most basic form of aeronautical navigation, and most casual Flight Simulator pilots use this method. You rely on a map, a good sense of direction, and good eyesight. You fly from landmark to landmark. Anything recognizable will work. A landmark can be a road, a river, or even Farmer Smith's barn. As long as you know where it is on the map or its relation to something else on the map, you can use it. Although pilotage tends to lead you on zig-zag courses all over the countryside, it generally works pretty well if you're not going too far.

The problem with pilotage is it doesn't work very well when:

- Visibility is poor. (If you can't see the landmarks.)
- Flying fast aircraft. (You: "Was that the road?" Co-pilot: "What road?")
- Flying at high altitudes. (*Everything* looks the same.)
- Flying in unfamiliar areas. (You'll tend to circle around quite a bit.)

Microsoft Flight Simulator 98

Flights Aircraft World Options Views Help

It's easy to call up a new map window. Press Shift +].

Views Help

Full Screen	ALT-ENTER
View Options...	
Instrument Panel	▶
New View	▶
View Mode	▶
Maximize View	W
Undock View	
Close View	]
✓ COCKPIT - View 01	

Cockpit   [
Virtual Cockpit
Spot Plane
Tower
Track
Map   NumLock

The New View option will also cause a new Map window to appear.

- Flying where there are no discernable landmarks (such as over large bodies of water or deserts).

Map View

Naturally, if you're going to fly by pilotage, you need a map. The Map view in Flight Simulator can be accessed by four methods. Two of them create new windows, and the other two just switch the current view to the Map.

- You can also create a new Map window from the New View option found on the View menu. This brings up a new map window exactly as if you pressed the Shift +].

  - The quickest way to view Map is by pressing the Shift +] keys. This will create a new map window. To close the window, press the] key or right-click the window and select Close Window from the pop-up menu.

  - To change a current view to Map, right-click any current view window, then select Map View from the pop-up menu. This will change the selected view window to Map View. To switch the view back to your original view, right-click the window again and select the view of your choice.

- You can also change a current view to Map by clicking View Options from the Views menu. Then on the View Options window, click the Map Radio button under Window Type. To switch the view back to your original view, go back to View Options and click the radio button of the view of your choice.

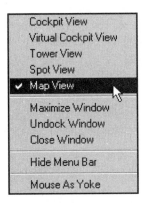

Flight Simulator 98 lets you easily "toggle" between views.

You have a couple of options concerning how you want to change map views.

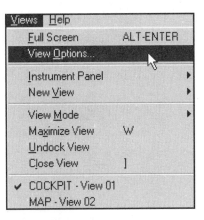

It stands to reason that before you can use the Map View Altitude feature, you must open a Map View.

Using Map is pretty straightforward. The map rotates based on your heading so the top of the map is always facing the direction you're flying in. All of the standard window option keys in Flight Simulator work: press the W key for full screen, the] key to close the window, the + key (plus sign) to zoom in, or the - key (minus sign) to zoom out. Additionally, there is a zoom feature exclusive to the Map View. This allows you to select the Map View Altitude in AGL increments. The benefit of this feature over the standard zoom options is it offers both greater range and finer adjustments.

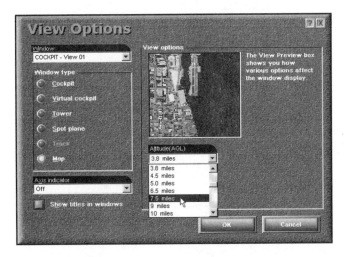

You'll get a taste of what your Map Altitude selections will look like from the View Preview box.

To access this Map View Altitude feature, a Map View must be open:

1. Click View Options from the Views menu.

2. On the View Options window, select Map from the Window drop-down list at the top right corner.

3. This will change the View Preview box in the center of the window to the current Map View. Directly below the View Preview box is the Altitude drop-down box. Select the altitude AGL you want to use and then click the OK button when you're finished. Note that the View Preview box will display what your Map Altitude selections will look like.

Dead Reckoning

There are many stories about how the term *dead reckoning* came about, but most seem to be one-liner jokes like "That's because if you reckon' wrong—you're dead." (The drummer gives a rimshot...*ba-bum bum.*)

But seriously, folks...*dead reckoning* seems to have roots in the military slang term *deduced reconnoitering*. Over the years, deduced reconnoitering was shortened to ded. recon. Then, as you can imagine, ded. recon. was easily butchered through verbal translations to *ded reconning.* Anyway, dead reckoning (or more accurately, *deduced* reckoning) literally means "reasoned guessing." Through the use of charts, a magnetic compass, true airspeed, and wind vectoring (velocity and direction), you calculate where you *should* be after a certain amount of flight time.

This works amazingly well. But the problem is, if you deviate from your course even a slight amount or if the wind changes and you don't realize it, it can put you miles from your desired destination.

Airspeed vs. Ground Speed

Back in Chapter Four we spoke a little about the difference between IAS (Indicated Air Speed) and TAS (True Air Speed). The only use for TAS other than for performance issues is for dead reckoning navigation. That's because if you know your true airspeed and the wind vector in relation to your desired flight path, you can calculate your ground speed. Maybe we should back up a bit.

It's a common misconception that TAS equals ground speed. This is only true if you're in level flight and there is zero wind. To give you two examples why this simplistic equation is flawed, you need only consider an airplane in a dive straight toward the ground. According to your ASI, your TAS will read something astronomically high (before your wings rip off, that is), but your ground speed will be 0 (zero). Granted, this is an extreme example, but it illustrates the point that TAS is unreliable for ground speed if you're climbing or descending.

As a second example, factor in some wind. As you know, your ASI only provides indicated airspeed. Although TAS is an IAS calculation corrected for pressure, altitude, and temperature, it applies only to your speed in relation to the air mass you're flying through. Because air is free to roam the face of the earth, your airspeed within that air mass has very little to do with ground speed (unless, of course, the air is perfectly still).

To better understand this, picture yourself walking up a down escalator. If you were an

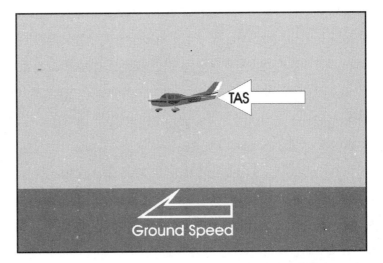

TAS only equals ground speed when you're in level flight and there is no wind.

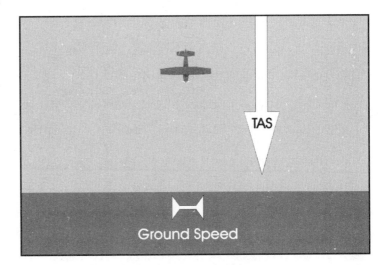

If you dive at the ground, your TAS will be very high, but your ground speed will be nearly 0 (zero).

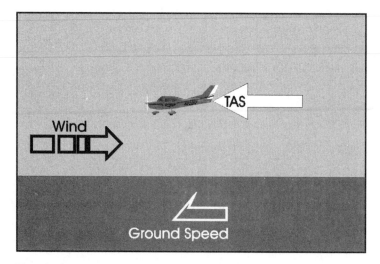

To calculate your ground speed in a direct headwind, subtract the wind speed from your TAS.

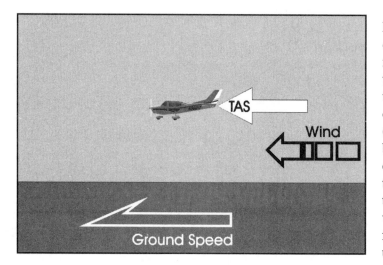

To calculate your ground speed in a direct tailwind, add the wind speed to your TAS.

airplane and the escalator belt/steps were the wind, depending on how fast you were climbing those steps (equivalent to your TAS), your ground speed (your speed in relation to the ground that the escalator is resting on) would be proportionately reduced. It works the same way with the wind. The bottom line: you can't rely on TAS as your absolute ground speed unless you're flying level and you calculate wind vector.

The next question is how is ground speed calculated? Well, you need two things to make the calculation—TAS and the wind vector. TAS comes from your ASI. (You set it to indicate TAS by disabling the IAS option on the Instrument tab under Preferences in the Options menu.) Wind vector information comes from ATIS. Unfortunately, unless the winds aloft (at altitude) equal the ground winds, you'll have to look up the winds in the Weather dialogue boxes.

Naturally, it's easy to calculate how the wind will affect your ground speed if the wind comes directly toward, or behind, your flight path. You'd simply subtract the wind speed in a direct headwind from your TAS or add the wind speed of a direct tailwind to your TAS to get your ground speed.

However, when the wind comes from another angle you must make additional calculations. The way to calculate how non-direct headwinds or tailwinds will affect your ground speed is to use a flight computer or, to a limited extent, a wind component graph.

To calculate the effect of a crosswind on TAS, find the wind velocity curve that meets the wind angle relative to your flight path and then read the corresponding headwind or tailwind on the scale to the left. Add (for tailwinds) or subtract (for headwinds) the number from your TAS to calculate your ground speed. For example, if you were flying heading 090 and there was a 20-knot crosswind coming from heading 130, your ground speed would be reduced in an amount equal to flying in a direct headwind of 15 knots. (090-130 = 40-degree angle.)

OK, it's easy to see that calculating ground speeds is a hassle, especially when you're trying to fly the airplane at the same time. Even if you have all of the calculations correct, there's still a lot that can go wrong. That's why most pilots don't rely solely on one form of navigation. They'll use some combination of pilotage, dead reckoning, and radio navigation. Let's look at radio navigation next.

Radio Navigation

Radio Navigation is simply navigating through the use of radio aids. It's the most accurate method of navigation of the three we've discussed. But pilotage and dead reckoning are still taught at the better flying schools. That's so you won't be caught up in the air totally lost if you lose your navigation radios. That's pretty rare, but if it ever happened to you, you'd be glad you learned some of the *older arts*. Enough philosophy—let's take a look at how radio navigation can help you.

Radio navigation is the most popular form of aeronautical navigation in the continental United States. In addition to being accurate, for the most part it doesn't require any complicated math or eagle eyesight like dead reckoning and pilotage do. When we first spoke about the navigation portion of The System,

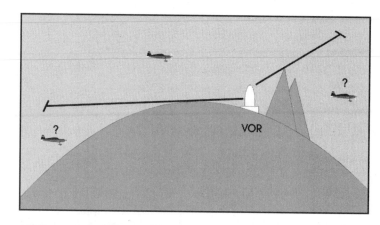

VOR transmissions are line of sight, so the curvature of the earth and physical obstructions limit their range.

the infrastructure we referred to is the network of VOR and NDB stations spread across the land.

The VOR System

VOR is an acronym for VHF (Very High Frequency) Omnirange Radio beacon. Pilot Help does a pretty good job of explaining what VORs are and how they work, so there's little reason to repeat that here. As great as it is, we should also mention the drawbacks of VOR technology. It is limited to your line of sight, and coverage is not worldwide.

VOR is a two-part system. The first part is the VOR transmitting stations, and the second part is the VOR receivers found in your instrument panels. Actually, a VOR receiver is also a two-part system as well. You have the receiver to tune and receive the signals and the indicator heads or indicator displays. Let's begin with the receivers.

Of all the aircraft in Flight Simulator, only the sailplane and the Camel are not equipped with radio navigation equipment. (The table labeled "Flight Simulator Radio Navigation Equipment By Aircraft" lists what radio navigation equipment is found on each aircraft in Flight Simulator.) VOR receivers are referred to as NAV radios. Tuning a NAV radio is very similar to tuning a COM radio, but there are a couple of differences. The biggest difference, of course, is that there are actually two NAV radios on all radio-navigation-equipped aircraft except for the Extra 300S. (Keeping weight to a minimum can yield an advantage in aerobatics.)

- To tune NAV frequencies by mouse, click the digit position of the number you want to change. When it is selected, it will change color from red to yellow. To increase the number, click to the right of the digit, and to decrease the number, click to the left of the digit.

- To tune NAV frequencies by keyboard, press N + the number of the NAV radio you want to tune. For example, to choose NAV 2, you would press N + 2. Each additional N key will cycle the selection one digit position to the right on the radio you've selected. When you've selected the digit you want to change, press the + key (plus sign) or the - key (minus sign) to increase or decrease the number.

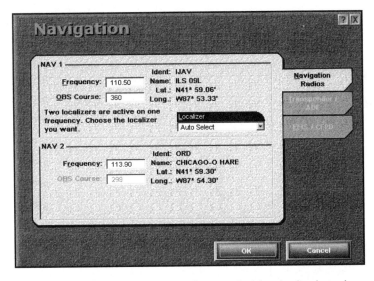

Frequencies on NAV radios can be tuned either by keyboard or mouse.

- To tune NAV frequencies from the menu, select Navigation from the Aircraft menu. Click the NAV 1 or NAV 2 Frequency boxes and type in the frequency. Click the OK button when you're finished.

Flight Simulator 98 Radio Navigation Equipment By Aircraft

Aircraft	XPDR	Equipment NAV head	NDB	DME
Bell 206B JetRanger	X	HSI & VOR	ADF	X
Boeing 737-400	X	HSI	RMI	X
Cessna 182RG		2 VOR	ADF	X
Cessna 182S	X	2 VOR	ADF	X
Extra 300S	X	VOR	ADF	X
Learjet 45	X	HSI	RMI	X
Schweizer 2-32				
Sopwith Camel				

A VOR indicator with glideslope needle.

A VOR indicator without a glideslope needle.

Indicator Heads

There are two kinds of NAV indicator heads modeled in Flight Simulator. The first is the familiar VOR indicator, and the second is the HSI (Horizontal Situation Indicator). Furthermore, VOR heads come in two flavors—with glideslope or without needles. Every aircraft in Flight Simulator has a VOR head with a GDI, unless it has an HSI as well (as in the case of the JetRanger).

The parts of the VOR indicator that you should be acquainted with are as follows:

- OBS—The Omni-Bearing Selector knob at the bottom left corner. This knob changes the VOR radial selection. You can select VOR radials with your mouse by clicking the OBS or through a menu by selecting Navigation from the Aircraft menu. Click the NAV 1 or NAV 2 OBS box and type in the new heading.
- CDI—The Course Deviation Indicator is the vertical needle that indicates whether you are to the right or the left of the selected radial. The CDI also acts as the localizer needle when the NAV is tuned to and receiving an ILS signal.
- Glideslope needle—When the NAV radio corresponding to the VOR indicator with a glideslope needle is tuned to and receiving an ILS signal, the glideslope needle will indicate whether you are above or below the glideslope.
- TO-FROM-NAV flag—This window is just to the right of center in a non-glideslope needle VOR head and in the 6 o'clock position next to the letters *NAV* on the glideslope version. In this little window, one of three flags will appear indicating certain conditions. An up arrow will indicate a TO VOR radial position, and a down arrow will indicate a FROM VOR radial position. The NAV flag is the little red and white, diagonally striped indicator that shows up when no valid VOR signals are being received. Two conditions will bring up this flag. The first is when there are no VOR stations in range or selected on the NAV radio; the

Note: *The OBS heading on NAV1 is what the autopilot slaves to when in NAV mode.*

second is when you are flying through what's known as the *zone of ambiguity*.

As ominous as the phrase zone of ambiguity may sound, it's merely the region directly above a VOR station. When you're flying there, the radials are so close together that the CDI moves randomly. Another name for this region is the *cone of confusion*. The zone of ambiguity is really shaped like a cone (it gets wider with altitude), and your CDI seems to get confused when you're inside this cone.

Anyway, be aware that when you get very close to a VOR station, your CDI will become unreliable. Rather than trying to chase a confused needle, just hold your heading until you pass the station. You'll know when that happens because the NAV flag will appear and disappear, and the TO flag that was showing will become a FROM flag.

This GS Flag means no valid glideslope signal is being received.

- GS Flag—GS stands for GlideSlope, and the GS flag shown in upper right figure indicates that no valid glideslope signal is being received. That means that, even though the glideslope needle may be moving, you can't trust it when the GS flag appears. The GS Flag window is in the same location as the TO-FROM-NAV window on a non-glideslope-indicating VOR (just right of center). You'll recognize it by the letters *GS* next to it. When a valid glideslope signal is being received, the letters *GS* will appear in the GS Flag window.

Let's move on to the HSI. An HSI is a combination glideslope—indicating VOR and a DG all rolled up in one. This conserves instrument panel space, and most pilots find it easier to use because you don't have to scan as many instruments to get the same information.

There are three versions of the HSI modeled in Flight Simulator—one is mechanical, and the other two are electronic. The mechanical version is found on the JetRanger.

The JetRanger's HSI is pretty simple to operate. The knob on the lower left is the OBS knob, and the knob on the lower right adjusts the DG heading bug. (Use this to set an autopilot heading in HDG mode.) The yellow arrow is the VOR radial course, and the yellow pointer around the circular scale is the DG bug. CDI information comes from the body of the yellow arrow, and GS

The upper VOR indicator shows a valid GS indication, and a TO flag. The lower VOR indicator shows a FROM flag.

This HSI is from the JetRanger.

The HSI in the 737 is very easy to read and understand.

The HSI of the 45 is complete, and extremely well-thought-out. (Kudos to the Learjet's designers.)

information is in the form of two pointers on the left and right side of the HIS, respectively. A NAV flag slides down in the top left corner when no valid VOR or ILS signals are being received.

Unfortunately, there don't seem to be any TO or FROM flags on the JetRanger's HSI. Some TO and FROM flags on real mechanical HSIs appear above and below the CDI scale that runs perpendicular to the radial course index arrow. On the other hand, flying heavy-duty IFR in a helicopter isn't something many will try, so this omission probably won't bother you.

The electronic HSIs on the 737 and LearJet 45 are more complete. The 737's HSI is read much the same way as the JetRanger's HSI. The yellow arrow is the VOR radial course, and the orange pointer around the circular scale is the DG bug. CDI information comes from the body of the yellow arrow, and GS information is shown just to the right—under the letters *GS*. TO and FROM arrows are indicated by gray triangles near the center of the radial course index arrow.

Essentially, the only difference between the 737's HSI and a completely mechanical HSI is the way you adjust the VOR radial course and DG heading. On both of the electronic HSIs in Flight Simulator, these variables are adjusted directly on the autopilot display. We'll talk about the autopilot a little more later, but you should know that you can click away at the course and heading numerical displays on the autopilot to change their values.

The best radio navigation indicator modeled in Flight Simulator is found on the Learjet 45. This HSI is really a hybrid that combines all of the navigation indicators into one display. Just like the 737's HSI, the yellow arrow is the VOR radial course, but instead of a pointer for a DG bug, your heading is listed numerically in the lower right corner under HDG. CDI information comes from the body of the yellow arrow, and GS information is shown just to the right of the AI. (Very slick!) TO and FROM arrows are indicated by gray triangles near the center of the radial course index arrow.

But perhaps the best part of the 45's HSI is that you're able to overlay VOR2 and ADF indicators on the same display. To display the green VOR2 arrow needle, click the button to the left of the slip indicator. To display the light gray ADF needle, click the button to the right.

DME

Recall that calculating ground speed is a major hassle. Radio navigation has helped reduce the need for those kinds of calculations through DME (Distance Measuring Equipment). The DME indicator (the fourth unit down on the Cessna 182S's radio stack) is slaved to NAV radio and picks up distance information from VOR-DME stations or VORTACs (VOR with TACAN-Tactical Air Navigation capabilities) on the UHF band.

You can select which VOR you want to slave to the DME by clicking the switch just to the left of the knob on the far right side of the transponder unit. Up is for NAV1, and down is for NAV2. DME information is displayed as the distance to the selected station in nautical miles and as ground speed in knots. That's right. It's all figured out for you already. (Isn't technology wonderful!) In fact, some DME displays will also calculate your ETA (estimated time of arrival) to the VOR station as well. Now how's that for lightening your cockpit workload?

Before you run out into the street cheering, there are a couple of things you should be aware of. First, when talking about DME, you have to discuss the concept of *slant range*. Slant range relates to the fact that DME measures in a straight line. In other words, the distance DME reports is the distance between your receiver and the station, not the distance on the ground (horizontal distance).

Slant range isn't a problem at low altitudes, but the higher you fly, the greater the error. On the other hand, slant range error does *decrease* the further away you are from the VOR. The second factor is time. Distance and speed calculations are only valid if you're flying directly toward or directly away from the selected station. Drawbacks notwithstanding, the DME

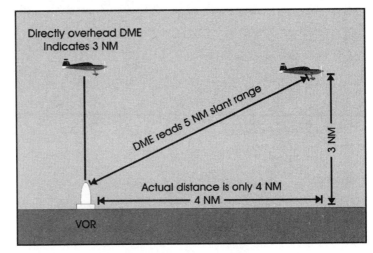

The distances that DME reports do not account for slant range.

is a great tool. As long as you're aware of the potential problems in its calculations, you'll be able to work with it and save yourself from doing a lot of math.

ADF

The ADF (Automatic Direction Finder) is the receiver component of an NDB (Non-Directional Beacon). An ADF is to an NDB what a VOR indicator is to a VOR station. Now that we've got that analogy out of the way, let's talk (alphabet) soup.

NDBs are generally found in wide-open areas. VORs are the navigation beacons of choice because they provide more intuitive directional information. However, NDBs are cheaper to set up and maintain. And they theoretically have a longer range. NDBs transmit on the ("oldie but goodie") AM radio band, and because NDB operates on low frequencies, it's not limited to line of sight operation.

The ADF system is divided into two parts—the radio receiver and the indicator head. Tuning the ADF is very similar to using COM1:

To tune the ADF, you follow most of the same steps you used in tuning the COM1 radio.

- To tune ADF frequencies with the mouse, click the digit position of the number you want to change. When it is selected, it will change color from red to yellow. To increase the number, click to the right of the digit, and to decrease the number, click to the left of the digit.
- To tune ADF frequencies by keyboard, press the A key. Each

additional A keypress will cycle the selection one digit position to the right on the radio you've selected. When you've selected the digit you want to change, press the + key (plus sign) or the - key (minus sign) to increase or decrease the number.

- To tune ADF frequencies from the menu, select Navigation from the Aircraft menu and then click the Transponder/ADF tab. After clicking the ADF Frequency box, type in the frequency. Click the OK button when you're finished.

This standard ADF indicator is found on all NDB—enabled Flight Simulator 98 aircraft, except for the Learjet 45 and Boeing 737-400.

There are two types of ADF indictors modeled in Flight Simulator—the standard ADF and the RMI (Radio Magnetic Indicator). The difference between an ADF and a RMI is similar to the difference between a VOR indicator and an HSI, only instead of a VOR radial course indication, you have an ADF needle.

Essentially, the RMI just adds a DG to the ADF. So instead of having to do math in your head to come up with a magnetic heading to a NDB (relative bearing + magnetic heading = magnetic heading), the RMI's outer ring automatically rotates like a DG so you can read magnetic headings directly. Although this may seem like a big advance in technology over an ADF, the old, standard ADF actually does the same thing. The only difference is you have to move the outer ring *manually* with the ADF's heading knob. (This is kind of a "poor man's" RMI.) So you really aren't stuck doing the math anyway.

The standard ADF indicator isn't found on Boeing's 737-400.

Remember that the Learjet's HSI also works as an RMI because the ADF needle is situated inside the HSI's DG. However, on the 737's RMI, a green needle shows VOR2 indications, and a yellow needle shows ADF indications. Although the RMI/VOR2 indicator is a separate unit, its roots in the Learjet system are apparent.

Like AM radio broadcasts, NDB signals are susceptible to static and other interference. Mountains have to been known to "bounce" NDB signals. (Erratic behavior around sunrise and sunset has been blamed on signals ricocheting off the ionosphere.) Another problem is that ADF needles tend to point toward lightning discharges as well. How can you trust these things with your virtual life?

In real life, in a commercial aviation environment, *all* radio navigation beacons must be identified. This includes VORs as well. All NDBs broadcast an audible Morse Code signal so they can be identified, and some even include a voice message. Unfortunately, in Flight Simulator you'll only receive the

Morse Code versions. The table labeled "Commands Used to Identify Radio Stations" lists the key commands that are used to identify radio navigation beacons, while the table labeled "Morse Code Alphabet" details the famous communications system. What you're supposed to listen for is the three-letter identifier of the beacon.

When you feel that the ADF indications of the NDB can't be trusted, fly while listening to the identify signal. As long as you hear the correct identifier, your ADF indications will be correct.

Commands Used to Identify Radio Stations

To Identify Station On	Keystroke
VOR1	Ctrl + 1
VOR2	Ctrl + 2
DME1	Ctrl + 3
DME2	Ctrl + 4
ADF	Ctrl + 5

Morse Code Alphabet

Letter	Code	Letter	Code
A	• -	N	- •
B	- • • •	O	- - -
C	- • - •	P	• - - •
D	- • •	Q	- - • -
E	•	R	• - •
F	• • - •	S	• • •
G	- - •	T	-
H	• • • •	U	• • -
I	• •	V	• • • -
J	• - - -	W	• - -
K	- • -	X	- • • -
L	• - • •	Y	- • - -
M	- -	Z	- - • •

Autopilot: Second-in-Command

The Cessna 182S, 182 RG, Learjet 45, and Boeing 737-400 are all equipped with autopilot. Learning to operate autopilot can relieve a lot of your cockpit workload. However, be aware that autopilot is only as effective as its operator—if you enter in the wrong information, autopilot will follow your instructions to the (bitter) end. Therefore, it's best to view autopilot as an assistant that requires constant monitoring.

The Bendix/King KAP 2-axis autopilot is found on both Cessnas, but the models 45 and 737 have different systems, both from each other and the Cessnas. Fortunately, all of the autopilot systems operate the same way, although the models 45 and 737 are a little bit more capable because they have throttle control.

Autopilot Functions by Airplane

Function	Cessna	Airplane 45	737
LVL	X	X	X
HDG	X	X	X
ATT	X	X	X
ALT	X	X	X
ASH		X	
MNH		X	
AAT			X
TO/GA			X
Yaw Damper	X	X	X

Here is a list that explains the abbreviations found on the autopilot dialogue windows and the front panels of the various autopilots:

- AP—Autopilot Master Switch engages/disengages the autopilot.
- HDG—Heading Hold will command the airplane to turn to the heading indicated by the DG bug.
- NAV—NAV1 Hold commands the airplane to turn to the heading indicated on NAV1 OBS.

The DG bug is the orange pointer that is adjusted by the knob at the lower right.

- APR—Approach Mode commands the airplane to follow an ILS localizer and glidescope that's selected on NAV1. (This will override all altitude holds.)
- REV—Back Course Mode tracks the reverse course selected on NAV1 OBS.
- ALT—Altitude Hold commands the airplane to hold the current altitude.
- UP—Up increases the numbers used for the vertical speed or altitude.
- DN—Down decreases the numbers used for the vertical speed or altitude.
- A/T—Auto Throttle arm
- SPD—(indicated) Airspeed Hold
- MACH—Mach Number Hold
- BC—Back Course is the same as REV.
- LVL—Wing Leveler
- Y/D—Yaw Damper
- ATT—Pitch and Bank Hold
- ASH—Air Speed Hold
- MNH—Mach Number Hold
- AAT—Arm Auto Throttle applies automatic throttle.
- TO/GA—Take Off/Go Around throttle (only functional if AAT is enabled)

As usual, there are three ways to activate the autopilot in Flight Simulator—by mouse, keyboard, or menu.

- To activate the autopilot with the mouse, click the Autopilot master switch or status indicator on the Autopilot panel. To change the selected heading, course, altitude, and other settings, find the number corresponding to the heading you wish to change. When you've selected it with your mouse, it will change color from red to yellow. To increase the number, click to the right of the digit. To decrease the number, click to the left of the digit.

Note: *Not all of the abbreviations on the face of the 737's autopilot correspond to the actual autopilot function. Quicktips (the text description of "hot" items that appear on screen) are correct, so you can rely on those.*

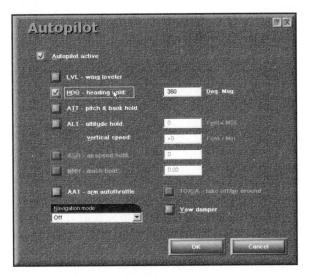

Note: *You must enable auto-pilot first in order to access autopilot functions from the Autopilot configuration window.*

- Press the key combinations for the autopilot functions you want to use.
- To activate and set the autopilot from the menu, select Autopilot from the Aircraft menu. Click the Autopilot Active box and then select the autopilot options you want enabled.

An autopilot is only as trustworthy as the information you enter into it.

Autopilot Commands

Action	Keystroke
Autopilot Master Switch	Z
Heading Hold	Ctrl + H
NAV 1 Hold	Ctrl + N
Approach Mode	Ctrl + A
Back Course Mode	Ctrl + B
Altitude Hold	Ctrl + Z
Wing Leveler	Ctrl + V
Yaw Damper	Ctrl + D
Localizer Hold	Ctrl + O
Airspeed Hold	Ctrl + R
Attitude Hold	Ctrl + T

Chapter Nine

JUST FOR FUN

After the hundreds of calculations, checklists, flight plans, and other pieces of data we've discussed in this book so far, it's easy to forget that flying is supposed to be *fun*. Although many of the more serious desktop pilots find the flight-planning aspects of aviation as enjoyable as barnstorming, there is no question that flying for the pure thrill of it appeals to just about everyone. And don't forget multiplayer flight. You can fly with up to seven other Microsoft Flight Simulator 98 pilots at the same time, and that opens a whole new world of opportunities for having fun.

Aerobatics

Aerobatics is about more than drawing lines in the sky with smoke. In essence, it's really all about perfecting your flying skills. Rather than spelling out step-by-step instructions for maneuvers, let's look at the Extra 300S and then discuss some general tips. Later on, we can look at some of the common pitfalls of specific maneuvers.

Extra 300S

The airplane of choice for aerobatics in Flight Simulator is the Extra 300S. Although it doesn't have flaps or retractable landing gear (features that some believe are standard on all high-performance airplanes), what it does have is a powerful engine and a tremendous roll rate (360 degrees/ sec.). What many people don't realize

Extra 300S.

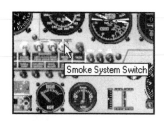

Click on the smoke control switch on the Extra 300S's instrument panel to turn on the smoke system.

is that modern aerobatics planes outperform military fighter aircraft in turn rate, roll rate, and G-tolerance. Who says civilian flying can't be exciting?

Here are some tips that may be of use to you when you're flying the Extra 300S:

- Use the video recorder to record your maneuvers (or use the instant replay feature). Then watch the replay from the tower or another external viewpoint. Turning on the smoke system can give you a better indication of your performance. To turn on the smoke system, press I on your keyboard or simply click with your mouse on the smoke control switch on the instrument panel. The smoke activation switch is the last switch on the right.

- Your AI will be useless most of the time during maneuvers because you'll see either all sky or all ground, so you'll need to use the outside horizon for attitude references. This means you'll need to switch views quite often.

Use the wing guides on the Extra 300 to help you keep your vertical climbs straight and true.

- Using the wing guides as references can help you with your vertical maneuvers. As long as the right angle is parallel to the horizon, you're traveling either straight up or down.

Practice Makes Perfect

There really is no substitute for practice. Competition aerobatics pilots strive for perfection, and perfection requires practice. Sorry, there are no shortcuts. However, because Flight Simulator looks and sounds so great, the hours spent boring holes in the sky will only add to your enjoyment.

One thing to keep in mind while practicing your aerial gymnastics is that flying aerobatics requires many different skills. Mastering only one or two

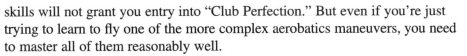

skills will not grant you entry into "Club Perfection." But even if you're just trying to learn to fly one of the more complex aerobatics maneuvers, you need to master all of them reasonably well.

Hand-eye coordination can get you only so far. What the experienced pilots have on their side is *knowledge*. Understanding how and why your airplane does what it does can help in several ways. You learn to keep the aircraft within its operating parameters and how to stay out of bad situations. Knowledge can also expand your repertoire of tricks and techniques. Put simply, you'll need to practice, but you'll also need to study a bit as well.

Energy Management

The most important skill an aerobatics pilot needs to learn, and fully understand, is energy management. In addition to the engine management skills we've discussed already, now you need to worry about energy management. In a nutshell, kinetic energy is your airspeed, and potential energy is your altitude. Potential energy is converted into kinetic energy by diving—thanks to gravity. And kinetic energy is converted into potential energy by climbing. Fortunately, poor energy management decisions, a very common blunder among new aerobatics pilots, are easy to correct.

Altitude and speed are functionally interchangeable, and you probably won't perform maneuvers at *nosebleed* (extremely high) altitudes. Therefore, in order to keep your energy at its highest, your only real option is to increase your kinetic energy before a maneuver, while maintaining your potential energy. Although all maneuvers will generally benefit from this extra energy, energy-robbing vertical maneuvers will benefit the most. That's because it's far better to have to get rid of excess energy near the bottom of a loop maneuver than it is to be left hanging at the top, like Wile E. Coyote, without any kinetic energy left. Just remember to perform all maneuvers at a higher airspeed if you're experiencing problems.

How much extra airspeed is enough? That really depends on the maneuver. Speed can also be too much of a good thing: you want to achieve enough speed to complete the stunt, but you should be careful not to lose control (or any airplane parts) due to excessive speed. Any maneuver that requires initial diving will not benefit as much from extra airspeed as those that require climbing initially. That's because the dive will trade altitude and gain airspeed anyway. So if you're at maximum airspeed before the dive, diving will most likely only cause you structural failures.

The best general advice is to keep as much excess airspeed as you can and quickly bleed off if you need to. Flying out on the edge is fine if you can handle it. Let's discuss some tips that will help you keep your energy high and your airplane in one piece.

On the Throttle

A couple of chapters back we spoke about how the throttle controls altitude and the elevator controls airspeed. We also demonstrated this during cruise when we allowed the aircraft to reach equilibrium. However, the whole point of aerobatics is to knock your airplane out of equilibrium to make it do things that it wouldn't normally do. Under those circumstances, the effects of throttle input aren't as obvious as they normally are. This causes many pilots to question the principle that the throttle controls airspeed and the elevator controls altitude.

Remember that if you are flying level and increase the throttle, your airspeed will rise. Aerodynamics tells us that when airspeed rises, so does lift. This means you will climb when your airspeed rises. Most pilots subconsciously recognize this and move the stick forward to keep the airplane level. Moving your elevator down will cause an increase in airspeed. So it's understandable that many believe if you increase throttle, your airspeed will go up. However, it's the down elevator they applied that actually caused that increase in airspeed. The increase in throttle caused a potential increase in altitude. Down elevator exchanged this potential altitude gain into airspeed.

What does this have to do with energy and aerobatics? Your joystick and rudder pedals direct your control surfaces (aileron, elevator, and rudder), and they should more or less follow a set pattern of movements to perform maneuvers in the sky. Your throttle, on the other hand (literally!), is what's used to keep your energy up as high as possible, in conjunction with what the stick is doing. Although the throttle doesn't require the precision that the control surfaces do (most of the time your throttle will be all the way on or completely off), do realize that your throttle will get a workout during aerobatics. You'll be pumping that thing on and off with almost as much activity as your joystick movements.

Getting back to our example of a maximum airspeed, high-energy, initial dive maneuver: because your joystick has to follow the pattern, you have no choice but to cut the throttle to avoid breaking your airplane into tiny pieces strewn across the countryside. The *cure* for our example situation is to slowly add throttle to keep the airplane near its performance edge, but don't cross over the red line on your ASI. You may get away with crossing the red line once or twice (if you have Aircraft Receives Damage From Stress enabled in the Crash/Damage tab of Aircraft Settings under the Aircraft menu). But if you do this more than a couple of times—well, don't say you weren't warned.

Control Patrol

It should go without saying that you need to be smooth on the stick. Well, actually *both* sticks—throttle and control. Although making

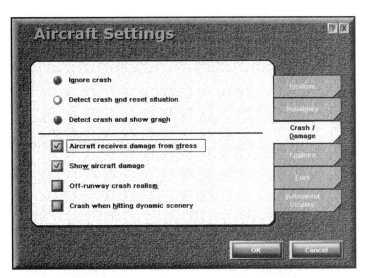

Unless you have the Aircraft Receives Damage From Stress option enabled, you won't have to worry about your airplane breaking apart during radical maneuvers.

many minor corrections is unavoidable, just try to be as smooth as possible with them. Being smooth is very important because, just as with auto racing, any control input beyond what is absolutely required for a winning performance bleeds off speed and energy.

Being smooth on the stick will help you avoid another pitfall as well. If you jerk the stick around, you run into the very real possibility of entering an accelerated stall. You may want that for some maneuvers, but be aware of it even if you don't.

We should also discuss the need to be smooth with the application and removal of power. The 300S has a high power-to-weight ratio. Couple that with its short wingspan, and the combination can cause havoc with the straight and smooth lines you're trying to fly through the sky. If you haven't picked up on it already, what we're talking about are *torque effects*. Be prepared to do the "rudder dance" when applying or reducing power. Sometimes torque effects and torque rolls are desirable. In those cases, of course, go ahead and mash the throttle through the firewall.

Torque effects are most noticeable when you make the transition from low to high power or vice versa. The more abrupt the transition, the more noticeable

the effects will be. And as you remember about takeoff and climbing power, when you factor in airspeed, the transition to high power at a low airspeed requires the most rudder input. However, be aware that the transition from high power to low power at a high airspeed also requires some rudder correction.

Da Rudder—Part Two

Aerobatics flying is the most rudder-intensive flight activity there is. In addition to having to be constantly pumping away on the rudder, you have to be accurate with it as well. But before we get to that, we should consider some of the physical aspects of rudder pedals.

Real-life aerobatics flying requires much more physical activity than most casual observers realize. To use another auto racing example, if you watch a Formula One race from a spectator's point of view, it looks like cars just move fast around the track. It looks easy. The drivers make racing seem so smooth. But in reality, the driver is in a cramped, hot, dirty environment getting his bones rattled. What's more, the spectator never sees the pedal dance going on inside .

This pretty much parallels what goes on in an aerobatics airplane's cockpit. So don't worry about what you look like doing it, just move the pedals as much as you need to. Let the spectators on the ground imagine that you're quite relaxed and merely making a few adjustments now and then.

Get over feeling self-conscious about the amount of physical body movement required to control the rudder during aerobatics. You know that the rudder mainly controls yaw; turns made solely by rudder input are possible. You press the pedal of the direction you want the nose to turn to, and it happens —simple and straightforward when you're upright and level. What tends to confuse people is what happens when you're not flying upright and level. (And that's pretty rare in aerobatics.)

When you're flying "knife-edge" (with wings perpendicular to the ground), your rudder is oriented in the same position that your elevator used to be in. This means that applying top rudder (top in relation to the ground) will cause your airplane to respond as if you were applying up elevator when flying upright and level. That's pretty intuitive, but what happens when you're inverted is another story entirely. Most aerobatics planes such as the Extra 300S feature symmetrical or semi-symmetrical airfoils. This is so the aircraft will fly pretty much the same while inverted as it does when it's right side up. Because either side of these airfoils will produce the same amount of lift, the only way to keep the wing flying is to increase its angle of attack—the angle of the wing chord line in relation to the oncoming airflow. This is why you need to keep the nose above the horizon while inverted, or you will lose altitude.

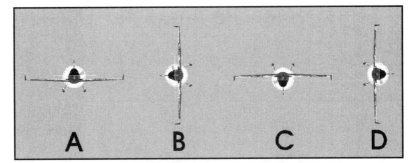

A slow roll to the left illustrates how the rudder behaves differently depending on your orientation. At point A your controls work normally. At point B, the right rudder acts like the up elevator. The rudder works like a rudder again at point C, but at point D the left rudder now works like the up elevator.

This concept can be illustrated by making a slow roll to the left. Begin the roll by applying left aileron. As the roll begins, you need to apply top (right) rudder to keep the nose above the horizon. That's because the position the rudder is in now makes it behave like the up elevator. Once you're inverted, the elevator works like an elevator again—but in exactly opposite directions (down is up and up is down), and the rudder returns to working like a rudder again.

The transition from inverted to upright flight requires that the top rudder keep the nose above the horizon. The problem is that even though you're still rolling to the left using the left aileron, the right rudder is no longer the top rudder—the left rudder is. This is because the designation "top" is based on its relation to the ground.

Finally, you should consider how much rudder needs to be used. The answer depends on three things: how far you want to move the nose of your airplane, your airspeed, and the power setting.

Naturally, the more rudder you apply, the more the nose will move, but its effectiveness and sensitivity will vary with your airspeed. It works exactly like your other flying surfaces—it becomes more effective as your airspeed increases, and more ineffective (softer) as your airspeed decreases. For example, if you want to move the nose of your airplane 5 degrees to the left, it may only take one-half left rudder input at a high airspeed, but at a slow airspeed, it may take full left rudder to achieve the same results.

Intermediate Aerobatic Maneuvers

Here are some intermediate aerobatics maneuvers that you can try. You may be able to do these, but the idea is to do them well. That means beginning and ending the maneuver at the same heading you started at, making all of the 45's (angle of climbs) straight, and all of your half-circles round. Gravity and airspeed will stretch the bottoms of your loops, and gravity plus the lack of airspeed will squash the tops of your loops as well.

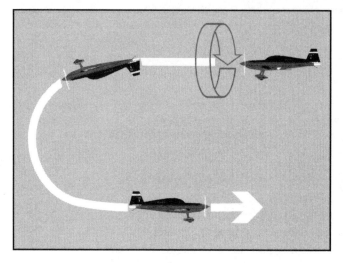

Split S.

Split S

The Split S is a simple maneuver that illustrates the effects of gravity on your airspeed and turn radius. If you have a hard time ending the maneuver at exactly 180 degrees from your starting heading, it's very likely that your initial roll is the culprit. Use the rudder to keep the nose in one spot during the initial roll. Reducing power after the roll will help keep your airspeed from increasing too much and will help keep the rest of the loop round.

Immelman

The Immelman is the exact opposite of the split S, and it presents a new set of problems. On your way up you'll lose

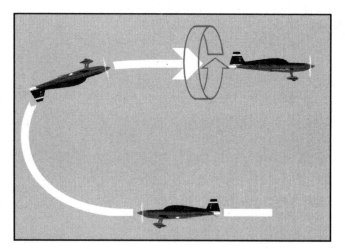

Immelman.

track of the horizon unless you use the side views. Rely on both distinct ground features and clouds as your reference markers to keep you on track. If you're not square on the first half of the loop, you'll lose your heading. Using a high-entry airspeed will help prevent stalling at the top when you have to initiate the roll. Also, use the rudder to keep the nose in one spot during the upright roll. That's where most pilots lose their heading.

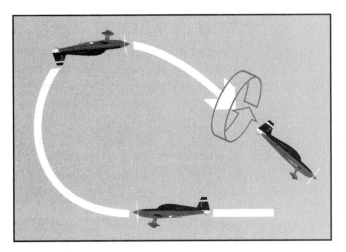

Half Cuban.

Outside Immelman

The Outside Immelman is exactly like the Immelman, except you begin it while inverted. (I hope you've digested your breakfast!) Enter with as much extra airspeed as you can, but be careful. The airframe won't take as many negative Gs as it will take positive Gs. Then hold the inverted position to gain a little speed before rolling to level.

Half Cuban

Enter the Half Cuban 8 with as much extra speed as you can. You're going to need it at the top for the roll. By cutting power on the downward section, you can help keep your altitude high. To do the Half Cuban 8 properly, you have to level out at the same altitude you started at as well.

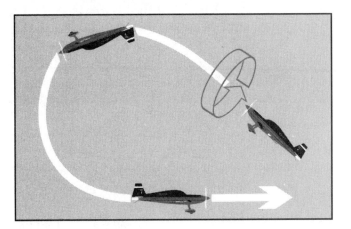

Reverse Half Cuban.

Reverse Half Cuban

The Reverse Half Cuban is to the Half Cuban what the Split S is to the Immelman. After the Half Cuban, this should be a piece of cake. Just keep the nose high on the rollover so you don't lose altitude.

Soaring

One aircraft that has always seemed to spark the imaginations of pilots old and new is the sailplane. As any sailplane pilot will tell you, soaring isn't gliding. Any airplane will glide with its engine off. The difference is that instead of just slowly descending to the ground (a glide), soaring is a sport where you use your skills to make use of atmospheric conditions to climb and remain aloft.

Some people describe soaring as being relaxing and challenging at the same time. It's also been referred to as the golf of the aviation world.

Schweizer 2-32 Sailplane.

Slope Dope

Slope soaring is easiest. When slope soaring, you can find lift fairly easily. Lift is generated on a slope thanks to the slope itself. Wind blows across the front of the slope causing the flow to move upward. Flying in this upwardly moving air mass will gain you altitude. So, as long as the wind keeps blowing, you'll have lift from the front edge of the slope.

As easy as slope soaring sounds, there are two things to watch out for. First, the air mass creating lift only exists near the slope. Move too far out in front of it, and you'll lose your lift. The effect is similar to what we've seen when a helicopter is making the transition to forward flight—only much stronger.

Second, you need to stay away from the back of the slope. As the air spills over the top of the slope, it folds over and creates a turbulent area that slope pilots call the *rotor*. You don't want to end up there. You'll lose all lift and will find yourself in for a very rough ride.

Avoid these problems by flying a circuit above and in front of the slope edge that always turns away from the slope. You can fly circles in one direction or, as most pilots prefer, in a Figure 8 pattern. Again, stay near the slope for lift. After you gain enough altitude, you can go wander about a little more.

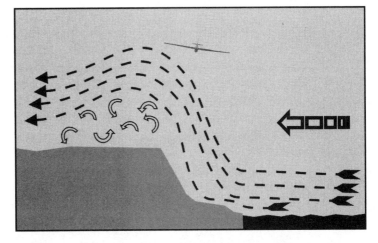

Lift is generated on a slope when wind blows across its front, causing the flow to move upward.

Thermal Hunting

The other type of soaring is called thermaling; you ride on rising columns of warm air known as *thermals*.

Warm air rises. Remember that warm air hurts engine performance and lift because it's less dense than colder air. The sun warms the air, but what most people don't realize is that only a tiny portion of the heat that's transferred to the atmosphere comes from the sunlight bouncing

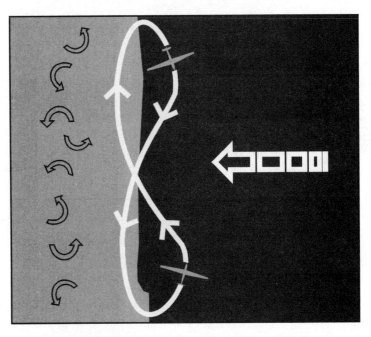

Always turn away from the slope. You can fly circles in one direction, but this Figure 8 pattern is preferred by most pilots.

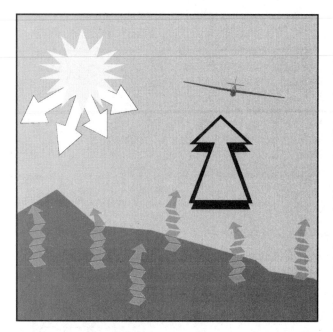

Thermals are created when the sun heats the earth and then the earth, in turn, heats the air.

directly on air molecules. Atmospheric heating results primarily when the sun heats the earth and then the earth transfers its heat to the atmosphere.

Of course, the hotter that a patch of earth becomes, the more it can warm the air above it. As you may recall from high school science class, lighter colors tend to reflect sunlight, and darker colors tend to absorb it. If you've ever sat in a car with a black exterior on a sunny day, you know exactly how this works. Well, it works the same way with the earth. Darker patches of earth generate more heat and stronger thermals, so that's what you look for.

What makes thermaling so difficult is that you can't see thermals themselves. Sure, you can see dark patches on the ground, but thermals are generally not very large. So finding them over dark patches of land isn't always easy. The way to detect that you're in a thermal is by watching your VSI and the horizon. You'll know you're in a thermal when your VSI indicates a climb even though you're flying more or less level. But finding a thermal once you fly smack in the middle of it is easy. There's another way to find them, too.

You're near a thermal when one wing rises without any control movement on your part. Let's say you're flying along and all of a sudden your airplane banks to the right. (The left wing rises.) That means your left wing has flown through the edge of a thermal.

OK, after you find a thermal, what do you do? Naturally, you want to stay within the thermal as long as possible to take "the elevator" up. Logically, there are only two ways you can do this. One is to fly really, really slowly, and the other is to circle around inside the thermal. And the best method of all is to combine the two maneuvers: to circle really, really slowly.

The best glide speed of the 2-32 Sailplane in Flight Simulator is 55 MPH (remember the Sailplane's ASI is in MPH). Flying at 55 MPH is a no-brainer, but don't forget that circling requires turning, and turning requires banking, and banking requires more lift. The stall speeds for the Schweizer 2-32 are listed in the table labeled "Schweizer 2-32 Sailplane Stall Speeds." Note that 55 MPH is really close to this aircraft's level stall speed, so be careful. Each time you stall, you lose energy and lose a little bit of the battle against gravity.

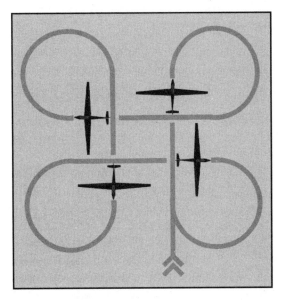

Making 270-degree turns will allow you to take advantage of the center of the thermal.

Schweizer 2-32 Sailplane Stall Speeds

Angle of Bank	Airspeed (MPH)
0°	52
30°	55
45°	57

Next let's discuss the final piece of the puzzle—how to circle. When novice thermal hunters find a thermal, they usually just attempt to make the smallest circle possible and hope for the best. The problem is that your turn radius at maximum glide speed is huge (because of the low angle of bank you have to adhere to). You can end up doing circles *around* a thermal and never even enter it.

One technique that works very well is known as the "270 rule." The idea is that if your wing flies through the edge of a thermal, turn away from the thermal and make a 270-degree turn. Then come back at the thermal. Although this goes against your natural instincts to turn *toward* the thermal, it really is the best tactic. At the low rate of turn you're flying, if you turn toward the thermal, most of the time you'll just end up flying around and around. All that will happen is that you'll get your wing bounced around once in while by the thermal if you're lucky. By consistently making 270-degree turns after each pass through the thermal, you'll be able to stay with it longer and also take advantage of the area of greatest lift in a thermal—the center.

Stupid Aircraft Tricks

Now we'll look at some silly things to try in Flight Simulator. Although they aren't on the same level of sophistication as the Challenges that come with Flight Simulator, the following ideas are challenging. But most of all they're fun. Testing skills and setting records has been a pastime since the first version of Flight Simulator. And after 15 years the tradition is still alive and well!

Although you'll no doubt try many...shall we say *unconventional* things with every aircraft in Flight Simulator, the traditional barnstorming aircraft is the Sopwith Camel. The Camel's low speed and simplicity make it easier to control. On the other hand, however, it's under-powered and fragile. This makes for an interesting balance that guarantees thrills and chills.

How Fast Can You Go?

This is usually one of the first things people do when they get their hands on a new airplane. "Crank 'er up and see what she'll do!" is the traditional cry. You can try to see how fast you can go with or without the Aircraft Receives Damage From Stress option enabled (in the Aircraft Settings option under the Aircraft menu). Compare your fastest speeds with those of your friends and see who really has the right touch.

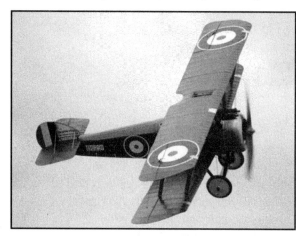

Sopwith Camel.

How High Can You Fly?

This is probably the second thing that people do when they get their hands on a new airplane. After you get tired of ripping the wings off your airplane by setting new speed records, take it up and set an altitude record. For an added challenge in the Learjet, enable Jet Engines Flameout on the Engine tab under the Aircraft Settings on the Aircraft menu. Here's one tip: just when you think you've reached as high as you can go, build up a little speed by lowering the nose and then pull up fast and try *zoom climbing*. You just might gain those extra few feet and set a new record.

Test Pilot

Scotty: "She can't take much more of this, Captain!"

Test Pilot is an extension of "How High Can You Fly." Take an airplane like the 182S or Camel to some impossibly high altitude using the slew functions.

(Press the Y key to enter slew and then F4 to climb. Press Y again when you're ready to start.) When you re-enter the flight, your aircraft will be tumbling out of control. Test your piloting skills by recovering to normal flight as fast as you can. One way to judge your performances is by noting at what altitude you are able to recover the aircraft. Naturally, the higher the altitude, the greater your skill.

Cessnas in S-P-A-C-E!

Microsoft

Flight Simulator 98

Replay: 23

Putting the wheels down is only part of the challenge.

Can You Make It?

This one's a hoot. Take off in any airplane with 1 percent of fuel (make sure you have the Engine Stops With No Fuel option selected) and see how high or how far you can fly. Then see if you can land in one piece. (Ground roll counts as well.) Keep track of your distance by using the coordinate display (Shift + Z).

737 Landing at Meigs

Try landing the 737 at Chicago's Meigs Field or some other airstrip that has an even shorter runway. Getting your wheels on the ground is only part of the challenge—trying to stop is where the fun begins. Hint: Try putting the engines in reverse.

Find Your Home and Buzz Your Neighbors!

One of the best parts about Flight Simulator is being able to do things you (or at least *most* of us) wouldn't try in real life. Finding your home from the air is a favorite activity for first-time pilots, but buzzing your house or your neighbors is frowned upon by the FAA.

Even if you live in one of the big cities that have been rendered in detail in Flight Simulator, you won't be able to find your actual house (unless you live in the Sears Tower or some other landmark building). Nevertheless, you can usually find the general area of where you live. The easiest way to do this is to take off from the airport nearest your home and then fly on a heading that will take you toward your house. Look for land features such as bodies of water, major highways, mountains, and hills to help you find the right general area.

New York City Taxi

Taxiing around New York's Kennedy Airport in a 737 isn't the most challenging thing in the world. It becomes interesting only if you try it going in reverse. Use the 737's reverse thrusters (press the F2 key a couple of times when in idle), differential braking (F11 and F12), plus individual engine control, and you'll have more than enough to keep you busy. For even more of a challenge, try entering the parking area and making a circuit around the airport—just don't forget to start the fare meter.

Taxi!

Formation Flying

When you have Dynamic Scenery (on the World menu) set to Normal or higher, you'll notice that, if you sit around at the end of a runway long

Flying through the gates of the Forbidden City is tricky, but not impossible.

enough, other aircraft will take off in front of you. To build up your flying skills, try playing "Follow the Leader" by trailing one of those aircraft into the air. Obviously, you won't have much luck following a Learjet 45 in your Cessna, but try following a Cessna in a Learjet 45. That's a challenge!

Storm the Palace Gates

Try flying a Sopwith Camel through the gates of the Forbidden City in Beijing, China. See how many gates you can fly through without becoming a stain on the wall. Hint: Just as with landings, the approach is the key.

One way to avoid paying a bridge toll.

Just a walk in the park—or is it?

Barnstorming Golden Gate in a Glider

Test your energy management and soaring skills by loading the Ridge Soaring Flight. Take your sailplane under the Golden Gate Bridge and then try to make it back to the ridge before you run out of altitude and airspeed.

Golden Gate Hopper

Sure, just about any novice pilot can fly under the Golden Gate Bridge in San Francisco, but flying *along* it is another story. Try flying the Golden Gate Bridge lengthwise using the Ridge Soaring world parameters. (Choose Select Flight from the Flights menu and then locate Sailplane Ridge Soaring from the list.) These settings will make it necessary to fly a crab angle the whole way through the bridge to counteract a heavy crosswind. Make it to the other side, and you'll win the respect and admiration of your fellow pilots.

Inverted Around New York City

This one gives a new meaning to the phrase "turning the city upside down." Flying between the buildings in New York City is challenging, but for even more excitement, try it while inverted. Use the Walk In The Park Flight and

turn the scenery complexity up to Dense, but be forewarned that your computer hardware will be in for a real workout.

Helicopter Loop

If you saw the movie *Blue Thunder*, trying to do a loop in a JetRanger is probably one of the first things you want to try. Even with the Aircraft Receives Damage From Stress option enabled, it's

Whirlybirds can fly in any direction, even upside down.

possible to loop—in Flight Simulator, at least. Just don't exceed VNE and use the collective to help reduce altitude loss at the top of the loop. If you lose too much airspeed on the way up, the aircraft will tend to tumble on the way down.

The City of Love Hover

To really put your helicopter hovering skills to the test, try hovering *inside* the Eiffel Tower in Paris, France. You won't be able to land on the platform inside, but just trying to keep your rotor blades from hitting the sides of the tower should keep you busy.

Hover lover.

Multiplayer Flying

Although it's doubtful that you'll get tired of flying Flight Simulator by yourself any time soon, there's a whole other facet of Flight Simulator that you can explore. If flying in real time with up to seven other pilots over the Internet sounds intriguing, read on.

Online Activities

Because Flight Simulator doesn't lock you into certain online flying activities, you're free to do anything you like. In addition to attempting "stupid aircraft tricks," other popular flight pastimes include formation flying, aerobatics challenges, and playing "Follow the Leader." But for serious desktop pilots, activities like air races around cities, flying as an observer/flight instructor, or trying your hand at airport traffic control make the multiplayer feature one of the most valuable in Flight Simulator 98.

Getting Connected

All connections are handled through Multiplayer Connect setup wizard found in the Multiplayer selection under the Flights menu. This wizard will take you step-by-step through the connection process, so rather than spend time rehashing those steps, let's just talk about the options available and provide some hints and insights into them.

The Multiplayer Connect setup wizard will take you through the connection process one step at a time.

Session Settings

Even though you'll be given the opportunity to change your Session Settings again before connecting, it's probably best to talk about it now. This way we'll be able to go ahead and incorporate discussion about connections.

Although the title Settings under the Multiplayer menu option (under the Flights menu) may give you the impression that this is where you set your modem commands and such, the actual name of the window is Session Settings, and this is where you configure your multiplayer game options.

Multiplayer Settings are broken down into two categories—Tracking and Visual Details. Tracking options help you keep track of the other players. It's a big world out there (in real life and in Flight Simulator because it models the whole world), so it's very easy to lose the (relatively) tiny airplanes of other players.

ADF lock to aircraft: Sets your ADF to point at the selected aircraft of another pilot.

DME lock to aircraft: Will present the distance between you and the selected aircraft on the DME.

Autopilot to aircraft: If you're totally lost, enabling this option can mean the difference between having fun or hours of frustration. Don't be afraid to set this on. Just make sure that if you're flying a faster aircraft, you don't fly into the other player.

Display Player Names: Superimposes the name of each player above his or her aircraft. This makes identification a snap.

The Visual Details options are used to send more detailed aircraft information to other players. The drawback to enabling this option is you may experience some slowdown in game speed.

At the bottom of the Session Settings window is the Set Flight

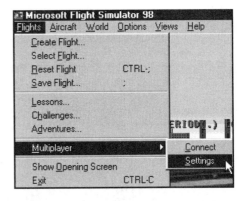

Session Settings are found under the Multiplayer menu option.

Note: *If you have one or more of the Tracking options enabled, you can cycle your target lock/selection through each available aircraft by pressing Ctrl + S on the keyboard.*

The Session Settings window is where multiplayer Tracking and Visual Details are configured.

Note: *The Visual Details setting won't affect individual Scenery Settings. So if one player has a scenery setting set to Dense and another player has it set to Sparse, the "Sparse" player won't have as many buildings to worry about as the other player. This can sometimes lead to the "Dense" player's seeing the other player fly though buildings when the "Sparse" player sees nothing in front of him or her.*

Conditions Now button. Depending on whether you are hosting or joining the session will dictate whether you can set or get flight conditions from the host. This features allows you to coordinate the various World settings (weather and time of day) between all of the players.

To Host or Not to Host

Other decisions you must make are whether you're going to host the multiplayer session or join someone else's session, and whether to join as a player or observer. Basically, the only difference between hosting and joining is who actually configures and starts the session. There is no game advantage or disadvantage to Internet, LAN, or serial connections, but with modem games the host does pay for the phone call. If you're calling long distance this may be an important consideration.

Player or Observer

Just as you might expect, a player can fly, and an observer can only watch. However, there are some other differences between these two modes that you should be aware of.

The Multiplayer Connect session setup screen is where you'll set your callsign and decide whether to host or join a game.

As an observer you can switch (ride along) with any of the other players' aircraft. Press Ctrl + Shift + S to cycle through available aircraft. If you begin a session as an observer, you can't change to player mode during that session.

To switch to observer mode after having started a session as a pilot, press Ctrl + Shift + O. When riding as an observer, Ctrl + Shift + D will lock your cockpit view in the aircraft you are observing.

Kinds of Connections

There are four types of connections that can be used to connect with other players in Flight Simulator 98. Each requires specific hardware, and some have other limitations as well. So let's talk about some of the general properties of each. Multiplayer connections in Flight Simulator are made by:

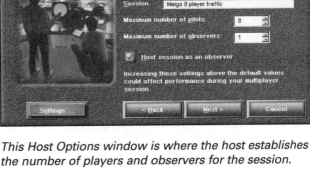

This Host Options window is where the host establishes the number of players and observers for the session.

IPX: This is for connecting via a IPX LAN network multiplayer games. Unless you already have an IPX LAN network setup, you'll want to use TCP/IP for Flight Simulator 98 network games. Naturally, NICs (Network Interface Cards) are required.

TCP/IP: (Transmission Control Protocol/Internet Protocol) is the language that Internet machines use to communicate. Because Windows 95 also uses TCP/IP for network connections, this is the multiplayer connection choice for both Internet play and most Windows 95 network play. Additional requirements include an Internet connection (and modem for dial-up service) and NICs for network play.

Modem: These connections are probably what most gamers are the most familiar with. Just as with most modem-enabled multiplayer games, you're limited to two players and have to deal with telephone line noise, phone toll charges, and generally the slowest connections of the four types offered by Flight Simulator 98. On the positive side, you don't

Tip: When you begin the setup wizard, you'll be asked to provide a callsign. Rather than just entering your name, sometimes adding the aircraft you'll be flying is a good idea. This way other players will instantly know what you're flying. Of course, this only works if you stay with the same aircraft throughout the session.

Tip: Observing flights is a great tool for learning. For the rookie, both watching and having an observer onboard can really help. Watching how things are done can drive home some lessons. But let's not forget that having a more experienced pilot in your aircraft talking (or typing) you through a maneuver or flight can also be extremely valuable.

There are four types of multiplayer connections to choose from in Flight Simulator 98.

need to be physically near your flight buddy, and you don't need a network or ISP (Internet Service Provider) to play together. A modem and serial cable (if external) are the only hardware requirements for a modem connection. Obviously, however, a telephone connection is required.

Serial: Playing over a serial cable connection—known as a null modem connection—has the same limitations as modem connections (only two players), but null modems are generally faster than modem connections. The disadvantage to them is that you need to be physically near the other player (a distance equal to or less than the length of the serial cable).

Flying on The Zone

One of the coolest things about the multiplayer capabilities in Flight Simulator 98 is the fact that you can fly with other players on the Microsoft Internet Gaming Zone. Besides being free, the appeal to flying on The Zone is it's a

Modem connection is probably the most familiar type of connection for gamers.

Null modem connections made via serial cable are generally faster than modem connections.

gathering place where (day or night) you can find other Flight Simulator pilots who also want to fly online. Here are some tips for flying on The Zone:

Chat first: Chat with other players before hosting or joining a game so you can coordinate starting locations and determine exactly what you'll be doing. If you close the Chat window, you can call it up again from the Flights menu under the Multiplayer selection or by pressing Ctrl + Enter. Note that Chat will be accessible only when you are connected to a multiplayer game.

Go For Latency: Consider only joining games with other players who have good (green) network latency indicators next to their names. These are visible on the player list on the right side of the game room screen. You can use the scroll bar to view the rest of the list if there are many players in the room.

The Name Game: When hosting a game it's often helpful to name your game something descriptive. Name the area where you'll be flying, how many players you'll host, and what type of activity will be taking place. Doing this will help attract like-minded players to your game.

Fly with other players on the Microsoft Internet Gaming Zone.

Consider only joining games with other players that have good (green) network latency indicators next to their names.

It makes sense to give your game a descriptive name.

Flight Simulator 98

Experiencing the SideWinder Force Feedback Pro

While first setting up this joystick, you'll realize that the Microsoft SideWinder Force Feedback Pro adds more realism than anything you can experience outside an airplane. In the Setup program, each button simulates a given force or event through special stick vibrations. You can experience the kick of a shotgun, the growl of a car engine, the blast of a laser cannon, and even the rumbling of a chainsaw (my personal favorite), among others. Merely sampling these was enough to convince me that adding this new stick was about to make my "virtual flying" experiences less "virtual" and more like true "flying." After Setup, I prepared a Cessna for take-off from Chicago's Meigs Field. With brakes secured, I increased the throttle and experienced a slight vibration from the joystick. After releasing the brakes and accelerating, I could feel the various imperfections along the runway: a bump here, a jerk there. As airspeed reached triple digits, I pulled the stick back and—wham!—the back tail gave the ground a firm kiss, the joystick responding with a yank forward. I lessened the angle of ascent, increased the flaps one notch and was surprised how "smooth" the air felt compared to the sensations of the bumpy runway.

At 3,000 feet I began to bank left, and the city skyline dominated the cockpit view. The stick offered resistance to the bank, but brute force overcame the joystick. Just as an experiment, I pulled the stick back all the way and watched the skyline turn into blue horizon. The nose and attitude rose while the speed dropped for a moment. Then a rapid-fire series of sounds followed: Snap! Wham! Sputter! Pop! The word "stalled" appeared in red toward the bottom of my view as I fought to regain control of the joystick. As I did, the plane leveled out, and I looked up only to be staring at the Sears Tower: more challenges... dead-ahead. I spotted two buildings of equal height in close proximity to each other. Ah...everything so far had been an ease to accomplish, so why not try flying through a space which

The challenge was on...

appeared to be smaller than my wingspan? I dropped attitude and leveled out, pointing directly at the gap between the two shiny skyscrapers. Seconds before impact I banked left to save my wings. The bank caused me to be pointed directly at the left building. With only a couple of seconds to react, I attempted to push the nose down, but the joystick's resistance was incredible. Finally, the plane responded to my strength. Unfortunately, though, I had over-corrected again—Splat! Crunch! Grind! Shake!—and I felt every bit of it with my new SideWinder Force Feedback Pro. Ouch!

Index

Inside Moves!

Microsoft® Windows® 95 has paved the way for a vividly exciting new generation of computer games. The *Inside Moves* series gives you expert tips, tricks, tactics, and strategies—some straight from the developers and not available anywhere else. Maximize the fun you have playing Microsoft and DreamWorks Interactive™ games with the Microsoft Press® *Inside Moves* series.

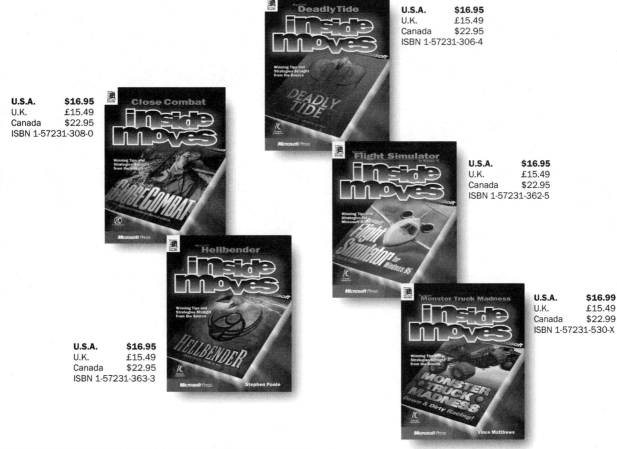

Deadly Tide
U.S.A.   **$16.95**
U.K.   £15.49
Canada $22.95
ISBN 1-57231-306-4

Close Combat
U.S.A.   **$16.95**
U.K.   £15.49
Canada $22.95
ISBN 1-57231-308-0

Flight Simulator
U.S.A.   **$16.95**
U.K.   £15.49
Canada $22.95
ISBN 1-57231-362-5

Hellbender
U.S.A.   **$16.95**
U.K.   £15.49
Canada $22.95
ISBN 1-57231-363-3

Monster Truck Madness
U.S.A.   **$16.99**
U.K.   £15.49
Canada $22.99
ISBN 1-57231-530-X

Microsoft Press® products are available worldwide wherever quality computer books are sold. For more information, contact your book or computer retailer, software reseller, or local Microsoft Sales Office, or visit our Web site at mspress.microsoft.com. To locate your nearest source for Microsoft Press products, or to order directly, call 1-800-MSPRESS in the U.S. (in Canada, call 1-800-268-2222).

Prices and availability dates are subject to change.

Microsoft®*Press*

IF YOU LIKED THE VIRTUAL, YOU'LL LOVE THE REALITY.

As a virtual pilot with Microsoft's amazingly realistic Flight Simulator, you've developed a "hands-on" feel for the challenge and fun of flying your own plane. Now, we challenge you to experience the next level – with a $35 discovery flight in a real Cessna aircraft. Imagine: for less than the cost of this software, you can take the controls and discover how easy it is to turn your virtual skills into real ones. Visit our website to find your nearest Cessna Pilot Center.

$35 DISCOVERY FLIGHT

COUPON NOT VALID UNTIL ACTIVATED.
Visit our website www.cessna.textron.com to activate your coupon today!

PLEASE ENTER YOUR ACTIVATION NUMBER HERE:_____

Once activated, this coupon entitles the bearer to one $35 discovery flight at a participating Cessna Pilot Center.

Valid only at locations in the U.S. and Canada. Must be 16 or older to redeem discovery flight coupon. Coupon expires 12/31/1998.

Cessna
A **Textron** Company